188469

GUIDE TO SPEECH TRAINING

Voice, Articulation, and Oral Reading

GEORGE W. HIBBITT

The City College of the City University of New York

and

RICHARD A. NORMAN

Barnard College, Columbia University

THE RONALD PRESS COMPANY • **NEW YORK**

Library of Congress Catalog Card Number 64–16617

Preface

The aim of this text is to supply practice material for voice, articulation, and oral reading. The authors have used many of these exercises in their teaching. The book will serve (1) to provide a text or exercise book for courses in voice and diction, (2) to present practice materials for individual as well as group work in speech improvement, (3) to assist the teacher in providing particular assignments for work in conferences and the language laboratory, and (4) to furnish a considerable amount of material for oral reading as well as for use in public-speaking classes.

The selections include various types of writing in both prose and poetry. These selections will interest students in the material itself and will help them to overcome, through practice, their particular problems in speech. Not all exercises will be of use to every student, because speech problems vary somewhat from individual to individual, but the teacher will be able to select from a wide variety of exercises those which fit the needs of a student at a particular time.

Although much of the practice material is designed to provide exercises for specific speech difficulties such as the omission, substitution, or addition of speech sounds, the hissing /s/, nasality, the dentalized /t/, etc., some of the material will serve many purposes. A reading exercise may provide material for interpretation and class discussion and at the same time fulfil a need for work in rhythm, intonation, and sentence stress, as well as for improvement in voice quality. Among the materials are exercises in the various sounds of American English. There are also exercises for securing support of tone, control of rate, variations in pitch, precision in articulation, and appropriate intonation. Exercises in difficult pronunciations include English and foreign words often used in conversation and writing. However, the main objective of this text has been to stress intelligibility of speech rather than to set up a prescriptive standard for all speakers of American English.

The authors have tried to bring the practice sentences and reading selections close to the student's reading and speaking experience so that from this text he can easily transfer the habits acquired to actual daily speech situations. Many of the examples come from the great record of English and American literature, but their choice has been based not on reputation in the literary world but rather on their usefulness for practice in speech work.

With this text, the student can never have the old excuse that he has no practice materials, nor will the instructor be left without sufficient material for class activities. However, the specific procedure for use of the book will, of course, depend upon the particular needs of the teacher and the student.

GEORGE W. HIBBITT
RICHARD A. NORMAN

New York City
April, 1964

Contents

PART I

EXERCISES IN VOICE QUALITY AND ARTICULATION

Chapter 1

Voice and Intelligibility

I. EXERCISES ON VOICE IMPROVEMENT

A. Development of Vocal Vigor

SUPPORT OF TONE: EXPLANATION

1.01 Support of tone means that the speaker has:

1. A sufficient amount of air in the lungs to vibrate the vocal bands
2. A steady stream of this air in vibration coming through the larynx, pharynx, mouth, and nasal cavities
3. A sufficient pressure on the expelled air so that the vibrations of the vocal bands give clear, sustained tone, without any obstruction, throughout the speech unit

With this support of tone, vowels, diphthongs, and sustained consonants such as *m, n, l,* and *z* reach the eardrum of the listener with precision and constant pressure. The mastery of this skill of control of tone is essential to well-articulated speech. Support of tone continues from the beginning of articulation to the end of the spoken unit, be that unit a phrase, a clause, or a complete sentence. Even at the moments when the pitch of the tone drops (usually toward the end of a sentence), the control of the tone by the speaker keeps the voice sustained and vibrant with no wobble or quaver.

SUPPORT OF TONE: DIRECTIONS

1.02 The muscles used in breathing alternate in tension and relaxation. The speaker working for support of tone fills the lungs with air and then, in speaking, exhausts that air slowly in the articulation of sounds. He learns to control the exhalation of air from the beginning of the unit of speech until the end. Soon this support of tone and the economical use of air become automatic.

1.03 To identify what happens in breathing, lie flat on a hard bed or on the floor as you might in a gymnasium. Place the heel of the palm of the hand against a correspond- ing hip bone. Let the palms and fingers rest flatly against the abdomen, just below the lowest ribs. The tips of the fingers may or may not touch, but notice the distance, if any, between the tips of the fingers of both hands.

Now, take a deep breath. The fingertips of both hands spread apart as you breathe air into the lungs and the ab- dominal wall moves outward. Let out the breath *slowly*. Notice that, as the air in the lungs diminishes, the distance between the fingertips dimnishes. In effective breathing for speech, the deep breath that moves the abdominal wall out- ward is more efficient than the breath quickly drawn into the lungs during which the chest cavity is raised.

The process of breathing for speech is similar to that used in swimming. In both processes, the object is to expend out- going air economically—in speaking, this economy strength- ens the voice and allows the speaker to reach the end of a phrase without gasping for additional breath or producing a quaver in the tone. In your exercises, control the exhalation of the breath by a steady contraction of the abdominal mus- cles through the use of pressure from below. If you do this, a sustaining column of air passes up through the "windpipe" to activate the vocal bands in the larynx, producing a sus- tained vocal tone.

1.04 Pronounce the vowel *a* as in *father* as a prolonged sound. This vowel is the same sound as that which the doctor asks you to say when he wants to look down into your throat. Hold this *a* sound; keep the pitch steady and the loudness constant. Listen carefully for any quaver or wobble in the tone. Sustain the spoken note in full open tone just as you would in singing. In all of your practice with the exercises, aim toward a feeling of openness and ease in speaking.

1.05 Count slowly from *one* through *five,* keeping the tone clear and full and the articulation open and easy. Whenever possible, hold the sound at the end of one word and allow it to glide, or blend, into the first sound of the word that follows.

One .... two .... three .... four .... five
or
Wunnnnnnnntooooooooothreeeeeeefourrrrrrrfivvvvvv

Now, using the same process, count through *seven;* keep the same objectives and the same control. Place your hand on the abdominal wall during the process. You will feel a contraction, a kind of "push," on each of the numbers as you say them. Next, blend the sounds one into another so that you do not have individual "push" at the initiation of each of the numbers.

One ... two ... three ... four ... five ... six ... seven

Next, count from one through ten on *one* breath. Continue to hold the sounds and to blend whenever possible.

One .. two .. three .. four .. five .. six .. seven .. eight .. nine .. ten

If you prefer, you may substitute the names of the letters of the alphabet—*A, B, C,* etc.—for the numbers.

1.06 Now, transfer the technique suggested in the preceding exercise to the speaking of short sentences. Sit erect or stand, but do not do so in any strained position. Do not pull back your shoulders, because such a distorted position tenses the muscles of the throat. These muscles need to be kept relaxed, so far as possible. The act of speaking requires the use of body muscles from the face to the feet.

EXERCISES

1.07 In speaking the following sentences, have a consciousness of the use of your entire body to integrate the exhalation of air with the initiation of spoken tone.

1. Good morning! Good afternoon! Good evening!
2. What time is it now?

3. Come back again tomorrow.
4. I'll take two more.
5. Give me one good reason.
6. Summer is coming.
7. Please sit down.
8. Try it again.
9. When will he be at home?
10. I've come to see Mr. Holmes.
11. He never answers the telephone.
12. They've gone to the movies.
13. John lives in Boston now.
14. The class meets at eleven A.M.
15. I've lost my gloves again.
16. They went to see A *Midsummer Night's Dream.*
17. He's studying Greek and Latin.
18. It's too hot in this room.
19. We ought to send him a telegram.
20. The assignment is not too long.

LONGER SENTENCES FOR CONTINUING THE VOCAL SOUND

1.08 Pay particular attention to the strength of your voice as it reaches the end of the sentence. The voice frequently weakens at this point, or becomes "toneless" or "scratchy." Don't allow it to fade away. Give the voice extra support as you approach the end of the sentence:

1. Hold on tightly! Watch the curves! Take a deep breath before the car goes down the slide!
2. Check all your measurements in Chemistry at least twice.
3. Write home every week; telephone once a month; and go home, if possible, every three months for a few days.
4. I haven't been to a concert or a theater since I have been here, but I have seen a number of second-rate TV shows.
5. Speech must be natural, easy, audible, and the pronunciations have to be consistent with the cultural standard of the community.
6. Papers typed for class reports must be read at least twice for errors before they are handed to the instructor.
7. Hello! How are you? I haven't seen you for some time. Where have you been?
8. The first day of the month, and nothing in the mail except bills!

9. Many people make the mistake of judging a person's personality to be an indication of his true character.
10. Extracurricular activities are non-academic responsibilities of the student. They carry no course credit in the registrar's records.
11. Admission to medical, dental, law, and other professional schools is based on course grades, personal recommendations, aptitude tests, and proof of good behavior during the four years of college.
12. There are so many cultural advantages to a city that many students are bewildered which ones to try first.
13. Gym takes too much time! Ten minutes to undress and dress; thirty-five for exercise; ten minutes, or more, to shower, and dress again; and then you get to the next class tired out and hungry.
14. Tomorrow we have a quiz. Monday a paper is due, and next Friday there is a Geology field trip for which a paper must be written by the following Wednesday.
15. To major in mathematics, a student should have calculus in his first year at college.
16. It was one o'clock before I finished studying, and then I had to write a paper for my nine o'clock class. You see how much sleep I had.
17. When Dad says "No" he means *probably,* unless it is about money, and then he really means "No."
18. Keep to the right on the highway and don't drive faster than forty miles an hour.
19. Before class, go over your notes of the last meeting. It will help considerably.
20. After college, I hope to go to graduate school or else get a $20,000-a-year job as an executive.

LONGER SELECTIONS FOR SPEAKING WITH STRENGTH AND CONTROL

1.09

1. The world is too much with us; late and soon,
   Getting and spending, we lay waste our powers:
   Little we see in Nature that is ours . . .
                          WILLIAM WORDSWORTH, "Sonnet."

2. Ever let the Fancy roam,
   Pleasure never is at home:

At the touch sweet Pleasure melteth,
Like to bubbles when rain pelteth;
Then let winged Fancy wander
Through the thought still spread beyond her:
Open wide the mind's cage-door,
She'll dart forth, and cloudward soar.

JOHN KEATS, "Fancy."

3. Tell me where is fancy bred
   Or in the heart or in the head?
   How begot, how nourished?
        Reply, reply.
   It is engend'red in the eyes,
   With gazing fed; and fancy dies
   In the cradle where it lies.
        Let us all ring fancy's knell;
        I'll begin it,—ding, dong, bell.
        WILLIAM SHAKESPEARE, *The Merchant of Venice,* III, ii.

4. Loveliest of trees, the cherry now
   Is hung with bloom along the bough,
   And stands about the woodland ride
   Wearing white for Eastertide.

A. E. HOUSMAN, "No. II," *A Shropshire Lad.*[*]

5. At length they all to merry London came,
   To merry London, my most kindly nurse,
   That to me gave life's first native source:
   Though from another place I take my name,
   An house of ancient fame.
   There when they came, whereas those bricky tow'rs,
   The which on Thames' broad aged back do ride,
   Where now the studious lawyers have their bowers,
   There whilom wont the Templar Knights to bide,
   Till they decay'd through pride:
   Next whereunto there stands a stately place,
   Where oft I gained gifts and goodly grace
   Of that great Lord, which therein wont to dwell,
   Whose want too well, now feels my friendless case:
   But Ah, here fits not well
   Old woes but joys to tell

Against the bridal day, which is not long:
Sweet Thames run softly, till I end my song.
EDMUND SPENSER, *Prothalamion*, 8.

6. I have neither the scholar's melancholy, which is emulation; nor the musician's, which is fantastical; nor the courtier's, which is proud; nor the soldier's, which is ambitious; nor the lawyer's, which is politic; nor the lady's, which is nice; nor the lover's, which is all these: but it is a melancholy of mine own, compounded of many simples, extracted from many objects; and indeed the sundry contemplation of my travels, in which my often rumination wraps me in a most humorous sadness—
WILLIAM SHAKESPEARE, *As You Like It*, IV, i.

7. A strikingly heavy proportion of the college men had gone to Harvard or Yale, or to such outposts of the New England educational tradition as Amherst, Brown, Williams, Dartmouth, and Oberlin.
RICHARD HOFSTADTER, "Idealists and Professors and
Sore-Heads. The Genteel Reformers,"
Columbia University Forum.*

8. The possibility of a lasting peace depended upon the successful outcome of the conferences over which these men presided. Wilson stated his expectations in a speech he made on arriving in France: "Friends, men, humble women, little children, we are here; we are here as your friends, as your companions, as your representatives . . ."
HENRY F. GRAFF and JOHN A. KROUT, *The Adventure
of the American People.*†

9. Suddenly the notes of the deep-laboring organ burst upon the ear, falling with doubled and redoubled intensity, and rolling, as it were, huge billows of sound. How well do their volume and grandeur accord with this mighty building! With what pomp do they swell through its vast vaults, and breathe their awful harmony through these caves of death, and make the silent sepulchre vocal!—
And now they rise in triumph and acclamation, heaving higher and higher their accordant notes, and piling sound on sound.
WASHINGTON IRVING, "Westminster Abbey."

10. Not much time will be gained, O Athenians, in return for the evil name which you will get from the detractors of the city,

* From *Columbia University Forum*, copyright 1962 by Columbia University.
† From *The Adventure of the American People*, copyright 1963 by Rand McNally & Co., now in its eighth printing.

who will say that you killed Socrates, a wise man; for they will call me wise, even though I am not wise, when they want to reproach you. If you had waited a little while, your desire would have been fulfilled in the course of nature. For I am far advanced in years, as you may perceive, and not far from death. I am speaking now not to all of you, but only to those who have condemned me to death. And I have another thing to say to them: You think that I was convicted because I had no words to the sort which would have procured my acquittal —I mean, if I had thought fit to leave nothing undone or unsaid. Not so; the deficiency which led to my conviction was not of words—certainly not. But I had not the boldness or impudence or inclination to address you as you would have liked me to do, weeping and wailing and lamenting, and saying and doing many things which you have been accustomed to hear from others, and which, as I maintain, are unworthy of me. I thought at the time that I ought not to do anything common or mean when in danger: nor do I now repent of the style of my defence; I would rather die having spoken in my manner, than speak in your manner and live.

PLATO, *The Apology*, translation by BENJAMIN JOWETT.

B. Securing a Sustained Tone

SUSTAINING A WELL-SUPPORTED TONE: EXPLANATION

2.01   After you have achieved a full tone, your next objective is to sustain that tone throughout a spoken idea. Within the sentence, groups of words expressing a thought or an aspect of a thought are held together by the sustained tone of the speaker. It is necessary, therefore, for the reader to examine a sentence to observe the units of meaning within it and, in his reading aloud, to bind together the parts that belong together. The guide mark for these segments of meaning is the slant line, /, placed before and after the segment that is to be spoken as a unit.

The effective speaker anticipates his pauses and has sufficient breath control to carry him through to the appropriate pauses. A firm, clear tone at the beginning of a sentence is not enough. That same clear, firm tone needs to be held throughout the entire utterance. The ability to sustain tone becomes automatic with most speakers.

Sustaining a Well-supported Tone: Directions

2.02   In the first exercises of this section, the slant lines indicate possible pauses in the flow of utterance. Unmarked passages follow in which you can work out your own scheme for reading sense groups. A single slant line, /, indicates a short pause. Two slant lines, / /, mean a longer pause or a complete stop.

In reading these passages, allow the final sounds of one word to run into the initial sounds of the next word. This process is called *blending*. This blending occurs most naturally if a final sound is an *m, n, ng, l, s,* or *sh,* or a vowel or diphthong. If you achieve proper blending, you will keep your speech from becoming choppy, jerky, or staccato. In working for blending, remember to articulate the sounds distinctly.

Marked Passages for Sense Groups

2.03

1. And the single question / now presented to the nation / is this /:/ shall a reactionary spirit / unfriendly to liberty / be permitted to subvert democratic-republican government / organized under constitutional forms /?/
   Governor Andrew, of Massachusetts, *Message to the Legislature,* January 5, 1861.

2. The Proposition is peace /./ Not peace through the medium of war /;/ not peace to be hunted through the labyrinth of intricate and endless negotiations /;/ not peace to arise out of universal discord, / fomented from principle, in all parts of the Empire /;/ not peace to depend on the judicial determination of perplexing questions / or the precise marking of the shadowy boundaries of a complex government /./ It is simple peace /;/ sought in its natural course and in its ordinary haunts /./
   Edmund Burke, *Speech Urging Conciliation with the Colonies,* 1775.

Unmarked Passages for Sense Groupings

2.04   Now indicate your own phrasing in the passages to follow. Then, paying attention to these marks, read the passages aloud with a sustained tone throughout the whole sense group.

1. I cannot do it; you cannot do it; no one, however skilled he is in government, can make reforms alone, unsupported, and without the greatest courage.

2. Take a No. 4 bus to Convent Avenue; transfer to a No. 3; and go to the end of that line. Then walk north three blocks until you reach DeKalb Avenue, and turn right.

3. She saved and saved and always saved, and then here and there, to this friend and to that, to one in her trouble and to the other in her joy in sickness, death, and weddings, or to make young people happy it always went, the hard earned money she had saved.

   GERTRUDE STEIN, "The Good Anna," from *Three Lives.* *

4. Let us acknowledge that you have a handsome profile City of New York, and get that over with.

   Long ago you were voted the most likely to succeed, and tonight the twelfth generation of Americans salutes you with the usual reference to your size, industry, accomplishments, glitter, and grandeur; also with special reference to the populace that takes you for its lawful address: the Manhattanese, Brooklynites, Astorians, Jamaicans, Bronxites, who think the rest of the world is all right to visit, but who wouldn't want to live anyplace but here.

   NORMAN CORWIN, "New York: A Tapestry,"
   Untitled and Other Radio Dramas.†

5. If there be any among us who would wish to dissolve this Union or to change its republican form, let them stand undisturbed as monuments of the safety with which error of opinion may be tolerated where reason is left free to combat it.

   THOMAS JEFFERSON, *First Inaugural Address, 1801.*

6. The King was in blue velvet, with diamond buttons; the hat was buttoned up with prodigious fine diamonds. The Queen was in black velvet, the Court being out of mourning only for that day. Princess Royal had white poudesoy [sic], embroidered with gold, and a few colours intermixed; the petticoat was very handsome, but the gown looked poor, it being only faced and robed with embroidery . . . The Prince of Wales was in mouse-coloured velvet, turned up with scarlet,

and very richly embroidered with silver; he dances very well, especially country-dances, for he has a great deal of spirit.

Mrs. Delany, "Birthday Ball of Queen Caroline, March
1, 1728," *The Autobiography and Correspondence
of Mary Granville, Mrs. Delany,* Vol. I.

7. I ran away from home with the circus,
Having fallen in love with Mademoiselle Estralada,
The lion tamer.
One time, having starved the lions
For more than a day,
I entered the cage and began to beat Brutus
And Leo and Gypsy.
Whereupon Brutus sprang upon me,
And killed me.
On entering these regions
I met a shadow who cursed me,
And said it served me right . . .
It was Robespierre!

Edgar Lee Masters, "Sam Hookey,"
Spoon River Anthology. *

8. Miss Helen Slingsby was my maiden aunt,
And lived in a small house near a fashionable square
Cared for by servants to the number of four.
Now when she died there was silence in heaven
And silence at her end of the street.
The shutters were drawn and the undertaker wiped his feet—
He was aware that this sort of thing had occurred before.
The dogs were handsomely provided for,
But shortly afterwards the parrot died too.
The Dresden clock continued ticking on the mantlepiece,
And the footman sat upon the dining-table
Holding the second maid on his knees—
Who had always been so careful while her mistress lived.

T. S. Eliot, "Aunt Helen," *Collected Poems 1909–1962.*†

9. If I told him would he like it. Would he like it if I told him.
Would he like it would Napoleon would Napoleon would
would he like it.

If Napoleon if I told him if I told him if Napoleon. Would he like it if I told him if I told him if Napoleon. Would he like it if Napoleon if Napoleon if I told him. If I told him if Napoleon if Napoleon if I told him. If I told him would he like it would he like it if I told him . . .

GERTRUDE STEIN, "If I Told Him a Completed Portrait of Picasso," *Portraits and Prayers.**

10.　　　I am certain that my fellow Americans expect that on my introduction into the Presidency I will address them with a candor and a decision which the present situation of our Nation impels. This is pre-eminently the time to speak the truth, the whole truth, frankly and boldly. Nor need we shrink from honestly facing conditions in our own country today. This great Nation will endure as it has endured, will revive and will prosper. So, first of all, let me assert my firm belief that the only thing we have to fear is fear itself—nameless, unreasoning, unjustified terror, which paralyzes needed efforts to convert retreat into advance. In every dark hour of our national life a leadership of frankness and vigor has met that understanding and support of the people themselves which is essential to victory. I am convinced that you will again give that support to leadership in these critical days.

FRANKLIN D. ROOSEVELT, *First Inaugural Address,* March 4, 1933.

11.　　　How far, in the name of heaven, O Catiline, do you mean to go before you cease abusing our patience? And furthermore, how long will that madness of yours make sport of us? To what lengths will you make a show of your unbridled audacity? Are you not disturbed, even a little, by the guard on the Palatine Hill by night; not at all by the patrols of the city guardians; not at all at the gathering together of the patriots; not at all that the place of holding the assembly has to be made most secure; not at all at the faces of these men here assembled? Do none of these have any effect on you? Do you not perceive that your plans are well known? Do you not see that your conspiracy is now held in check and understood by the information known to all men present? What did you do last night, what the night before last—where were you, who was called to plot with you, what plan did you concoct of which you think any one of us is unaware?

CICERO, *First Oration Against Catiline.*

12.　　　With malice toward none, with charity for all, with firmness in the right, as God gives us to see the right, let us strive

---

* From "If I Told Him a Completed Portrait of Piscasso" from *Portraits and Prayers* by Gertrude Stein. Copyright 1934 by The Modern Library, Inc.

on to finish the work we are in, to bind up the nation's wounds, to care for him who shall have borne the battle and for his widow and his orphan; to do all which may achieve and cherish a just and lasting peace among ourselves and with all nations.

ABRAHAM LINCOLN, *Second Inaugural Address,* March 4, 1865.

13. Whereas Dr. Jonathan Swift, Dean of St. Patrick's, Dublin, hath been credibly informed, that, on Friday the 13th of this instant February, a certain person did, in a public place, and in the hearing of a great number, apply himself to the Right Honourable the Lord Mayor of this city, and some of his brethren, in the following reproachful manner: "My lord, you and your city can squander away the public money, in giving a gold box to a fellow who hath libelled the government!" or words to that effect.

Now, if the said words, or words to the like effect, were intended against him the said Dean, and as a reflection on the Right Honourable the Lord Mayor, aldermen, and commons, for their decreeing unanimously, and in full assembly, the freedom of this city to the said Dean, in an honourable manner, on account of an opinion they had conceived of some services done by him the said Dean to this city, and to the kingdom in general—the said Dean doth declare, That the said words, or words to the like effect, are insolent, false, scandalous, malicious, and, in a particular manner perfidious. . . .

JONATHAN SWIFT, "Advertisement by Dr. Swift in his Defense Against Joshua, Lord Allen, February 18, 1729," *The Prose Works of Jonathan Swift, D.D.*

14. The most perfect work of poetry, says our master Aristotle, is tragedy. His reason is, because it is the most united; being more severely confin'd within the rules of action, time, and place. The action is entire, of a piece, and one, without episodes; the time limited to a natural day; and the place circumscribed at least within the compass of one town, or city. Being exactly proportion'd thus, and uniform in all its parts, the mind is more capable of comprehending the whole beauty of it without distraction.

JOHN DRYDEN, "Discourse Concerning Satire."

15. As soon as nature has made a mountain, she seems to regret it and she begins to tear it down. Then, once she has torn it down, she makes another—perhaps, as here, precisely where the former mountain had once towered. Speed the action up as in those movies of an opening flower, and the landscape of

the earth would seem as insubstantial and as phantasmagorical as the cloudscape of a thundery afternoon.

Joseph Wood Krutch, *Grand Canyon.* °

16.   For my Religion, though there be several Circumstances that might perswade the World I have none at all, (as the general scandal of my Profession, the natural course of my Studies, the indifference of my Behaviour and Discourse in matters of Religion, neither violently Defending one, nor with that common ardour and contention Opposing another;) yet, in despite hereof, I dare without usurpation assume the honourable Stile of a Christian.

Sir Thomas Browne, *Religio Medici,* Part I.

17.   Englishwomen, from the educational point of view, could give nothing until they approached forty years old. Then they become very interesting—very charming—to the man of fifty. The young American was not worth the young Englishwoman's notice, and never received it. Neither understood the other. Only in the domestic relation, in the country—never in society at large—a young American might accidentally make friends with an Englishwoman of his own age, but it never happened to Henry Adams. His susceptible nature was left to the mercy of American girls, which was professional duty rather than education as long as diplomacy held its own.

Henry Adams, *The Education of Henry Adams.*†

18.   A great painter, a great man, is born great—born for ever. No other person can ever approach or liken himself in the *slightest degree* to him. A man is born a painter as a hippopotamus is born a hippopotamus; and you can no more *make* yourself one than you can make yourself a giraffe. Moreover a great man's work always tells more in advancing him than other people's, so that the older other people are, the *farther they are off from* the great men . . .

John Ruskin, *Letters on Art and Literature,* 1854.

19.   It little profits that an idle king,
By this still hearth, among these barren crags,
Match'd with an aged wife, I mete and dole
Unequal laws unto a savage race,
That hoard, and sleep, and feed, and know not me.
I cannot rest from travel; I will drink

Life to the lees. All times I have enjoy'd
Greatly, have suffer'd greatly, both with those
That loved me, and alone; on shore, and when
Thro' scudding drifts the rainy Hyades
Vext the dim sea.

ALFRED, LORD TENNYSON, "Ulysses."

20.   Pausing again for a moment, she [Queen Elizabeth] continued in a deeper tone. "To be a king and wear a crown is a thing more glorious to them that see it than it is pleasant to them that bear it. The cares and troubles of a crown I cannot more fitly resemble than to the drugs of a learned physician, perfumed with some aromatical savour, or to bitter pills gilded over, by which they are made more acceptable or less offensive, which indeed are bitter and unpleasant to take."

LYTTON STRACHEY, Elizabeth and Essex.*

C. Reinforcing the Vocal Tone

LOUDNESS AND REINFORCEMENT OF TONE: EXPLANATION

3.01 The first responsibility of the speaker is to be heard. Usually he tries to accomplish this end by speaking loudly, but loudness, in time, tires the speaker and bores the listener. Means other than mere loudness achieve audibility and intelligibility and do not weary speaker or listener.

Composers of music use the notations *ppp* and *fff* to indicate the degree of softness or loudness expected in the playing of their music. Nevertheless, even if a passage is marked *ppp*, the composer expects every note of it to be heard distinctly by everyone in the audience. The speaker manages his own degrees of softness or loudness, and he, like the composer, must keep in mind that, whenever he "drops his voice," he must still be intelligible. He must have efficient control of his breathing and articulating mechanisms and, where possible, be able to adjust the resonating cavities, to send the sound distinctly to the ear of the remotest listener. Intelligibility of communication requires an adequate level of loudness suited to the size of the room, the number of lis-

* From *Elizabeth and Essex* by Lytton Strachey, published by Harcourt, Brace & World, Inc.

teners, and, on certain occasions, the system of sound transmission over which the speech is carried.

3.02   Loudness is not a measure of acoustic energy. If you say the words *hit* and *hot* with equal loudness, the measurable acoustic energy of the vowel in *hot* is considerably greater than that of the vowel in *hit*. One reason for this is that, in articulating the vowel /ɑ/ * of *hot*, the resonating cavity of the mouth is more open than it is for the vowel /ɪ/ in *hit*. If a speech tone enters the resonating cavities, it sets in vibration the air within the cavities and the tone reissues from the cavities with greater energy than when it entered. If, however, the tone meets with any obstruction in the cavities, such as mucus in the nasal passages, then it is said to be *damped*. You have experienced in your own speech the difference between a damped and a resonant, or reinforced, speech sound. When you have a cold, and the resonating cavities are stopped up, the tone is damped, but, when your head is clear, you usually experience resonant tone. You may even feel the vibrations of resonance in your nasal cavities.

3.03   Some resonating cavities change either their shape or their texture or both in the process of articulation. Those that do so are in the mouth and pharynx (a resonating area at the back of the throat). The jaws vary the size of the opening into the mouth; so also does the positioning of the tongue. In some positions, the tongue is soft in texture, as for the /ɔ/ in *call*, but it may be tensed, as for the /i/ in *be*. The insides of the cheeks can also change tension during articulation. The walls of the pharynx can be stretched and thus enlarged and the muscles tensed. When the muscles are relaxed, the pharynx resumes its normal aperture. These variations change the resonance of the speech tone. You can very easily illustrate this possibility by stretching and relaxing these cavities by yawning. By this process you can estimate the differences in the size of the opening into the throat area and the degree of tension at various moments.

In all of the exercises for resonance, direct the tone toward the hard palate, the bony part of the roof of the mouth.

---

* Symbols between slant lines are from the International Phonetic Alphabet. See pages 46–48.

When the sound strikes that solid area, it bounces off it and reaches the outer air without any damping. Thus, the hard palate becomes a sounding board in your speaking.

EXERCISES FOR REINFORCEMENT OF TONE: DIRECTIONS

3.04 Sit firmly in a chair, or stand erect. Do not be stiff and tense, but maintain some muscular tonus, necessary for all speaking. Breathe deeply. On exhaling, let the air pressure come from below in a slow, steady, controlled impulse. Avoid quick, short gasps.

Say the vowel *a* as in *father* at *ppp,* and then gradually increase in loudness to *fff* but without a quaver in the tone. Do not force a loud sound; instead, try to open up the resonating cavities throughout the procedure so that you begin to feel the sound in those cavities.

The following sentences are constructed with speech sounds that can be easily reinforced, or resonated in the particular cavities of the mouth, nose, and pharynx. The "front" of the mouth is the area of the gum ridge and the hard palate; the "back" of the mouth is the area of the pharynx; and the "nasal" cavities are those of the nasal passages. Do not allow any of these sounds to be muffled or damped. Keep them clear and sustained.

FRONT

3.05

1. Fat, black cats sat on the rafters.
2. They managed to track back and find the facts of the matter.
3. Careful dentists check each tooth for cavities.
4. Sleet fell on the streets and made driving dangerous.
5. She glared wide-eyed at the diamond bracelet, and then said "Thanks."

NASAL

3.06

1. Many moons ago, those who saw her in all her beauty were made mad, or mildly mixed up.

2. Naught now frightened the mountain lion on the mesa.
3. On the wings of night, she flew toward Reno, the law, and freedom.
4. *Bing-bang, ping-pong* broke the morning silence of the dawn patrol.
5. Tomato plants need plenty of sun and the warm earth.

BACK

3.07

1. The yawl was caught in a bad squall off Long Island.
2. Hold the Fourth of July open for other engagements.
3. Harvest on a large farm is no holiday.
4. The sloop was marooned in a calm backwater harbor.
5. A bull in a china shop can run up a large bill for the owner.

GENERAL EXERCISES FOR REINFORCEMENT OF TONE

3.08

1. one, TWO, THREE!
2. On your marks! Get Set! GO!
3. Right, left! Right, left! Right, left!
4. Forward . . . . . MARCH!
5. Right, FACE! About, FACE!
6. Going, going, GONE!
7. If at first you don't succeed, try, try again.
8. Keep going as long as you can, please.
9. Ouch! The water's hot!
10. Don't tell me they've made another touchdown!
11. Fight the good fight! Defend the right!
12. Tippecanoe and Tyler too!
13. Say it again, and say it louder—and smile.
14. Down the hatch, brother, down the hatch, I say.
15. Oh, what a beautiful morning—or is it morning?
16. God for Harry, England and St. George!
17. Sail on, O Ship of State, sail on!
18. Here's to the Queen of the May, and I'll add of June, July, and August, too.
19. Hail, hail, the gang's all here.
20. It was seven feet high, four feet wide, and three feet thick, and weighed twenty-one hundred pounds. And my, what it cost!

Longer Selections for Reinforcement of Tone

3.09 Practice reading the following exercises in a full, firm voice, keeping in mind all the advice in the previous sections, from **1.01** on.

1. Now strike the Golden Lyre again;
   A louder yet, and yet a louder Strain.
   Break his Bands of Sleep asunder,
   And rouse him like a rattling peal of thunder.
   > John Dryden, "Alexander's Feast."

2. A thousand hearts are great within my bosom.
   Advance our standards! set upon the foes!
   Our ancient word of courage, fair Saint George,
   Inspire us with the spleen of fiery dragons:
   Upon them; Victory sits on our helms.
   > William Shakespeare, *Richard the Third,* V, iii.

3. Away, away, my steed and I
      Upon the pinions of the wind,
      All human dwellings left far behind;
   We sped like meteors through the sky,
      When with its crackling sound the night
      Is chequer'd with the northern light.
   > Lord Byron, "Mazeppa."

4. Hear the tolling of the bells,
   Iron bells!
   What a world of solemn thought their melody compels!
   > Edgar Allen Poe, "The Bells."

5. Oh, to be in England
   Now that April's there,
   And whoever wakes in England
   Sees, some morning, unaware,
   That the lowest boughs and the brushwood sheaf
   Round the elm-tree bole are in tiny leaf,
   While the chaffinch sings on the orchard bough
   In England—now!
   > Robert Browning, "Home Thoughts from Abroad."

6. Over the mountains
   And over the waves
   Under the fountains
   And under the graves;

Under floods that are deepest,
Which Neptune obey,
Over rocks that are steepest,
Love will find out the way.

ANONYMOUS

7. O Mighty-Mouth'd inventor of harmonies,
    O skill'd to sing of Time and Eternity,
    God-gifted organ-voice of England,
        Milton, a name to resound for ages:

ALFRED, LORD TENNYSON, "Milton."

8. Fifteen men on the Dead Man's Chest—
        Yo-ho-ho, and a bottle of rum!
    Drink and the devil had done for the rest—
        Yo-ho-ho, and a bottle of rum!

ROBERT LOUIS STEVENSON, *Treasure Island.*

9. The tide rises, the tide falls,
    The twilight darkens, the curlew calls;
    Along the sea-sands damp and brown
    The traveller hastens toward the town,
    And the tide rises, the tide falls.

HENRY WADSWORTH LONGFELLOW, "The Tide Rises, The
Tide Falls," *Ultima Thule.*

10. The splendour falls on castle walls
        And snowy summits old in story;
    The long light shakes across the lakes,
        And the wild cataract leaps in glory.

    Blow, bugle, blow, set the wild echoes flying,
    Blow, bugle; answer, echoes, dying, dying, dying.

ALFRED, LORD TENNYSON, *The Princess.*

11. All the bells of heaven may ring,
    All the birds of heaven may sing,
    All the wells on earth may spring,
    All the winds on earth may bring
        All sweet sound together.

ALGERNON SWINBURNE, "A Child's Laughter."

12. Desire! Desire, I have too dearly bought
        With price of mangled mind thy worthless ware;
    Too long, too long asleep thou hast me brought
        Who should my mind to higher things prepare.

But yet in vain thou hast my ruin sought,
　In vain thou mad'st me to vain things aspire,
　In vain thou kindlest all thy smoky fire
For virtue hath this better lesson taught,
　Within myself to seek my only hire,
　Desiring naught but how to kill desire.

Sɪʀ Pʜɪʟɪᴘ Sɪᴅɴᴇʏ, "Desire."

13. The melting voice through mazes running;
　Untwisting all the chains that tie
　The hidden soul of harmony.

Jᴏʜɴ Mɪʟᴛᴏɴ, *L'Allegro.*

14. . . . there lies at this moment in Newgate, under sentence to be burnt alive, a girl just turned fourteen; at her master's bidding, she hid some white-washed farthings behind her stays, on which the jury has found her guilty, as an accomplice with her master in the treason. The master was hanged last Wednesday; and the faggots all lay ready—no reprieve came till just as the cart was setting out, and the girl would have been burnt alive on the same day, had it not been for the humane but casual intereference of Lord Weymouth. Sir, we are taught to execrate the fires of Smithfield, and we are lighting them now to burn a poor harmless child for hiding a white-washed farthing! And yet this barbarous sentence, which ought to make men shudder at the thought of shedding blood for such trivial causes, is brought as a reason for more hanging and burning.

Sɪʀ Wɪʟʟɪᴀᴍ Mᴇʀᴇᴅɪᴛʜ, *Speech in the
House of Commons,* May 13, 1777.

II. EXERCISES FOR INTELLIGIBILITY OF SPEECH

A. Articulating the Flow of Speech

Aʀᴛɪᴄᴜʟᴀᴛɪᴏɴ ᴡɪᴛʜ Eᴀsᴇ ᴀɴᴅ Aɢɪʟɪᴛʏ: Eхᴘʟᴀɴᴀᴛɪᴏɴ

4.01 Precision and accuracy of articulation of vowels, diphthongs, glides, and consonants depend upon the conscious coordination of the muscles involved in the production of the sounds of speech. These muscles include those in the throat attached to the bony structure of the chest and terminating in the lower jaw; the tongue, a single muscle from its root to its tip in the front of the mouth; the muscles for raising and lowering the soft palate (velum); the lips; and many smaller muscles within the facial area. All of these muscles work in coordination with the muscles used in breathing. In speaking with ease and agility, the integration of the action of all of these muscles is performed unconsciously. The speaker who consciously uses these muscles in practice will notice their existence as he never has before.

4.02 The speaker who has accuracy of articulation is aware of the proper sounds to be uttered and makes the necessary muscular adjustments easily and quickly. He realizes that some alphabetical letters are silent in pronunciation. For example, no /b/ is sounded in *plumb;* no /t/ occurs in the pronunciation of *soften;* no /l/, in *half.* In some words, the spelled letters have no correspondence to sound, such as the *-ed* in *asked,* the *c* in *ocean,* and the *s* in *has.* Precision in articulation does not mean, therefore, articulation that slavishly follows the letters of the alphabet. (See Section III, on *Assimilation.*) It does not mean sounding every letter in every word, but it does mean uttering those that are sounded in general good usage.

BLENDING

4.03 In all exercises, wherever possible, blend the final sound of a word into the adjacent oncoming sound. This blending does not mean, however, fusing sounds to form unintelligible clusters of vowels and consonants. An analogy may be made to a "wet paper" watercolor wherein one color runs into an adjacent color unless it is stopped by some dry spot on the paper. Much the same process occurs in speaking or reading aloud; one word blends into the next word unless a stop consonant (such as /t/, /d/, /p/, /b/, etc.) or a break in the sense checks the blending.

The purpose of blending is to consolidate, wherever it is possible, the words of a sense group into a unit of meaning. This continuity of sound is possible when a nasal sound such as /m/ or /n/ ends the word. Then, the sound can be prolonged into the initial sound of the next word. The same continuity is obtained with final sounds such as /s/, /z/, /l/, /f/, and /v/. Keep in mind that continuity of sound requires sufficient breath for a sustained tone so that the speaker finishes the end of the phrase or sentence without a quaver in the tone.

SENTENCE EXERCISES FOR EASE, AGILITY OF ARTICULATION, AND BLENDING

4.04 Be sure to articulate the consonants clearly; get good firm support of tone to the end of the sense group. Observe blending wherever the opportunity occurs.

1. Put toothpicks in each of the frankfurters.
2. Keep pulling on the rope to stretch it tightly.
3. The shadows of the late afternoon helped the other team.
4. We packed everything you had asked us to bring.
5. By twisting the top of the jar instead of pulling on it, you save a great deal of strength.
6. Choose any book you want from the list; read it thoroughly; then write a paper of three hundred words about it.
7. Twinkle, twinkle little star, do you wonder what we are?
8. Cincinnati, Chattanooga, Columbus, and Chicago have little in common except that their names are all spelled with the same initial consonant.
9. The children's playroom was a shambles of toys, boxes, and scattered crayons.
10. Handle carefully. Use no hooks. Keep this side up.
11. Wisteria and trumpet vines send their tendrils under the shingles and clapboards.
12. Yukon, Yokohama, Yalta, Yukatat, and Yakima are also names of telephone exchanges.
13. Before she sold the Chevrolet, she had already bought a Buick.
14. The contract can be terminated in writing, by either one of the parties, before the 10th of January of next year.
15. In the medieval university, games of ball were suspect, and dancing was considered the invention of the devil.
16. Phonemics and phonetics are different disciplines in the scientific investigation of the sounds of speech.
17. The MacDonalds, the MacFerrits, and the MacPhersons were Highland neighbors, but they were not friends.

18. The Penobscot Valley is inhabited by sturdy New England people, not Indians.
19. A quart of milk, please; fifty cents worth of cheese; a chicken for broiling; and a dozen eggs.
20. Whatever direction one turns in San Francisco, he has a pleasant view; and each view has its own weather either of fog or sunshine; but, if is of fog, it is sure to be a most beautiful fog.

Consonant Combinations for Agility

4.05 Speakers have more difficulties with some consonants than with others. Below are listed some of the consonant combinations that present some of those difficulties. Form the consonants precisely, but, at the same time, get ease and assurance in their pronunciation.

Here are some pairs of words wherein the presence or absence of a sound makes a difference in meaning:

ducks—ducts	toughs—tufts
wax—waxed	mass—masts
acts—axe	gasps—grasps
tracks—tracts	risks—wrists
graphs—grafts	masked—massed

Sentences with Consonant Combinations

4.06

1. He asked if he had the receipts for the bill.
2. He bathes the baby whenever he acts as nursemaid.
3. We missed the facts that masked his action.
4. The fifth-graders played basketball with the sixth-graders.
5. The length of a basketball player's legs is not an indication of the strength of the muscles.
6. The myths of the Goths are some of the ghosts of literature.
7. Since he had already quit ten times, it was hard to get him to work there again.
8. As soon as the horse dropped into second position in the race, the rider lost his spirit for winning.
9. He drank the waters for his health's sake.
10. He builds well who builds for years to come.

11. He tried to bequeath the estate to his friends, but, since the butler ruled him with an iron hand, he left it all to the butler's second wife.
12. The Picts clothed themselves with heavy animal skins in winter, but in summer they painted their bodies.
13. Three-hundredths of the land was left to the corporation of the city, for the benefit of the citizens.
14. The pests that infect city houses are not eliminated by regular use of an insecticide.
15. There is no way in which to cover dishonest tracks by writing tracts on "Honesty."
16. Who but the very rich and some Africans have seen the cataracts of the Victoria Falls?
17. The masts of the anchored craft in the little harbor of Newport waited for the fog to lift.
18. Five-twelfths of the amount was held back by the decree of the court.
19. When he grasped me, I gasped. It was none other than Beelzebub himself.
20. A good crop yields forty casks of wine; but we have had poor crops in recent years and have been able only to raise enough grapes for a few fifths.

LONGER EXERCISES: EASE, ARTICULATION, AND BLENDING

4.07 In the following passages, keep in mind the sustained tone, the agility of muscles, and the smooth blending necessary for good speaking. The sounds must be sharp and distinct; but do not sound pedantic or as if you felt that every syllable had to have equal emphasis with the others.

1. To be rougher and tougher
   Strengthened and lengthened
   More assured and less sanguine,
   I drink goat's milk with black bread
   For breakfast and supper,
   But for dinner a beefsteak
   A good fire and rich old ale.

   ANONYMOUS

2. Boot, saddle, to horse, and away!
   Rescue my castle before the hot day
   Brightens to blue from its silvery grey
   Boot, saddle, to horse, and away!

Ride past the suburbs, asleep as you'd say;
Many's the friend there, will listen and pray
"God's luck to gallants that strike up the lay—
Boot, saddle, to horse, and away!"

ROBERT BROWNING, "Cavalier Tunes."

3.   Over the sea our galleys went,
With cleaving prows in order brave
To a speeding wind and a bounding wave,
A gallant armament:
Each bark built out of a forest-tree
Left leafy and rough as first it grew.
And nailed all over the gaping sides,
Within and without, with black bull-hides,
Seethed in fat and suppled in flame,
To bear the playful billows' game:
So, each good ship was rude to see,
Rude and bare to the outward view,
But each upbore a stately tent
Where cedar pales in scented row
Kept out the flakes of dancing brine,
And an awning drooped the mast below,
In fold on fold of the purple fine,
That neither noontide nor starshine
Nor moonlight cold which maketh mad,
Might pierce the regal tenament.

ROBERT BROWNING, *Paracelsus*, IV.

4.   Trochee trips from long to short;
From long to long in solemn sort
Slow Spondee stalks; strong foot! yea ill able
Ever to come up with Dactyl trisyllable.
Iambics march from short to long;—
With a leap and a bound the swift Anapaests throng;
One syllable long, with one short at each side,
Amphibrachys hastes with a stately stride;—
First and last being long, middle short, Amphimacer
Strikes his thundering hoofs like a proud high-bred Racer.

SAMUEL TAYLOR COLERIDGE, "Metrical Feet."

5.   When the hounds of spring are on winter's traces,
The mother of months in meadow plain
Fills the shadows and windy places
With lisp of leaves and ripple of rain;

And the brown bright nightingale amorous
Is half assuaged for Itylus,
And the Thracian ships and the foreign faces,
  The tongueless vigil, and all the pain.
>   ALGERNON CHARLES SWINBURNE, "Atalanta."

6. So it fell on a time King Arthur said unto Merlin, My barons
   will let me have no rest, but needs I must take a wife, and I
   will none take but by the counsel and by thine advice. It is
   well done, said Merlin, that ye take a wife, for a man of your
   bounty and noblesse should not be without a wife. Now is
   there any that ye love more than another? Yea, said King
   Arthur, I love Guenever the king's daughter, Leodegrance of
   the land of Cameliard, the which holdeth in his house the
   Table Round that ye told he had of my father Uther. And
   this damosel is the most valiant and fairest lady that I know
   living, or yet that ever I could find.
>   SIR THOMAS MALORY, *Le Morte D'Arthur,*
>   Book III, Chapter 1.

7. After every storm, whether stirred up by his private rashness
   or by a world-wide revolution, Goya, the successful egoist, always emerged on top, his vitality, his creative energy and his
   prestige undisturbed. Such ability and imposing self-regard
   might perhaps have equipped him for a political career, rising
   from a district leadership to a ministry of state, but he gained
   equivalent worldly success and he won it as an artist.
>   A. PHILIP MCMAHON, "Goya, the First Modern,"
>   *The Arts,* August, 1926.

8. When you're lying awake with a dismal headache, and repose
     is taboo'd by anxiety,
   I conceive you may use any language you choose to indulge in,
     without impropriety;
   For your brain is on fire—the bedclothes conspire of usual
     slumber to plunder you:
   First your counterpane goes, and uncovers your toes, and
     your sheet slips demurely from under you;
   Then the blanketing tickles—you feel like mixed pickles—so
     terribly sharp is the pricking,
   And you're hot, and you're cross, and you tumble and toss till
     there's nothing 'twixt you and the ticking.
   Then the bedclothes all creep to the ground in a heap, and you
     pick 'em all up in a tangle;
   Next your pillow resigns and politely declines to remain at its
     usual angle!

Well, you get some repose in the form of a doze, with hot eye-
balls and head ever aching,

But your slumbering teems with such horrible dreams that
you'd very much better be waking;

For you dream you are crossing the Channel, and tossing about
in a steamer from Harwich—

Which is something between a large bathing machine and a
very small second-class carriage—

And you're giving a treat (penny ice and cold meat) to a party
of friends and relations—

They're a ravenous horde—and they all came on board at
Sloane Square and South Kensington Stations.

And bound on that journey you find your attorney (who started
that morning from Devon);

He's a bit undersized, and you don't feel surprised when he
tells you he's only eleven.

Well, you're driving like mad with this singular lad (by the
by, the ship's now a four-wheeler),

And you're playing round games, and he calls you bad names
when you tell him that "ties pay the dealer";

But this you can't stand, so you throw up your hand, and you
find you're as cold as an icicle,

In your shirt and your socks (the black silk with gold clocks),
crossing Salisbury Plain on a bicycle:

And he and the crew are on bicycles too—which they've somehow or other invested in—

And he's telling the tars all the particulars of a company he's
interested in—

It's a scheme of devices, to get at low prices all goods from
cough mixtures to cables

(Which tickled the sailors), by treating retailers as though they
were all vegetables—

You get a good spadesman to plant a small tradesman (first
take off his boots with a boot-tree),

And his legs will take root, and his fingers will shoot, and they'll
blossom and bud like a fruit-tree—

From the greengrocer tree you get grapes and green pea,
cauliflower, pineapple, and cranberries,

While the pastrycook plant cherry brandy will grant, apple
puffs, and three-corners, and Banburys—

The shares are a penny, and ever so many are taken by
Rothschild and Baring,

And just as a few are allotted to you, you awake with a shudder
despairing—

You're a regular wreck, with a crick in your neck, no wonder
you snore, for your head's on the floor, and you've needles
and pins from your soles to your shins, and your flesh is
a-creep, for your left leg's asleep, and you've cramp in your
toes, and a fly on your nose, and some fluff in your lung,
and a feverish tongue, and a thirst that's intense, and a
general sense that you haven't been sleeping in clover;

But the darkness has passed, and it's daylight at last, and the
night has been long—ditto ditto my song—and thank
goodness they're both of them over!

W. S. GILBERT, *Iolanthe,* II.

B. Determining Rate of Speaking

RATE OF SPEAKING AND RATE OF COMPREHENSION:
EXPLANATION

5.01 The aim of every speaker or reader is to be understood by his listeners. If, however, he speaks or reads too
rapidly or too slowly for the comprehension of the listener,
his purpose will be lost. Articulation, projection, and phrasing are important, but, if the flow of speech is too rapid or
too slow, the speaker will lose the attention of the listener,
and excellence in these factors will go for nothing.

The nature of the material read, or spoken, determines,
in great part, the rate of utterance. No one would, consciously, rush through a reading of the Twenty-third Psalm,
nor would one presume to slow down the tempo of one of
the patter songs of Gilbert and Sullivan. Many Americans
assume that native speakers of Italian, Russian, Spanish, etc.,
speak those languages rapidly. They make this judgment
largely because the combinations of sounds in those languages are unfamiliar to them. Indeed, if a speaker of English speaks on a difficult subject, or one unfamiliar to his
audience, he may be thought by some to be speaking at an
incomprehensible rate.

5.02 How rapidly do you speak? It would be well for
you to find out so that, by comparison with standard rates,
you will be able to gauge whether or not you are speaking

too fast or too slowly. In adjusting your rate to standard rates of comprehension, you will find, if you are a rapid speaker, that slowing down will, at first, be uncomfortable for you, and you will have the impression that you are speaking too slowly. Conversely, if you are a slow speaker, speeding up will produce the impression that you are racing your speech. You should try to adjust your speaking rate to the limits found to be best suited for the comprehension of American audiences.

5.03   The most convenient way of determining rate of speaking is to estimate the rate of words you speak a minute. The method is, at best, a rough estimate, but it will serve our present purpose.

The first step in this process is to select material from the daily newspaper, or from current magazines, that you think approaches your sentence length and vocabulary. Do not select editorials from the newspaper, as they do not usually represent the type of sentence structure or vocabulary used in speaking. It would be preferable to select a news item or a sports account from the newspaper, or an informal expository article from a magazine.

5.04   After you have selected your material, read it aloud for fifteen seconds. Check your timing with the second hand of your watch or with a school clock. Count the number of words you read in this fifteen seconds. Multiply this number by four, and you have an estimate of the number of words you speak a minute. Take another sample from the same material. Determine your rate for that sample. Get several more estimates from other materials. You might well have a page in your notebook with estimates such as the following:

Estimate No.	Words per Minute	Kind of Material
1	330	Sports page
2	272	Columnist
3	140	Novel
4	186	Book review
5	210	Baseball game
6	190	News story
7	220	Obituary
7	1558	

From these seven estimates, your average of words per minute would be 222.1.

EXERCISES FOR TESTING RATE

5.05   If you want to find out your rate more readily than by the above procedure, read aloud one of the following selections, in which the words have been numbered in bold type. Numerals have been counted as they would be spoken.

1.   The new gymnasium, to be built over the rocks of Morningside Park, will fulfill a dream of over half a century.
          The building, which will [25] follow the natural terrain
of the park, will contain five floors of facilities. Approaching
the Morningside Drive level, the visitor will be led over a [50]
landscaped entrance court directly into the vestibule and lobby
of the gymnasium which will house the athletic trophies.
          Approximately 3,200 spectators will be [75] seated in the
double-tiered stands of the main gymnasium. Measuring 150'
× 120', the cleared main floor [100] will be used for various
activities of the physical education program.
          The $2,000,000 swimming pool wing will be able to ac-
commodate about 1,200 [125] spectators for a variety of
aquatic sports. The wing will contain a swimming and water
polo tank with six seven-foot-wide racing lanes, a [150] separate diving pool with two springboards and diving platforms
at fifteen and thirty feet, and a fifty meter above[175]-deck
glass walled Olympic training and teaching tank.
                              The Columbia Daily Spectator, New York,
                              Wednesday, May 23, 1962.

2.   It seems incredible, nevertheless it is true: By splitting the
latest of their interminable Sunday double-headers at the Stadium, the Yankees yesterday crawled back [25] into first place.
          With homers by Tom Tresh and Hector Lopez accounting
for five runs, they beat the Los Angeles Angels, 6–3, in the
[50] first game. The Angels won the second game, 12–5.
          And so this is the situation in the American League race:
          The Angels, who won [75] two of four here, have moved
into second place only three points behind the Yankees.
          By losing twice, the Cleveland Indians dropped to third
and [100] a virtual tie with the Minnesota Twins.
          The first four teams in the American League are grouped
within half a game and 12 percentage points. [125] A spread
of 3½ games covers the first seven clubs.

What will happen from now on is anybody's guess, but the proud [150] champions certainly expected nothing like this when the season began.

At flood tide, there were 34,618 customers in the [175] Stadium yesterday and those who stayed to the finish witnessed some notable events.

New York Herald Tribune, July 2, 1962. TOMMY HOLMES.

3.   The superliner United States will pass this week the tenth anniversary of her record-breaking maiden voyage when the 51,988[25]-gross-ton ship sets a speed mark by sailing across the Atlantic Ocean in 3 days 10 hours and 40 minutes. The mark still stands unchallenged [50] with little likelihood in this era of jet planes of any ship attempting to surpass it.

There will be no ceremonies marking the anniversary. The [75] big ship sailed Friday in routine manner with 1,755 passengers for Southhampton and Le Havre with few in the capacity [100] list aware that a decade has elapsed since their ship set her amazing record.

Indeed, the United States has set several other marks in her [125] first ten years of service on the popular North Atlantic runs. For one thing, she has clocked 1,605,000 miles [150] without a serious breakdown in the vast machinery that not only keeps her going but also furnishes air conditioning and hundreds of other comforts for [175] her passengers and crew.

The only delays encountered during her 226 round trips across the Atlantic and two West Indian cruises [200] were at her home pier at 46th St. and the Hudson River during the maritime strikes. Otherwise the huge ship has gone in and out [225] of the port with regularity of clockwork.

New York Herald Tribune, July 1, 1962. WALTER HAMSHAR.

4.   The Footprint

It happened one day, about noon, going towards my boat, I was exceedingly surprised with the print of a man's naked foot on the shore, [25] which was very plain to be seen in the sand. I stood there like one thunderstruck, or as if I had seen an apparition. I [50] listened, I looked around me, I could hear nothing, nor see anything. I went up to a rising ground, to look farther. I went up [75] the shore, and down the shore, but it was all one; I could see no other impression but that one. I went to it again [100] to see if there were any more, and to observe if it might not be my fancy; but there was no room for that, for [125] there was exactly the very print of a foot—toes, heel, and every part of a foot. How it came thither I knew not, nor [150] could in the least part imagine. But after innumerable fluttering thoughts, like a man perfectly confused and out of myself, I came home to my fortification, [175] not feeling, as we say, the ground I went on, but terrified to the last degree, looking behind me at every two or three steps, [200] mistaking every bush and tree, and fancying every stump at a distance to be a man; nor is it possible to describe how many various [225] shapes affrighted imagination represented things to me in, how many wild ideas were found every moment in my fancy, and what strange, unaccountable whimsies came [250] into my thoughts by the way.

DANIEL DEFOE, Robinson Crusoe.

5.06 Scientists and radio and TV broadcasters have investigated the rate at which people listen and comprehend. In the visual, face-to-face situation in movies and TV, that rate of comprehension is from 150 to 190 words a minute. In purely aural communication such as that by radio and telephone, the rate is somewhat lower.

Compare your rate of speaking with the rate of listener comprehension. If your figures tell you that you were too rapid, slow down. Make several more estimates to be sure that you have found the rate that suits—not yourself—but your listeners.

SUGGESTIONS TO KEEP IN MIND

5.07 In working for an appropriate rate of speaking, remember to keep these fundamentals in mind:

1. Pause at the ends of thought or sense groups. These breaks allow you to take a breath and also may permit your listener to catch up with you.
2. Clearly articulate all vowels and diphthongs, as well as consonants.
3. When they occur at the end of the word, blend such sounds as /m/, /n/, /l/, /s/, and /z/ into the beginning of the next word.
4. Vary your rate of speaking occasionally, according to your subject matter or your material. As a general rule, the more difficult the subject matter, the slower the rate at which it is given.

EXERCISES FOR PRACTICE ON RATE AND COMPREHENSION

5.08 In the first of the following selections, pauses have been indicated for your guidance. In all of the selections, remember to sustain your tone, articulate intelligibly, blend, and watch your rate.

1. Let no one marvel that Michelangelo loved solitude,/ for he was devoted to art,/ which claims man for himself alone;/ and because those who study must avoid society/ the minds of those who study art are constantly preoccupied,/ and those who consider this to be eccentricity are wrong,/ for he who would do well must avoid cares and vexations/ since genius demands thought,/ solitude/ and comfort,/ and a steadfast mind.

> Giorgio Vasari, *The Lives of the Painters,*
> *Sculptors and Architects,* translated by A. B. Hinds.*

2. "I was an infant when my mother went
    To see an atheist burned. She took me there.
    The dark-robed priests were met around the pile;
    The multitude was gazing silently;
    And as the culprit passed with dauntless mien
    Tempered disdain in his unaltering eye,
    Mixed with a quiet smile, shone calmly forth;"

> Percy Bysshe Shelley, *Queen Mab.*

3.   I was afterwards of a party at Sadler's-wells, where I saw such tumbling and dancing upon ropes and wires, that I was frightened and ready to go into a fit—I tho't it was all inchantment; and believing myself bewitched, began to cry—You know as how witches in Wales fly upon broom-sticks; but here was flying without any broom-sticks, or thing in the varsal world, and firing of pistols in the air, and blowing of trumpets, and swinging, and rolling of wheel-barrows upon a wire . . . no thicker than a sewing thread; that, to be sure, they must deal with the devil!

> Tobias Smollet, *Humphrey Clinker.*

Exercises for Determining Speaking Rate on Special Topics

5.09   Here is another method for determining your speaking rate: Look over the following list of topics. Choose one of them, and make a brief outline of what you would want to cover in a short talk on that subject. Think for a while about your talk. Then, if you have a recording machine in the language laboratory or at home, make the speech

---

* From *The Lives of the Painters, Sculptors and Architects,* Vol. 4, by Giorgio Vasari, published by E. P. Dutton & Co., Inc., Everyman's Library.

from your outline. Do not write out your speech, but speak from the notes you made. After you have recorded the speech, play it back and count the words you speak during any fifteen-second period of it. Multiply this figure by four for an estimate of your rate of words uttered per minute. Take several fifteen-second samples from your speech. The average of these various samples will give you a more accurate estimate of your rate of speaking when you use notes.

1. Describe the most efficient way to hold a certain golf club.
2. Explain what is meant by a "bicameral" legislature.
3. Present some proposals for increasing or decreasing the extracurricular activities at your school.
4. Formulate an argument for or against a liberal arts education.
5. Explain one of the following games: football, baseball, basketball, hockey, tennis.
6. Describe the registration process at your school.
7. Explain the law of supply and demand.
8. Indicate the reasons why our government should attempt to send men to the moon.
9. Present a program for reducing juvenile delinquency in your neighborhood.
10. Discuss the question of whether or not a social debut is necessary for a young girl.

C. Phrasing of Sense Groups

EXPLANATION

6.01 The comprehension of spoken English requires that the words be expressed in groups rather than pronounced as separate units. Meaning, in English, is carried by the phrase and is in this respect unlike, for example, Chinese. If the words are uttered individually, carved, so to speak, one from another, the listener has difficulty in putting together those words that belong to a central idea. The responsibility for this grouping of words rests with the speaker or reader.

PHRASING AND PUNCTUATION

6.02 Many speakers believe that they simplify the problem of pausing in reading aloud by a rule of thumb that says,

"Pause, or take a breath, at a mark of punctuation." It is not well to follow this rule blindly. For example, in reading aloud the sentence *The flag is red, white, and blue,* no pause is necessary at the commas. However, main marks of punctuation such as the semicolon, the colon, the period, and other *final* marks of a sentence usually require a pause.

ILLUSTRATIONS

6.03   The breaks (pauses, or holding of sounds) occur at the beginning and at the end of sense groups or word clusters. The moment of pause may sometimes be so short that the ear can barely distinguish it. The break between sense groups may also be signaled by the prolongation of the last sound in one sense group, which is held momentarily before the sounding of the first sound in the sense group that follows.

An illustration may make this clearer.

1. *Take eight steps backward;/ turn to the right,/ and bow to your partner/./*

In this sentence, the breaks are marked; they will be momentary silences, because both *backward* and *right* end in consonants that cannot be prolonged to the next sense group. The period represents, of course, a final pause.

2. *The law is definite in this matter/;/ it requires specific evidence/ and, in addition, / /proof/./*

Here, instead of momentary pauses, the last sound of *matter* can be prolonged into the *it* of the next sense group, the last sound in *evidence* prolonged into the *and* of the next sense group, and the final *n* in *addition* held a bit until the *p* in *proof* is pronounced.

6.04   In Section 2.03 may be found the system of indicating pauses. In the numbered selections that follow, breaks are indicated by combinations of slant lines and punctuation:

   / indicates a short pause or a prolongation of a sound.
   / / indicates a longer pause and may be the equivalent of a
      semicolon (/;/).

/:/ indicates a long pause.
/./ indicates a complete stop used for the end of a sentence
or at the beginning of a list of items.

The use of this system is illustrated in the following selections:

1. Today's weather map / is expected to show a high pressure / off the mid Atlantic coast / with a ridge extending southwest / to the Gulf of Mexico /./ A trough of low pressure / is due to run from the upper Great Lakes west-southwestward / to the central plains through the Rockies to the central Pacific coast /./ An area of high pressure / is likely from the northern plains to the upper Mississippi valley / / while centers of low pressure / are predicted in the central Rockies and in the central plains region /./

New York Herald Tribune, September 13, 1962.

It is well to remember that pauses, or breaks, do not necessarily come at the end of punctuated segments of the sentences, nor do they necessarily come at the ends of lines of poetry. Applying the same techniques to a passage from Milton's *Il Penseroso,* we have a reading that looks like this:

2. Or let my lamp/ at midnight hour,
Be seen in some high lonely tow'r,/
Where I may oft out-watch the Bear,
With thrice great Hermes,/ or unsphere
The spirit of Plato to unfold
What worlds,/ or what vast regions hold
The immortal mind that hath forsook
Her mansion in this fleshly nook:

D. Precision of Articulation in the Flow of Speech

EXERCISES IN PHRASING

6.05 Before reading aloud the following sentences, indicate the breaks you should make, by using the previously explained system of slant lines. See that your reading corresponds to your markings.

1. In the early morning, before breakfast, Henry brought a basket of apples picked from his own trees.

2. Sir Thomas More, though beset with personal and political problems, kept a calmness of thought and action at variance with the hotheads around him.

3. It was a dark and damp cell for an innocent man, darker and damper than needed for even the most guilty murderer.

4. No one knew the answer to the problem; no one tried even to find the answer.

5. I had told him not to do it, and what did he do? He did the very same thing over.

6. His wife had failed to light the fire in the furnace, and when he got home the place was an icebox, so you know what happened.

7. The dress had been marked down from $75 to $25, and, though you know I am impoverished, you also know what I did about it.

8. The big grasshopper made one tremendous jump across the sidewalk and then found nothing there and jumped back again where he had been.

9. Big game such as the elephant, rhinoceros, and water buffalo is found in Africa at the present time, but no one knows how long man will allow these animals to exist.

10. The thermometer registered zero, but there was a bright sun in the sky, and that indicated that the column of mercury would rise.

11. On a hot, humid night, a thick, fluffy down pillow is uncomfortable.

12. All unnecessary lights must be extinguished at least by eleven P.M., unless special permission has been secured from the Officer of the Day.

13. The judge looked solemn, and he spoke authoritatively, but the jury noticed that he frequently took a drink of buttermilk.

14. The top peaches on the tree, the peaches that are the most difficult to reach, are often the best for eating.

15. The sand dunes along the eastern shore of Lake Michigan are ideal for romping children and serve the older ones for sand skiing.

16. Football games in hot weather are unbearable for the team, the spectators, and the purse, because one has to drink too much lemonade and a girl's flowers always wilt.

17. Someone told him to stop picking blueberries from the bushes because he would leave none for the birds, but he

didn't do it and kept on picking so that he had blueberries for breakfast every morning in season and the birds had none.

18. The beach chair was painted pink for no reason except that there was a can of pink paint in the shed and the New England habit of saving dominated; it was for that reason, I guess, that the chair never dried all summer long.

19. The teacher named Hazel Smith tried to get the attention of the class without success, because Gladys Schmergerholzer had come to school with an entirely new fancy hairdo that caught all eyes and some hearts.

20. Everyone who has been in Washington, D.C., wants to see a senator or, if not a senator, a representative, but he has a better chance to see one if he stays home and sits by the television set during the days of electioneering.

LONGER SELECTIONS

6.06

1.   Prosperity and peace introduced the distinction of the *vulgar* and the Ascetic Christians. The loose and imperfect practice of religion satisfied the conscience of the multitude. The prince or magistrate, the soldier or merchant, reconciled their fervent zeal and implicit faith with the exercise of their profession, the pursuit of their interest, and the indulgence of their passions: but the Ascetics, who obeyed and abused the rigid precepts of the Gospel, were inspired by the savage enthusiasm which represents man as a criminal, and God as a tyrant. They seriously renounced the business and the pleasure of the age; abjured the use of wine, of flesh, and of marriage; chastised their body, mortified their affections, and embraced a life of misery, as the price of eternal happiness.

EDWARD GIBBON, *The Decline and Fall
of the Roman Empire,* Chapter 37.

2.   Happiness lies not in the mere possession of money; it lies in the joy of achievement, in the thrill of creative effort.

Joy and moral stimulation of work no longer must be forgotten in the mad chase of evanescent profits. These dark days will be worth all they cost us if they teach us that our true destiny is not to be ministered unto but to minister to ourselves and to our fellow-men.

FRANKLIN D. ROOSEVELT, *First Inaugural
Address,* March 4, 1933.

3.   You say we are sectional. We deny it. That makes an
issue and the burden of proof is upon you. You produce your
proof and what is it? Why, that our party has no existence in
your section—gets no votes in your section. The fact is sub-
stantially true; but does it prove the issue? If it does, then in
case we should, without change of principle, begin to get
votes in your section, we should thereby cease to be sectional.
You cannot escape this conclusion; and yet are you willing
to abide by it? If you are you will probably soon find that we
have ceased to be sectional, for we shall get votes in your section this very year.

ABRAHAM LINCOLN, Cooper Union Speech, 1860.

4. The pure contralto sings in the organ loft,
    The carpenter dresses his plank, the tongue of his foreplane
        whistles its wild ascending lisp,
    The married and unmarried children ride home to their
        Thanksgiving dinner.
    The pilot seizes the king-pin, he heaves down with a strong
        arm,
    The mate stands braced in the whale-boat, lance and harpoon
        are ready,
    The duck-shooter walks by silent and cautious stretches,
    The seasons are ordain'd with cross'd hands at the altar,
    The spinning-girl retreats and advances to the hum of the
        big wheel . . .

WALT WHITMAN, "Song of Myself," Section 15.

5.   It is not only highly desirable, but necessary, that there
should be legislation which shall carefully shield the interests
of wage-workers, and which shall discriminate in favor of the
honest and humane employer by removing the disadvantages
under which he stands when compared with unscrupulous
competitors who have no conscience, and will do right only
under fear of punishment.

THEODORE ROOSEVELT, Address at
State Fair of Minnesota, 1901.

6. As I went down the hill along the wall
        There was a gate I had leaned at for the view
        And had just turned from when I first saw you
    As you came up the hill. We met. But all
    We did that day was mingle great and small
        Footprints in summer dust as if we drew
        The figure of our being less than two

But more than one as yet. Your parasol
  Pointed the decimal off with one deep thrust.
And all the time we talked you seemed to see
  Something down there to smile at in the dust.
(Oh, it was without prejudice to me!)
  Afterward I went past what you had passed
Before we met and you what I had passed.

                ROBERT FROST, "Meeting and Passing." *

7.   The white people have no right to take the land from the Indians, because they had it first; it is theirs. They may sell, but all must join. Any sale not made by all is not valid. The late sale is bad. It was made by a part only. Part do not know how to sell. It requires all to make a bargain for all. All red men have equal rights to the unoccupied land. The right of occupancy is as good in one place as in another. There cannot be two occupations in the same place. The first excludes all others.

      TECUMSEH, *Speech at Vincennes on the Sale of Land to*
                      Governor Harrison, 1813.

8. At the round earth's imagin'd corners, blow
Your trumpets, Angels, and arise, arise
From death, you numberless infinities
Of souls, and to your scatter'd bodies go,
All whom the flood did, and fire shall o'erthrow,
All whom war, dearth, age, agues, tyrannies,
Despair, law, chance, hath slain, and you whose eyes,
Shall behold God, and never taste death's woe.
But let them sleep, Lord, and we mourn a space,
For, if above all these, my sins abound,
'Tis late to ask abundance of thy grace,
When we are there; here on this lowly ground,
Teach me how to repent; for that's as good
As if thou hadst seal'd my pardon, with thy blood.

               JOHN DONNE, *Holy Sonnets,* VII.

9.   I must now beg to ask, sir, whence is this supposed right of the states derived? Where do they find the power to interfere with the laws of the Union? Sir, the opinion which the honorable gentleman maintains is a notion founded in a total misapprehension, in my judgment, of the origin of this gov-

---

* From *Complete Poems of Robert Frost.* Copyright 1916, 1921 by Holt, Rinehart & Winston, Inc. Copyright renewed 1944 by Robert Frost. Reprinted by permission of Holt, Rinehart & Winston, Inc.

ernment, and of the foundation on which it stands. I hold it
to be a popular government, erected by the people; those who
administer it responsible to the people and itself capable of
being amended and modified, just as the people may choose
it should be. It is as popular, just as truly emanating from
the people, as the state governments. It is created for one
purpose; the state governments for another. It has its own
powers; they have theirs. There is no more authority with
them to arrest the operation of a law of Congress, than with
Congress to arrest the operation of their laws. We are here
to administer a constitution emanating immediately from the
people, and trusted by them to our administration. It is not
the creature of the state governments.

> DANIEL WEBSTER, *Reply to Hayne*, 1830.

10. Then quickly from the foughten field he sent
Ulfius, and Brastias, and Bedivere,
His new-made knights, to King Leodogran,
Saying, "If I in aught have served thee well,
Give me thy daughter Guinevere to wife."

Whom when he heard, Leodogran in heart
Debating—"How should I that am a king,
However much he holp me at my need,
Give my one daughter saving to a king
And a king's son?"—lifted his voice, and call'd
A hoary man, his chamberlain, to whom
He trusted all things, and of him required
His counsel: "Knowest thou aught of Arthur's birth?"

Then spake the hoary chamberlain and said:
"Sir King, there be but two old men that know;
And each is twice as old as I; and one
Is Merlin, the wise man that ever served
King Uther thro' his magic art, and one
Is Merlin's master—so they call him—Bleys,
Who taught him magic; but the scholar ran
Before the master, and so far that Bleys
Laid magic by, and sat him down, and wrote
All things and whatsoever Merlin did
In one great annal-book, where after-years
Will learn the secret of our Arthur's birth."

> ALFRED, LORD TENNYSON, "The Coming of Arthur,"
> *Idylls of the King.*

Chapter 2

American-English Sounds: Consonants, Vowels, Diphthongs

I. REPRESENTATION OF THE SOUNDS OF SPEECH

A. Spellings and Sounds

7.01 The International Phonetic Alphabet (hereafter referred to as the IPA) is one of several systems of notation for the sounds of speech by which one symbol of the alphabet indicates one and only one sound in speech. The spelling of English words confuses rather than clarifies, and the letters of the Roman alphabet do not carefully distinguish sounds. The *a* in *father* is one sound, but the *a* in *man* is another, and the *a* in *all* is still another sound. The *c* in *ocean* differs from the *c* in *cake* and the *c* in *cease. I read* may be either present or past tense, but, when this is put into the symbols of the IPA, there is no confusion: /aɪ rid/ and /aɪ rɛd/.

Below are given the symbols of the IPA, with key words to illustrate the sounds. In the next column are the diacritic symbols of *Webster's Third New International Dictionary,* and in the third column the symbols of *The American College Dictionary.*

The symbols of the IPA distinguish between the *voiced* consonants such as /b/, /d/, and /g/, in which the vocal bands are in vibration, and the *unvoiced,* or *voiceless,* consonants such as /p/, /t/, and /k/, in which the vocal bands are *not* in vibration. This difference between voiced and voiceless is indicated in the text. The IPA has several unfamiliar symbols such as the Old English *thorn*, ð, to indicate the voiced *th* in *then;* the Greek *theta*, θ, for the voiceless *th* in *thin;* and the mathematics integral sign, ʃ, to represent the voiceless sound of *sh* in *should.* The IPA also includes the *schwa*, ə, to represent an unstressed vowel, and the newer dictionaries use this symbol.

The IPA is perhaps the most widely used and internationally recognized of the systems of notation used to represent the sounds of speech. It can be easily assimiliated and is used for your reference in the pages to follow. The complete chart of the IPA includes modifications for many sounds and symbols for languages other than English. These marks and symbols are not necessary for the use of this text.

B. IPA Symbols and Diacritic Marks

7.02   *The Sounds Heard in American English.*

IPA symbol Consonants		Usual spelling equivalents	Equivalent diacritic marking in Webster's Third New International Dictionary	Equivalent diacritic marking in The American College Dictionary
p	p	(*pipe*), pp (*upper*)	p	p
b	b	(*bib*), bb (*rubber*)	b	b
t	t	(*toot*), tt (*little*)	t	t
d	d	(*dead*), dd (*riddle*)	d	d
k	k ck q	(*lake*), c (*cool*), (*luck*), ch (*chasm*), (*quiet*)	k	k
g	g gh	(*game*), gg (*rugged*), (*ghost*)	g	g
f	f ph gh	(*fine*), ff (*differ*), (*phonograph*), (*rough*)	f	f
v	v	(*vase*), f (*of*)	v	v
θ	th	(*think*)	th	th
ð	th	(*that*)	*th*	t͟h

IPA Symbols and Diacritic Marks (Cont.)

IPA symbol Consonants		Usual spelling equivalents	Equivalent diacritic marking in Webster's Third New International Dictionary	Equivalent diacritic marking in The American College Dictionary
s	s sc c	(*say*), ss (*miss*), (*scene*), sch (*schism*), (*lace*)	s	s
z	z s	(*zero*), zz (*fuzzy*), (*news*), ss (*dissolve*)	z	z
ʃ	sh ssi ci	(*she*), s (*sugar*), (*fission*), ti (*ration*), (*vicious*), ch (*chandelier*)	sh	sh
ʒ	si z j	(*vision*), su (*leisure*), (*azure*), ge (*rouge*), (*rajah*)	zh	zh
r	r	(*rim*), rr (*worry*)	r	r
w	w	(*way*), u (*quiet*)	w	w
ʍ or hw	wh	(*whey, when*)	hw	hw
j	y u	(*yes*), (*unite*), ie (*view*)	y	ū, y
h	h	(*head*)	h	h
m	m	(*mad*), mm (*dimmer*)	m	m
n	n	(*now*), nn (*winner*)	n	n
ŋ	ng	(*sing*)	ŋ	ng
l	l	(*like*), ll (*silly*)	l	l
tʃ	ch	(*chime*), tu (*creature*)	ch	ch
dʒ	j	(*just*), ge (*budge*)	j	j

Vowels

i	e ee ei	(*he*), ea (*tea*), (*meet*), ie (*field*), (*receive*)	ē̵, ē	ē
ɪ	i u ie	(*is*), y (*myth*), (*business*), (*sieve*)	i	ĭ
e *	a ea	(*name*), ey (*they*), (*steak*), ai (*bait*)	ā	ā
ε	e a	(*set*), ea (*bread*), (*care*), ai (*stair*)	e	ĕ

IPA Symbols and Diacritic Marks (Cont.)

IPA symbol Vowels		Usual spelling equivalents	Equivalent diacritic marking in Webster's Third New International Dictionary	Equivalent diacritic marking in The American College Dictionary
æ	a	(*man*), au (*aunt, laugh*— in most dialects)	a	ă
ɑ	a	(*palm*), ea (*heart*)	ä	ä
ɔ	a ou o	(*all*), au (*fault*), (*ought*), aw (*flaw*), (*fort*)	ȯ	ô
o †	o ou	(*no*), ow (*slow*), (*soul*), oa (*boat*)	ō	ō
ʊ	u o	(*full*), oo (*foot*), (*wolf*), ou (*would*)	u̇	o͝o
u	u ou ew	(*crude*), oo (*noose*), (*through*), o (*do*), (*threw*)	ü	oo
ɜ, ɝ ††	u i	(*urn*), o (*worm*), (*fir*), ea (*earn*)	ə̄	û
ʌ	u ou	(*sun*), o (*love*), (*rough*), oo (*blood*)	¦ə, ə̧	u
ə, ɚ §	a e o	(*around, total*), (*enough, hover*), (*actor*), u (*circus*), etc.	ə	ə

Diphthongs

ɔɪ	oy	(*boy*), oi (*toil*)	ȯi	oi
aɪ	i ei	(*line*), ie (*lie*), (*height*), y (*try*)	ī	ī
aʊ	ou	(*pouch*), ow (*how*)	au̇	ou

* Often pronounced as a diphthong, as in *may, prey*, etc.

† Often pronounced as a diphthong, as in *go* and *no*.

†† If *r* coloration is used on the stressed vowel, as in "hurt" and "affirm," the symbol ɝ is used.

§ If *r* coloration occurs on the vowel, as in "never" and "confirmation," the symbol ɚ is used.

Syllabic Identification. In phonetic transcription, the accenting mark (ˈ) precedes, and is *above*, the syllable to be stressed. This is called primary stress, as in məˈnɑtənəs (*mo-*

notonous) or əˈkaʊntəbl (*accountable*). Secondary stress marks are placed in front of, and *below*, the syllable to be stressed, as in ˌʌndɚˈstændɪŋ (*understanding*) and ˈsɛkrəˌtɛrɪ (*secretary*).

II. EXERCISES ON THE CONSONANTS

A. Plosive Consonants

EXPLANATION

8.01 An easy way to remember the plosive sounds is to associate them with the word *explosion*. Actually, these sounds are made by momentarily stopping the breath stream in the mouth and then releasing it quickly as in a little explosion. These sounds are also called *stops* and sometimes *explosives*. In articulating them, be certain the air is released sharply from the articulators. The plosive sounds give firmness to speech and, when well articulated, aid greatly in intelligibility.

BILABIAL PLOSIVES /p/, /b/

8.02 The bilabial plosives are made by impounding the air momentarily behind the closed lips and then releasing it sharply in a sort of puff. In making the /p/, the vocal bands are not in vibration at the closure of the lips; in making the /b/, the vocal bands are in vibration at the closure of the lips and continue to vibrate until the lips open for the "explosion." The /p/ and /b/ sounds are not exploded when they occur in final position in a word.

SHORT SENTENCES FOR PRACTICE

8.03 Say the following sentences with firm articulation of the consonant sounds:

1. Penny wise—pound foolish.
2. Billy bought apples, bananas, and peaches at the fruit store.
3. These paper boxes are products of Japan.

4. There is an appalling amount of poverty in Naples.
5. The orchestra played Von Suppe's *Poet and Peasant* overture.
6. The boy ordered two pieces of apple pie.
7. The battle of Blenheim is famous in British history.
8. The purchase price of the property was about a million dollars.
9. The little boy stuck a pin in the big, red balloon.
10. Peter paid a high price for the picture.
11. He stooped to pick up the baby's bib from the floor.
12. Some people regard pumpkin pie as the perfect dessert for the festive board.
13. The bastion was bombed during the battle.
14. I have the impression that he expects to pick someone's pocket soon.
15. The passers-by were captivated by the East Indian's performance of rope tricks.

LONGER SELECTIONS

8.04   Here are additional practice selections for firm articulation of the /p/ and /b/ sounds. (Care should be taken not to overasperate by sending out too much air, so that the /p/ sounds like /ph^h/ and the /b/ like /bh^h/.)

1. Mankind have ever been prone to expatiate in the praise of human nature. The dignity of man is a subject that has always been the favorite theme of humanity. They have declaimed with that ostentation, which usually accompanies such as are sure of having a partial audience: they have obtained victories, because there were none to oppose.
   OLIVER GOLDSMITH, *The Citizen of the World,* Letter CXV.

2. To be a pedestrian in Moscow takes the nerves of a jet pilot, the spilt-second timing of a bullfighter and a poker player's gift of bluff.
   HOWARD NORTON, *Only in Russia.**

3. "Papa is a preferable mode of address," observed Mrs. General. "Father is rather vulgar, my dear. The word Papa, besides, gives a pretty form to the lips. Papa, potatoes, poultry, prunes, and prism, are all very good words for the lips: especially prunes and prism. You will find it serviceable, in the formation of a demeanour, if you sometimes say to yourself in

* From *Only in Russia* by Howard Norton. Copyright 1961, D. Van Nostrand Co., Inc., Princeton, N.J.

company—on entering a room, for instance—Papa, potatoes, poultry, prunes and prism, prunes and prism."

CHARLES DICKENS, *Little Dorrit,* Book II, Chapter 5.

4. The barge she sat in, like a burnish'd throne,
   Burn'd on the water. The poop was beaten gold;
   Purple the sails, and so perfumed that
   The winds were love-sick with them. The oars were silver,
   Which to the tune of lutes kept stroke, and made
   The water which they beat to follow faster,
   As amorous of their strokes. For her own person,
   It beggar'd all description: she did lie
   In her pavilion—cloth-of-gold of tissue—
   O'er-picturing that Venus where we see
   The fancy outwork nature.

   WILLIAM SHAKESPEARE, *Antony and Cleopatra,* II, ii.

5. I chatter over stony ways,
      In little sharps and trebles,
   I bubble into eddying bays,
      I babble on the pebbles.

   ALFRED, LORD TENNYSON, "The Brook."

6. Beauty sat bathing by a spring,
      Where fairest shades did hide her;
   The winds blew calm, the birds did sing,
      The cool streams ran beside her.

   ANTHONY MUNDAY, "Beauty Bathing."

7. He thought he saw a Buffalo
      Upon the chimney piece:
   He looked again, and found it was
      His Sister's Husband's Niece.
   "Unless you leave this house," he said,
      "I'll send for the police."

   LEWIS CARROLL, "The Gardener's Song."

8. When I was a beggarly boy
      And lived in a cellar damp,
   I had not a friend or a toy,
      But I had Aladdin's lamp;
   When I could not sleep for the cold,
      I had fire enough in my brain,
   And builded, with roofs of gold,
      My beautiful castles in Spain!

   JAMES RUSSELL LOWELL, "Aladdin."

9. Booth led boldly with his big bass drum—
   (Are you washed in the blood of the Lamb?)
The Saints smiled gravely and they said: "He's come."
   (Are you washed in the blood of the Lamb?)

Vachel Lindsay, "General William Boooth
Enters into Heaven." *

10. My words fly up, my thoughts remain below.
Words without thoughts never to Heaven go.

William Shakespeare, *Hamlet*, III, iii.

11. Life's a pudding full of plums.

W. S. Gilbert, *The Gondoliers*, I.

12. How much better is it to weep at joy than to joy at weeping.

William Shakespeare, *Much Ado About Nothing*, I, i.

13.   The world is filled with the proverbs and acts and winkings of a base prudence, which is devotion to matter, as if we possessed no other faculties than the palate, the nose, the touch, the eye and ear; a Prudence which adores the Rule of Three, which never subscribes, which never gives, which seldom lends, and asks but one question of any project—Will it bake bread?

Ralph Waldo Emerson, "Prudence," *Essays*, First Series.

14. Silvered is the raven hair,
   Spreading is the parting straight,
Mottled the complexion fair,
   Halting is the youthful gait,
Hollow is the laughter free,
   Spectacled the limpid eye—
Little will be left of me
   In the coming by and by!

Fading is the taper waist,
   Shapeless grows the shapely limb,
And although severely laced,
   Spreading is the figure trim!
Stouter than I used to be,
   Still more corpulent grow I—
There will be too much of me
   In the coming by and by!

W. S. Gilbert, *Patience*, II.

---

* From "General William Booth Enters into Heaven" by Vachel Lindsay, published by The Macmillan Co.

15. Americans and foreigners alike have been prone to describe our townscapes as haphazard, formless or the products of accident. Nothing could be farther from the truth. Although not often beautiful, each street or district of our towns reflects some premeditation or planning on the part of an individual or a group, whether it be a home-owner, a banking institution, an individual corporation or a town government.

CHRISTOPHER TUNNARD and HENRY HOPE REED, JR.,
*American Skyline.**

LINGUA-ALVEOLAR (tongue to gum ridge) PLOSIVES

8.05 Among the most troublesome of the plosive sounds are the /t/ and /d/, called lingua-alveolar sounds. They are properly articulated by touching the tip of the tongue to the alveoli or upper gum ridge, just above the upper front teeth. However, they are sometimes *improperly* made by placing the tip or blade of the tongue on the upper teeth (as in Spanish *t* and *d*), by overaspirating the sounds so that a rush of air accompanies their articulation, or by making them affricate sounds (that is, making a /t/ sound like /ts/ as in the substandard pronunciation "tsen" for "ten" or a /d/ sound like /dz/ as in the substandard "dzear" for "dear").

The /t/ and /d/ sounds should be articulated with a sort of light plucking motion, touching the tongue tip to the upper gum ridge. Practice this sort of movement; be careful not to send out any breath or to use any voice as you do it. Now try a /t/ sound with a slight amount of air emitted as you make the plucking motion. Say *tee-too-toe-ta, tie-toy-tay-taw*. Next, add voice to the /t/ sound, but do not increase the amount of air sent out during the articulation. Say *do-dee-die-dow, day-doy-dah-daw*.

SENTENCES FOR PRACTICE

8.06 Practice the articulation of the /t/ and /d/ in the following sentences:

1. Ted doesn't know what he's going to do today.
2. They had two seats for the City Center.

* From *American Skyline* by Christopher Tunnard and Henry Hope Reed, Jr., published by The New American Library. Copyright © 1956 by Christopher Tunnard and Henry Hope Reed, Jr.

3. Tom invited her to a dance on Tuesday.
4. The Purdue team made two touchdowns in the second quarter.
5. Terry was prevented from lighting the taper.
6. Twelve men entered the tournament.
7. Quantity is not synonymous with quality.
8. *Cat on a Hot Tin Roof* is the title of a play by Tennessee Williams.
9. Time and tide wait for no man.
10. Tea for two, and two for tea.
11. Don't talk too much.
12. "Ten Cents a Dance" and "Tiptoe Through the Tulips" were popular tunes some time ago.
13. Ten and ten and two are twenty-two.
14. The motor was defective and had to be replaced.
15. I must write to her tonight.
16. They ought to be contented now.
17. He was seated to the right of the speaker.
18. Tad would stop at nothing to win his point.
19. I don't think I can mend it.
20. The painting was sold to the highest bidder for over two million dollars.

SENTENCES FOR PRACTICE: /n/ plus /d/ and /t/

8.07 Practice articulation of /n/ plus /d/ and /n/ plus /t/ in the following sentences. Be sure you articulate both consonants where they occur in sequence.

1. The candidate bounded to the platform to make another campaign speech.
2. They banded together to resist the propaganda of the opposition party.
3. Glenda planned to cross the Atlantic by air last winter.
4. The lawyer maintained that the entire case of the prosecution was fraudulent.
5. I went over in my mind the startling events of the week end.
6. We abandoned any hope for reaching the goal of the fund drive.
7. I didn't understand all his ranting and raving.
8. There are many advantages to having painting as a hobby.

9. The student was reprimanded for placing a lantern on the veranda of the president's house.
10. A midterm test is mandatory in the fundamental courses.

SENTENCES FOR PRACTICE: /t/ and /d/ plus /n/

8.08 Practice the articulation of /d/ plus /n/, and /t/ plus /n/, in the following sentences. Articulate these consonants one immediately after the other without letting a vowel come between them. Form the /d/ and /t/ sounds with your tongue, and then release the air for the /n/ through the nose.

1. He stuffed a wad of cotton in his left ear.
2. Eton College is one of England's most famous "public" schools.
3. She couldn't understand why the conductor wouldn't take her transfer.
4. Norton didn't have the strength to straighten out his affairs.
5. Isn't the garden lovely in the rain?
6. The dog was maddened by the clawing of the frightened kitten.
7. I hadn't eaten snails before my first visit to France.
8. She was saddened by the news that her candidate had been beaten in the election.
9. I can't seem to pardon his leaden sense of humor.
10. Here comes Santa Claus laden with gifts!

SENTENCES FOR PRACTICE: /t/ and /d/ plus /l/

8.09 Practice now the /t/ and /d/ sounds followed by the /l/. Be sure you articulate a /t/ or a /d/ where necessary. As with /d/ plus /n/ and /t/ plus /n/, put the tongue in position for the /d/ or /t/, and release the air over the sides of the tongue, in this case for the /l/. Do not insert a vowel between the /t/ or /d/ and the /l/, as in "bottell" for *bottle.*

1. The men fought a battle over the bottle.
2. He received a medal for his bravery in battle.
3. The total head of cattle numbered a little over thirteen hundred.

4. Glottal sounds impress most people as unpleasant.
5. I hope they'll settle their differences with little or no battling.
6. That's a pretty kettle of fish!
7. It'll be certain to put him on his mettle.
8. The title of the play was *The Hurdle*.
9. The badlands of the Dakotas are not very fertile.
10. Myrtle had noodle soup as part of a hot lunch.

Longer Selections

8.10 Practice reading aloud the following selections. Articulate light but firm /t/ and /d/ sounds.

1. Men have died from time to time, and worms have eaten them, but not for love.
   WILLIAM SHAKESPEARE, *As You Like It*, IV, i.

2. Silence does not always mark wisdom. I was at dinner some time ago, in company with a man, who listened to me and said nothing for a long time; but he nodded his head, and I thought him intelligent. At length, towards the end of the dinner, some apple dumplings were placed on the table, and my man had no sooner seen them, than he burst forth with "Them's the jockeys for me!"
   SAMUEL TAYLOR COLERIDGE, *Table Talk, 1836.*

3. A man should be careful never to tell tales of himself to his own disadvantage. People may be amused and laugh at the time, but they will be remembered, and brought out against him upon some subsequent occasion.
   JAMES BOSWELL, *Life of Samuel Johnson*, Vol. II.

4. "Oh, for a trap, a trap, a trap!"
   Just as he said this, what should hap
   At the chamber door but a gentle tap?
   ROBERT BROWNING, *The Pied Piper of Hamlin.*

5. An Englishman fears contempt more than death; he often flies to death as a refuge from its pressure; and dies when he fancies the world has ceased to esteem him.
   OLIVER GOLDSMITH, *The Citizen of the World*, Letter IV.

6. Dew sat on Julia's hair
      And spangled too,
   Like leaves that laden are
      With trembling dew;

Or glitter'd to my sight
  As when the beams
Have there reflected light
  Danced by the streams.
    ROBERT HERRICK, "Upon Julia's Hair Filled with Dew."

7. Tweedledum and Tweedledee
  Agreed to have a battle;
For Tweedledum said Tweedledee
  Had spoiled his nice new rattle.
Just then flew down a monstrous crow,
  As black as a tar-barrel;
Which frightened both the heroes so,
  They quite forgot their quarrel.
    LEWIS CARROLL, *Through the Looking Glass.*

8. Hear the loud alarum bells—
  Brazen bells!
What a tale of terror, now their turbulency tells!
  In the startled ear of night
  How they scream out their affright!
    Too much horrified to speak,
    They can only shriek, shriek,
      Out of tune . . .
    EDGAR ALLAN POE, "The Bells."

9. The day is done, and the darkness
  Falls from the wings of Night,
As a feather is wafted downward
  From an eagle in his flight.
    HENRY WADSWORTH LONGFELLOW, "The Day Is Done."

10. Eye of newt and toe of frog,
Wool of bat and tongue of dog,
Adder's fork and blind-worm's sting,
Lizard's leg and howlet's wing,
    WILLIAM SHAKESPEARE, *Macbeth,* IV, i.

11. Time travels in diverse paces with diverse persons. I'll tell
you who Time ambles withal, who Time trots withal, who
Time gallops withal, and who he stands still withal.
    WILLIAM SHAKESPEARE, *As You Like It,* III, ii.

12. Keeping time, time, time,
In a sort of Runic rhyme,

To the tintinnabulation that so musically swells
From the bells, bells, bells, bells,
   Bells, bells, bells—
From the jingling and the tinkling of the bells.
Edgar Allan Poe, "The Bells."

13. Passions are liken'd best to floods and streams:
   The shallow murmur, but the deep are dumb;
So, when affection yields discourse, it seems
   The bottom is but shallow whence they come.
They that are rich in words, in words discover
That they are poor in that which makes a lover.
Sir Walter Raleigh, "The Silent Lover."

14.   It is a common practice with those who have outlived the susceptibility of early feeling, or have been brought up in the gay heartlessness of dissipated life, to laugh at all love stories, and to treat the tales of romantic passion as mere fictions of novelists and poets.
Washington Irving, "The Broken Heart,"
The Sketch Book.

15. Daughters of Time, the hypocritic Days,
Muffled and dumb like barefoot dervishes,
And marching single in an endless file,
Bring diadems and fagots in their hands.
To each they offer gifts after his will,
Bread, kingdoms, stars, and sky that holds them all.
Ralph Waldo Emerson, "Days."

16. Were I to take an iron gun,
And fire it off towards the sun;
I grant 'twould reach its mark at last,
But not till many years had passed.
But should that bullet change its force,
And to the planets take its course,
'Twould never reach the *nearest* star,
Because it is so *very* far.
Lewis Carroll, "Facts."

17. For just experience tells, in every soil,
That those who think must govern those who toil;
Oliver Goldsmith, The Traveler.

18. Weep not, my wanton, smile upon my knee;
When thou art old there's grief enough for thee.
Robert Greene, "Sephestia's Lullaby."

19. A little stream best fits a little boat;
     A little lead best fits a little float;
     As my small pipe best fits my little note.
     A little meat bests fits a little belly,
     As sweetly Lady, give me leave to tell ye,
     This little pipkin fits this little jelly.
                 ROBERT HERRICK, "A Ternary of Littles, upon a Pipkin
                                         of Jelly Sent to a Lady."

LINGUA-VELAR PLOSIVES

8.11 The /k/ and /g/ sounds are called lingua-velar (tongue to soft palate) plosives, because, in articulating them, the back part of the tongue is raised to press momentarily against the velum, or soft palate. The sound is emitted with a quick withdrawal of the tongue from the area. In English, these sounds should not be articulated with the tongue placed too far back on the soft palate. This latter placement causes a rather harsh, "gutteral" sound.

SENTENCES FOR PRACTICE

8.12 Say the following sentences for practice in making the /k/ and /g/ sounds:

1. The coliseum was crowded with people.
2. Chekov's play *The Sea Gull* is not a comedy.
3. The harpsichord is a keyboard instrument played by the plucking of the strings.
4. The cattle were crossing the road when the car came towards them.
5. Greengage plums grow in a temperate climate.
6. Actions speak louder than words.
7. Great oaks from little acorns grow.
8. The girls wanted more extracurricular activities.
9. The colonel gave orders for the big guns to go into action.
10. The cake broke apart at the first attempt to cut it.
11. The congressmen agreed to adjourn in late August.
12. The dog dragged a broken toy along the garden path.
13. The Keystone Cops were a creation of Mack Sennett.
14. He groped for his gun in the dark.

LONGER SELECTIONS

8.13 Here are several selections of prose and poetry that contain the /k/ sound, and its voiced equivalent, the /g/ sound:

1. How'er it be, it seems to me,
       'Tis only noble to be good.
   Kind hearts are more than coronets,
       And simple faith than Norman blood.
           ALFRED, LORD TENNYSON, "Lady Clara Vere de Vere."

2. As good almost kill a man as kill a good book; who kills a man kills a reasonable creature, God's image; but he who destroys a good book kills reason itself.
           JOHN MILTON, *Areopagitica.*

3. A drunken Congressman said to Horace Greeley one day: "I am a self-made man." "Then, sir," replied the philosophical Horace, "the fact relieves the Almighty of a great responsibility."
   Anonymous, "Self-Made," *Modern Eloquence,* Vol. XII.

4. Weep no more, nor sigh, nor groan,
   Sorrow calls no time that's gone;
   Violets plucked, the sweetest rain
   Makes not fresh nor grow again.
           JOHN FLETCHER, *The Queen of Corinth,* III, ii.

5. He thought he saw a Rattlesnake
       That questioned him in Greek;
   He looked again, and found it was
       The Middle of Next Week.
   "The one thing I regret," he said,
       "Is that it cannot speak!"
           LEWIS CARROLL, "The Gardener's Song."

6. A widow kept a Favourite Cat,
       At first a gentle creature;
   But when he was grown sleek and Fat,
   With many a Mouse, and many a Rat,
       He soon disclos'd his nature.
           JONATHAN SWIFT, "The Widow and Her Cat."

7. I can set a braggart quailing with a quip,
       The upstart I can wither with a whim;

He may wear a merry laugh upon his lip,
  But his laughter has an echo that is grim!
When they're offered to the world in merry guise,
  Unpleasant truths are swallowed with a will—
For he who'd make his fellow creatures wise
  Should always gild the philosophic pill!
                    W. S. GILBERT, *The Yeomen of the Guard*, I.

8. And, ev'n while fashion's brightest arts decoy,
   The heart distrusting asks, if this be joy.
                    OLIVER GOLDSMITH, *The Deserted Village*.

9. Mastiff, greyhound, mongrel grim,
   Hound or spaniel, brach, or lym,
   Or bobtail tike or trundle-tail,
                    WILLIAM SHAKESPEARE, *King Lear*, III, vi.

10. "My mother bids me bind my hair,"
    And not go about such a figure;
    It's a bother, of course, but what do I care?
    I shall do as I please when I'm bigger.
                    LEWIS CARROLL, "Those Horrid Hurdy-Gurdies."

11.   The more one contemplates the cliché, the more one be-
    comes aware of what an exasperating medium language can
    be. It is quicksilver. It is alchemy, constantly changing baser
    materials to better, and vice versa. The painter knows where
    he is with his colors—they are unchanging, as are the sculp-
    tor's wood and stone, and the various materials of the archi-
    tect. But the writer deals with living stuff, and words, or the
    combinations we make of them, assume lives of their own, and
    die, even before our eyes.
        Certain sights and sounds, however often repeated, re-
    main always arresting or beautiful. The crescent moon, cas-
    cading water, the evening star, the first flush of day in the
    east, bells over summer fields—of these we never tire. But
    words, perhaps our greatest creation, are corrupted by time
    and use.
                    J. DONALD ADAMS, "Speaking of Books," *New York Times
                        Book Review*, October 27, 1957.*

12. I shall speak much more gently to you, my dear child, though
    you don't like Gothic architecture. The Grecian is only proper
    for magnificent and public buildings. Columns and all their

beautiful ornaments, look ridiculous when crowded into a closet of a cheesecake-house.

Horace Walpole, *Selected Letters of Horace Walpole.*

13. Conversation is only possible when men's minds are free from pressing anxieties. Their lives must be reasonably secure and they must have no grave concern about their souls. They must attach importance to the refinements of civilization. They must value courtesy, they must pay attention to their persons (and have we not also been told that good prose should be like the clothes of a well-dressed man, appropriate but unobtrusive?), they must fear to bore, they must be neither flippant nor solemn, but always apt; and they must look upon "enthusiasm" with a critical glance.

W. Somerset Maugham, *The Summing Up.**

For Impromptu Talk

8.14 Talk briefly about a book you are reading for another course. As you talk, be aware of the necessity for making light, clear plosive sounds. Watch particularly your tongue placement for the /t/ and /d/ sounds.

B. Fricative Consonants: Explanation

9.01 Fricative consonants are made with some degree of friction, because the outgoing breath stream is partially restricted in passing over the articulators. The fricative sounds include the /f/ and /v/ sounds; the voiceless /θ/ and voiced /ð/ *th* sounds; the /s/ and /z/ sounds; the /ʃ/ and /ʒ/ sounds, as in *shame* and *azure,* respectively; the /h/ sound; and the /j/ sound, as in *ye.* In making these sounds, the articulators (tongue, lips, etc.) must be in precise placement, or there will be distortion.

Labio-Dental Fricatives

9.02 In making the /f/ sound and the voiced equivalent, the /v/, the lower lip touches the edge of the upper teeth, and the air is sent through the surrounding openings of the teeth.

---

* From *The Summing Up* by W. Somerset Maugham. Copyright 1938 by W. Somerset Maugham. Reprinted by permission of Doubleday & Co., Inc.

9.03 Say the following sentences to practice the placement of the tongue for the /f/ and /v/ sounds:

1. The foreigners fought their way through the London fog.
2. The leaves of that tree don't fall until November.
3. After his vacation, he flew back to Nevada.
4. Various proposals were advanced to prevent inflation.
5. Frank walked down Fifth Avenue to Fortieth Street.
6. They saw a revival of the film *Love from a Stranger.*
7. His chief hobby was making home movies.
8. The fashion model wore mauve-colored gloves.
9. The Vikings lived in Scandinavia.
10. French is often thought to be the language of lovers.
11. The vicious attack brought a vow of vengeance.
12. *Vile Bodies* is the title of a novel by Evelyn Waugh.
13. Stones fell off the fence into a deep ravine.
14. Jeff decided to laugh off his discomforts in learning to drive.
15. Lavender, violet, and saffron are all famous shades of color.

LONGER SELECTIONS

9.04 Here are some practice selections containing a number of /f/ and /v/ sounds:

1. False words are not only evil in themselves, but they infect the soul with evil.
   > PLATO, *Phaedo.* Translated by BENJAMIN JOWETT.

2. Who o'er the herd would wish to reign,
   Fantastic, fickle, fierce, and vain?
   Vain as the leaf upon the stream,
   And fickle as the changeful dream;
   Fantastic as a woman's mood,
   And fierce as Frenzy's fever'd blood.
   Thou many-headed monster-thing,
   O who could wish to be thy king?
   > SIR WALTER SCOTT, *The Lady of the Lake,*
   > Canto V, Stanza XXX.

3. Fear is one of the passions of human nature, of which it is impossible to divest it. You remember that the Emperor

Charles V, when he read upon the tomb-stone of a Spanish nobleman, "Here lies one who never knew fear," wittily said, "Then he never snuffed a candle with his fingers."

JAMES BOSWELL, *Life of Samuel Johnson,* Vol. II.

4. Westward the course of empire takes its way;
    The first four acts already past,
A fifth shall close the drama with the day;
    Time's noblest offspring is the last.
BISHOP BERKELEY, "On the Prospect of Planting Arts
and Learning in America."

5. At thirty, man suspects himself a fool;
Knows it at forty, and reforms his plan;
At fifty chides his infamous delay,
Pushes his prudent purpose to resolve;
In all the magnanimity of thought
Resolves; and re-resolves; then dies the same.
EDWARD YOUNG, "Night Thoughts."

6. Elysium is as far as to
    The very nearest room,
If in that room a friend await
    Felicity or doom.

What fortitude the soul contains,
    That it can so endure
The accent of a coming foot,
    The opening of a door!
EMILY DICKINSON, "Elysium Is as Far as to." *

7. He that is down needs fear no fall;
    He that is low, no pride;
He that is humble ever shall
    Have God to be his guide.
JOHN BUNYAN, "The Shepherd Boy Sings in the Valley
of Humiliation."

8. Venus, take my votive glass:
Since I am not what I was,
What from this day I shall be,
Venus, let me never see.
MATTHEW PRIOR, "The Lady Who Offers Her
Looking-Glass to Venus."

* From *The Complete Poems of Emily Dickinson,* published by Little, Brown & Co.

9. Come live with me, and be my love
    And we will all the pleasures prove,
    That valleys, groves, hills and fields,
    Woods or steepy mountain yields.
                              CHRISTOPHER MARLOWE, "The Passionate
                                        Shepherd to His Love."

10. They who have no other trade but seeking their own fortune,
    need never hope to find her: coquette-like she flies from her
    close pursuers, and at last fixes on the plodding mechanic,
    who stays at home, and minds his business.
        OLIVER GOLDSMITH, *The Citizen of the World,* Letter LXX.

11. Revenge triumphs over death: love slights it; honour aspireth
    to it; grief flieth to it; . . .
                              FRANCIS BACON, "Of Death."

12. Friends, who set forth at our side,
    We, we only are left!
    With frowning foreheads, with lips
    Sternly compress'd, we strain on,
    Falter, are lost in the storm.
                              MATTHEW ARNOLD, "Rugby Chapel."

13. True, in old age we live under the shadow of Death, which,
    like a sword of Damocles, may descend at any moment, but
    we have so long found life to be an affair of being rather
    frightened than hurt that we have become like the people who
    live under Vesuvius, and chance it without much misgiving.
        SAMUEL BUTLER, *The Way of All Flesh,* Chapter 6.

14. Fill ev'ry glass, for wine inspires us,
    And fires us,
        With courage, love, and joy.
        Women and wine should life employ.
    Is there ought else on earth desirous?
                              JOHN GAY, *The Beggar's Opera,* II, i.

15. When lovely woman stoops to folly,
        And finds too late that men betray,
    What charm can soothe her melancholy?
        What art can wash her guilt away?
        OLIVER GOLDSMITH, *The Vicar of Wakefield,* Chapter 24.

16. There was a Door to which I found no Key:
    There was a Veil through which I might not see.
        EDWARD FITZGERALD, *The Rubaiyat of Omar Khayyam.*

17. All we have gained then by our unbelief
    Is a life of doubt diversified by faith,
    For one of faith diversified by doubt:
    We call the chess-board white,—we call it black.
            ROBERT BROWNING, "Bishop Blougram's Apology."

LINGUA-DENTAL FRICATIVES

9.05 In making the two *th* sounds that occur in English (the /θ/ as in *think* and the /ð/ as in *then*), the tip of the tongue is placed lightly against the upper teeth and the air is pushed out over the tongue tip.

SENTENCES FOR PRACTICE

9.06 Say the following sentences, making sure that you articulate a true fricative sound and not a plosive.

1. Was that the one you wanted?
2. Do these things belong to them?
3. This is the cloth I chose.
4. Send them on Thursday.
5. The wind drove them hither and thither.
6. They went bathing at South Beach.
7. The thermos is there on the table.
8. Call them at three o'clock.
9. He thrust his hand through the opening.
10. The theater reopened on the thirty-first.
11. They walked farther and farther into the woods.
12. There was a throng of people on the dock.
13. They sell summer clothing at the other counter.
14. He thought he'd go on Thursday.
15. They counted three thousand three hundred and thirty votes.
16. This is the wrong thermometer.
17. Thelma is going home for Thanksgiving.
18. They took a path through the forest.

PHRASES

9.07 Read aloud the following phrases. Use in sentences those with which you seem to have trouble.

that Thursday, what thing, but think, eight thousand, that theft, what theater, bought three, not thankful, quite thin, at the, set the, hit them, bite the, eat them, but they, sit there, write this, caught them, hurt the, not then, hard thing, red thorn, said Thursday, third thing, loud thunder, need three, fine thought, own things, ten theaters, one thief, Elizabeth sold, worth something, fourth section, tenth soldier, both sorts, South Side, hearth-stone, twelfth sailor, breathe slowly, with sauce

Longer Selections

9.08 Here are some practice selections of prose and poetry that contain the $/\theta/$ and $/\eth/$ sounds:

1. The hag is astride
   This night for to ride;
      The devil and she together:
   Through thick and through thin,
   Now out and then in,
      Though ne'er so foul be the weather.
   Robert Herrick, "The Hag."

2. He that travelleth into a country, before he hath some entrance into the language, goeth to school, and not to travel.
   Francis Bacon, "Of Travel."

3. There was a time when meadow, grove, and stream,
   The earth, and every common sight,
      To me did seem
      Apparelled in celestial light,
   The glory and the freshness of a dream.
   It is not now as it hath been of yore;—
      Turn wheresoe'er I may,
      By night or day,
   The things which I have seen I now can see no more.
   William Wordsworth, "Ode, Intimations of Immortality."

4. It is computed, that eleven thousand persons have, at several times, suffered death, rather than submit to break their eggs at the smaller end.
   Jonathan Swift, *Gulliver's Travels*, Chapter 4.

5. 'Beauty is truth, truth beauty,—that is all
   Ye know on earth, and all ye need to know.'
   John Keats, "Ode on a Grecian Urn."

6. I will talk of things heavenly, or things earthly; things moral, or things evangelical; things sacred, or things profane; things

past, or things to come; things foreign, or things at home; things more essential, or things circumstantial; provided that all be done to our profit.

JOHN BUNYAN, *The Pilgrim's Progress*, Part I.

7. From too much love of living,
       From hope and fear set free,
    We thank with brief thanksgiving
       Whatever gods may be
    That no life lives forever;
    That dead men rise up never;
    That even the weariest river
       Winds somewhere safe to sea.

ALGERNON SWINBURNE, "The Garden of Proserpine."

8. The end and the means, the gamester and the game—life is made up of the intermixture and reaction of these two amicable powers, whose marriage appears beforehand monstrous, as each denies and tends to abolish the other. We must reconcile the contradictions as we can, but their discord and their concord introduce wild absurdities into our thinking and speech.

RALPH WALDO EMERSON, "Nominalist and Realist,"
Essays, Second Series.

9. I know my soul hath power to know all things,
       Yet she is blind and ignorant in all
    I know I'm one of nature's little kings,
       Yet to the least and vilest things am thrall.

SIR JOHN DAVIES, "Man."

10. Theophilus Thistle, the successful thistle sifter, in sifting a sieve full of unsifted thistles, thrust three thousand through the thick of his thumb. Now if Theophilus Thistle, the successful thistle sifter, in sifting a sieve full of unsifted thistles, thrust three thousand thistles through the thick of his thumb, see that thou, in sifting a sieve full of unsifted thistles, thrust not three thousand thistles through the thick of thy thumb. Success to the successful thistle sifter.

ANONYMOUS, *Practical Elocution.*

POSTDENTAL FRICATIVES

9.09 In making the /s/ sound and its voiced equivalent, the /z/ sound, the tip of the tongue is pulled back slightly from the region of the upper gum ridge and the air is sent in a thin, narrow stream over the tongue tip. Remember to keep the tongue high and slightly retracted in making these sounds. Do *not* prolong them; their production requires little air pressure.

WORDS FOR PRACTICE

9.10 Practice putting the following words in meaningful sequences. Do not be content merely to read the list.

Initial /s/— seat, sit, set, sat, sot, soot, suit, seed, sad, soothe, sawed, search, sum, side, soil, south
stole, strap, stop, stream, star, stroke
slope, sloppy, sleeve, slaw, slight
small, smirk, smack, smile, smell
sneer, snail, snow, sniff, snide
swell, swift, swallow, swim, swear

Medial /s/—hasten, listen, parson, costly, lastly, history, cloister, isolate, aspen, loosely, lists, mists, fasts, fists, insists

Final /s/— miss, mess, mass, moss, kiss, less, horse, helps, halts, kits, kites, loss, cats, Keats, mats, nets, drafts, snaps, caps

Initial /z/— zeal, zim, zealous, Zachary, Xerxes, Xavier

Medial /z/—husband, loser, closing, causing, spasm

Final /z/— words, needs, beds, cabs, loves, leaves, kings, wrongs, kegs, begs, rears, cheers, bores

PHRASES AND SENTENCES

9.11 Practice saying the following sequences:

take a seat
sit down
set the table
sat on a tack
soot on the windowsill
silly sot
tailor-made suit
sing me no sad songs

soothe the spirit
sawed a table leg
search for something
sum it all up
toilers of the soil
south side of town
strap of a dress
small snowfall

1. She suffered a great loss.
2. "The Eve of St. Agnes" is by Keats.

3. He's studying history and other social sciences at school.
4. This is a bus stop.
5. Stealing is against the law.
6. We seemed to go faster and faster.
7. There was a stream in the pasture.
8. Her husband closed the heavy door with great ease.
9. He pounds his fists against the posts.
10. He's read *The Wizard of Oz* six times.
11. Sam knew the names of many Byzantine emperors.
12. It's a mystery what costume she'll wear.
13. He loves to hear the leaves rustling.
14. The baseball season begins in April.
15. Most sightseers seldom relax.
16. The audience liked the last scene best.

LONGER EXERCISES

9.12   The following reading selections should provide useful practice in working for correctly articulated /s/ and /z/ sounds:

1. The distant sounds of music, that catch new sweetness as they vibrate through the long-drawn valley, are not more pleasing to the ear, than the tidings of a far distant friend.
   OLIVER GOLDSMITH, *The Citizen of the World*, Letter LVI.

2. When to the sessions of sweet silent thought
      I summon up remembrance of things past,
   I sigh the lack of many a thing I sought
      And with old woes new wail my dear time's waste.
               WILLIAM SHAKESPEARE, Sonnet, XXX.

3. Some books are to be tasted, others to be swallowed, and some few to be chewed and digested; that is, some books are to be read only in parts; others to be read but not curiously; and some few to be read wholly, and with diligence and attention.
               FRANCIS BACON, "Of Studies."

4. How sweet the moonlight sleeps upon this bank!
   Here will we sit and let the sounds of music
   Creep in our ears. Soft stillness and the night
   Become the touches of sweet harmony.
           WILLIAM SHAKESPEARE, *The Merchant of Venice*, V, i.

5. To sit in solemn silence in a dull, dark dock,
   In a pestilential prison, with a life-long lock,
   Awaiting the sensation of a short, sharp shock,
   From a cheap and chippy chopper on a big black block!
   W. S. GILBERT, *The Mikado*, I.

6. There is something in the character and habits of the North
   American savage, taken in connection with the scenery over
   which he is accustomed to range, its vast lakes, boundless
   forests, majestic rivers, and trackless plains, that is, to my
   mind, wonderfully striking and sublime. He is formed for the
   wilderness, as the Arab is for the desert. His nature is stern,
   simple, and enduring; fitted to grapple with difficulties, and
   to support privations.
   WASHINGTON IRVING, "Traits of Indian Character," *The Sketch Book*.

7. Burly, dozing humble-bee,
   Where thou art is clime for me.
   Let them sail for Porto Rique,
   Far-off heats through seas to seek;
   I will follow thee alone,
   Thou animated torrid-zone!
   Zigzag steerer, desert cheerer,
     Let me chase thy waving lines;
   Keep me nearer, me thy hearer,
     Singing over shrubs and vines.
   RALPH WALDO EMERSON, "The Humble-Bee."

8. Poetry is certainly something more than good sense, but it
   must be good sense, at all events; just as a palace is more
   than a house, but it must be a house, at least.
   SAMUEL TAYLOR COLERIDGE, *Table Talk*.

9. So smooth, so sweet, so silvery is thy voice,
   As, could they hear, the damned would make no noise,
   But listen to thee, (walking in thy chamber)
   Melting melodious words to lutes of amber.
   ROBERT HERRICK, "Upon Julia's Voice."

10. Follow a shadow, it still flies you;
    Seem to fly it, it will pursue:
    So court a mistress, she denies you;
    Let her alone, she will court you.
    Say, are not women truly, then,
    Styled but the shadows of us men?
    BEN JONSON, "The Shadow."

11. For, if once a man indulges himself in murder, very soon he comes to think little of robbing; and from robbing he comes next to drinking and sabbath-breaking, and from that to incivility and procrastination. Once you begin upon this downward path, you never know where you are to stop.

> THOMAS DE QUINCEY, "Murder Considered
> as One of the Fine Arts."

12. Augustus, a few minutes before his death, asked his friends who stood about him, if they thought he had acted his part well; and upon receiving such an answer as was due to his extraordinary merit, "Let me then," says he, "go off the stage with your applause"; using the expression with which Roman actors made their exit at the conclusion of a dramatic piece.

> JOSEPH ADDISON, *A Citizen's Diary.*

13. Shrewd Simon Short sewed shoes. Seventeen summers' storms and sunshine, saw Simon's small, shabby shop standing staunch, saw Simon's selfsame sign still swinging, silently specifying: "Simon Short, Smithfield's sole surviving shoemaker. Shoes sewed and soled superfinely." Simon's spry sedulous spouse, Sally Short, sewed shirts, stitched sheets, and stuffed sofas. Simon's six stout sturdy sons—Seth, Samuel, Stephen, Saul, Shadrach, and Silas, sold sundries. Sober Seth sold sugar, starch, spices; simple Sam sold saddles, stirrups, screws; sagacious Stephen sold silks, satins, shawls; skeptical Saul sold silver salvers, silver spoons; selfish Shadrach sold shoe strings, soaps, saws, skates; slack Silas sold Sally Short's stuffed sofas.

> ANONYMOUS, *Practical Elocution.*

14. There was no need, false woman, to encrease
My misery with hopes of happiness
This scorn at first had to my Love and me
But Justice been; now it is Cruelty.
Was there no way his constancy to prove,
But by your own inconstancy in Love?

> SIR GEORGE ETHEREGE, *The Comical Revenge;*
> *or, Love in a Tub,* V, i.

15. Is it not a shame to make two chapters of what passed going down one pair of stairs? For we are got no farther yet than to the first landing, and there are fifteen more steps down to the bottom . . .

> LAURENCE STERNE, *The Life and Opinions of Tristram
> Shandy,* Book IV, Chapter 10.

16. Sixteen singing boys
       In cottas spotless white
     Shining faces all
       But shoes that are a fright.

ANONYMOUS.

17. The sun rose red and fiery, a sure sign
       Of the continuance of the gale: to run
     Before the sea until it should grow fine,
       Was all that for the present could be done:
     A few tea-spoonfuls of their rum and wine
       Were served out to the people, who begun
     To faint, and damaged bread wet through the bags,
     And most of them had little clothes but rags.

LORD BYRON, Don Juan, Canto II, Stanza LXII.

18. The world is known to us through many senses, not just
     hearing, smell, vision and, at close range, touch and taste.
     Aristotle recognized these five, setting a pattern that has been
     followed for more than two thousand years. Like men before
     him, Aristotle was impressed by small numbers. Five senses
     fitted into a magic series: one True Cause, two Sexes, three
     Graces, four Humors. Today, the chain continues. Every
     Irishman can name Six Counties. We refer to the seven won-
     ders of the world, the eight notes in an octave, the cat's nine
     lives. Such numbers are handy, even if oversimplified.

LORIS and MARGERY MILNE, The Senses of
Animals and of Men.*

FOR IMPROMPTU UTTERANCE

9.13 Include in your practice on /s/ and /z/ sounds
some impromptu talk during which you are particularly
careful to place the tongue correctly for the articulation of
these sounds. Some suggestions follow for short talks in the
course of which you might alert yourself to these sounds:

1. Describe any difficulty you have had or are having at
    present with /s/ and /z/ sounds.
2. What types of deviation of the /s/ sound have you
    noticed in your class? Do they annoy you? Why?

3. Indicate some of the inferences that are often made when one hears an individual with a hissing /s/, or a *th* substitution for /s/ or /z/, or a "slushy" /s/.

LINGUA-PALATAL FRICATIVES

9.14 The voiceless /ʃ/ sound, as in *shock* and *hush,* and the voiced /ʒ/ sound, as in *rouge* and *measure,* are formed by placing the front of the tongue somewhat farther back and slightly lower than for the /s/ and /z/ sounds. The tongue is also less grooved and the lips more rounded than for the /s/ and /z/ sounds.

SHORT SENTENCES

9.15 Read aloud the following sentences, and listen for your errors:

1. She was shocked to see a shark so close to the shore.
2. Shirley was sure the silk dress was not in fashion.
3. The Shah of Persia has visited Washington.
4. It was a great pleasure to look up at the azure sky.
5. *Measure for Measure* is a play by Shakespeare.
6. His garage is located on Ocean Street.
7. Parisian fashions have high prestige.
8. She shuddered at the memory of the vicious attack.
9. The shadow of suspicion fell on the young Russian.
10. We should give all of our attention to the issue.
11. He suffered several lesions as the result of the crash.
12. Many men wish that they had more of leisure and less of rushing in their lives.
13. The treasure was found in a cache buried in the sand.
14. He casually mentioned that the ship would sail in a short time.
15. The shoeshine boy was not at his usual stand.
16. Some people consider having a massage a luxury.

LONGER SELECTIONS

9.16 The following selections should provide practice material for the articulation of the /ʃ/ and /ʒ/ sounds:

1. Ships that pass in the night, and speak each other in passing,
   Only a signal shown and a distant voice in the darkness;

So on the ocean of life, we pass and speak one another,
Only a look and a voice, then darkness again and a silence.
                    HENRY WADSWORTH LONGFELLOW, "Elizabeth,"
                              Tales of a Wayside Inn.

2. There was an old man who said, "Hush!
   I perceive a young bird in this bush!"
   When they said—"Is it small?" He replied—"Not at all!
   It is four times as big as the bush!"
                    EDWARD LEAR, *A Book of Nonsense.*

3. Where'er you walk, cool gales shall fan the glade;
   Trees, where you sit, shall crowd into a shade;
   Where'er you tread, the blushing flowers shall rise,
   And all things flourish where you turn your eyes.
                    ALEXANDER POPE, "Summer Pastorals."

4. I with borrow'd silver shine,
   What you see is none of mine.
   First I show you but a quarter,
   Like the bow that guards the Tartar:
   Then the half, and then the whole,
   Ever dancing round the pole.
                    JONATHAN SWIFT, "On the Moon."

5. Bacchus' blessings are a treasure,
   Drinking is the soldiers' pleasure:
   Rich the treasure;
   Sweet the pleasure;
   Sweet is pleasure after pain.
                    JOHN DRYDEN, "Alexander's Feast."

6. Shakespeare was of us, Milton was for us,
   Burns, Shelley, were with us—they watch from their graves!
                    ROBERT BROWNING, "The Lost Leader."

7. Swift as a shadow, short as any dream,
   Brief as the lightning in the collied * night,
   That, in a spleen, unfolds both heaven and earth,
   And ere a man hath power to say "Behold!"
   The jaws of darkness do devour it up:
   So quick bright things come to confusion.
      WILLIAM SHAKESPEARE, *A Midsummer Night's Dream,* I, i.

* Collied: blackened.

8. She was a good deal shocked; not shocked at tears,
      For women shed and use them at their liking;
   But there is something when man's eye appears
      Wet, still more disagreeable and striking:
   A woman's tear-drop melts, a man's half sears,
      Like molten lead, as if you thrust a pike in
   His heart to force it out, for (to be shorter)
   To them 't is a relief, to us a torture.
          LORD BYRON, *Don Juan,* Canto V, Stanza CXVIII.

9. Each time of year has its special meaning. As the seasons
   cycle past they offer repetitions of pleasures we have known:
   the welcome warmth of spring sunshine, the fragrances of
   summer flowers, the fruits of autumn, the lively flames of
   burning logs crackling in the fireplace on a winter night. We
   think of the world greening under April's showers, of July
   picnics, of October foliage and of the pure glistening white-
   ness of fresh snow reflecting a January sun.
          LORIS and MARGERY MILNE, *The Senses of*
          *Animals and of Men.**

10. Now air is hushed, save where the weak-ey'd bat,
    With short shrill shriek flits by on leathern wing,
    Or where the beetle winds
    His small but sullen horn,
           WILLIAM COLLINS, "Ode to Evening."

GLOTTAL FRICATIVE

9.17 In the formation of the glottal fricative, or /h/
sound, the vocal bands are close enough together to cause
friction but not voicing. In actuality, the articulators assume the position for the vowel to follow, so there is no one
set position for the /h/.

PRACTICE SENTENCES

9.18 Practice reading aloud the following sentences. Be
sure that you sound an /h/ where it is necessary in acceptable
pronunciation and omit it where it has been dropped from
usual pronunciation.

1. He hoped to reach the top of the hill by half past ten.
2. Heaven help an honest man among thieves.

---

* From *The Senses of Animals and of Men* by Loris and Margery Milne.
Copyright © 1962 by Loris and Margery Milne. Reprinted by permission
of Atheneum Publishers.

3. We shall have hot weather in August, whether we like it or not.
4. A holiday was decreed, to pay homage to the hero.
5. The herb garden was a haven on a humid day.
6. Humility is often the hallmark of the great man.
7. A sense of humor is a mark of humanity.
8. How did Henry get the cut on his forehead?
9. He saw her carrying a huge bouquet.
10. He was very humble in accepting the honor offered to him.
11. Harold received a picture postcard of a penitentiary, with the message on the back: "Having a wonderful time. Wish you were here."
12. That road is closed to vehicular traffic on holidays.
13. Two hogsheads of wine proved a heavy load to lift.
14. Home is where the heart is.
15. How far is it from here to Harrisburg?

PHRASES

9.19 Pronounce the following phrases in the manner approved in your geographical area. Be sure to articulate the preliminary /h/ in words like *whether* and *which*, in areas in which this pronunciation is preferred.

Where are you going?	Which way?	Why not?
white sales	What's new?	whether or not
while away	wheel barrow	whale steak
wheat germ	old wheeze	whistling in the dark
a whim of the moment	whine about	whip up
whirl around	whittle down	whisper in her ear
huge task	human being	humane practice
humble pie	humid weather	sense of humor
rich hues	herb garden	abhor a vacuum

LONGER EXERCISES

9.20 Here is some practice material for pronunciation of the /h/ sound:

1. Happy the man, and happy he alone,
   He who can call today his own;
   He who, secure within, can say,
   "Tomorrow, do thy worst, for I have lived today."
   JOHN DRYDEN, *Imitation of Horace*, Book III.

2. He who has no hands
   Perforce must use his tongue;
   Foxes are so cunning
   Because they are not strong.
                    RALPH WALDO EMERSON, "Orator."

3. The devil hath not, in all his quiver's choice
   An arrow for the Heart like a sweet voice.
                    LORD BYRON, *Don Juan,* Canto XV, Stanza XIII.

4. A gentleman who had been very unhappy in marriage, married immediately after his wife died: Johnson said, it was the
   triumph of hope over experience.
                    JAMES BOSWELL, *Life of Samuel Johnson,* Vol. II.

5. Now hatred is by far the longest pleasure;
   Men love in haste, but they detest at leisure.
                    LORD BYRON, *Don Juan,* Canto XIII, Stanza XIII.

6. This is that Lady Beauty, in whose praise
   Thy voice and hand shake still,—long known to thee
   By flying hair and fluttering hem,—the beat
   Following her daily of thy heart and feet,
   How passionately and irretrievably,
   In what fond flight, how many ways and days!
                    DANTE GABRIEL ROSSETTI, "Soul's Beauty."

7. How easy it is to make a tragedy into a farce, and to slip from
   the sublime to the ridiculous. Burke did this when, in the
   course of a debate in the House of Commons in 1793, he drew
   a dagger from his breast and threw it on the floor of the House,
   saying: "That is what you are to obtain from an alliance with
   France." In the French chamber such an act would have produced great excitement, but at Westminster it only provoked
   ridicule. "The gentleman has brought his knife," said Sheridan, "but where is the fork?"
                    ANONYMOUS, "Oratorical Cutlery,"
                    Modern Eloquence, Vol. X.

C. Affricate Sounds

10.01 Affricates are combinations of the plosive sounds
/t/ and /d/ with the fricative sounds /ʃ/ and /ʒ/. These
combinations function and sound as if they were single units.
They are written /tʃ/, as in *church,* and /dʒ/, as in *judge.*

Short Sentences

10.02 Practice reading aloud the following sentences, making sure that you can sound both the plosive and the fricative elements of each affricate:

1. Each teacher gave an achievement test to the children.
2. Chaucer lived in the fourteenth century.
3. James was a soldier in the Foreign Legion.
4. It would be cheaper to junk the old furniture than to re-condition it.
5. The doctor urged us to get flu injections.
6. Rich foods are often indigestible for lunch.
7. George has a very vivid imagination.
8. Many people try to eat with chopsticks in a Chinese restaurant.
9. The judge lectured the jury on their responsibilities in trying to arrive at a just decision.
10. Revenge is a major cause of crimes of passion.
11. Marjorie endured the jibes of her chums with cheerful resignation.
12. The general ordered his troops to march into battle.
13. Many housewives dislike the idea of strangers in their kitchens.
14. Did George Washington chop down a cherry tree with his little hatchet?
15. Jerry got a chill at the tennis match.
16. You don't have to be rich to collect etchings.
17. French is generally thought of as a language of beauty and charm.
18. The car lunged to a stop at the edge of the cliff.

Longer Selections

10.03 The following selections are designed to provide practice material for the affricate sounds:

1. The world has grown so bad
   That wrens make prey where eagles dare not perch
   Since every Jack became a gentleman,
   There's many a gentle person made a Jack.
   WILLIAM SHAKESPEARE, *Richard the Third,* I, iii.

2. Age, that lessens the enjoyment of life, increases our desire of living. Those dangers, which in the vigor of youth we had learned to despise, assume new terrors as we grow old. Our caution increasing as our years increase, fear becomes at last the prevailing passion of the mind; and the small remainder of life is taken up in useless efforts to keep off our end, or provide for a continuous existence.
OLIVER GOLDSMITH, The Citizen of the World,
Letter LXIII.

3. Ploffskin, Pluffskin, Pelican jee,—
   We think no Birds so happy as we!
   Plumpskin, Ploshskin, Pelican jill,
   We think so then, and we thought so still!
EDWARD LEAR, "The Pelican Chorus," Nonsense Songs.

4. If to do were as easy as to know what were good to do, chapels had been churches and poor men's cottages princes' palaces.
WILLIAM SHAKESPEARE, The Merchant of Venice, I, ii.

5. The hungry Judges soon the Sentence sign,
   And wretches hang that Jurymen may Dine.
ALEXANDER POPE, The Rape of the Lock, Canto III.

6. "I'll be judge, I'll be jury," said cunning old Fury: "I'll try the whole cause, and condemn you to death."
LEWIS CARROLL, Alice's Adventures in Wonderland.

7. Dear, beauteous Death! the jewel of the just,
       Shining nowhere, but in the dark;
   What mysteries do lie beyond thy dust,
       Could man overlook that mark!
HENRY VAUGHAN, "They Are All Gone."

8. Yet he was jealous, though he did not show it,
   For jealousy dislikes the world to know it.
LORD BYRON, Don Juan, Canto I, Stanza LXV.

9. The general attention had been entirely directed from himself to the person in the carriage, and he was quite alone. Rightly judging that under such circumstances it would be madness to follow, he turned down a bye-street in search of the nearest coach-stand, finding after a minute or two that he was reeling like a drunken man, and aware for the first time of a stream of blood that was trickling down his face and breast.
CHARLES DICKENS, Nicholas Nickleby, Chapter 32.

10. Haste thee nymph, and bring with thee
    Jest and youthful Jollity,
    Quips and Cranks, and wanton Wiles,
    Nods, and Becks, and Wreathed Smiles,
    Such as hang on *Hebe's* cheek,
    And love to live in dimple sleek;

    JOHN MILTON, *L'Allegro.*

11. He always was one for a jeer and a jest,
    And was given to iconoclasm;
    His smile was sardonic, and he seemed to suggest:
    "Let others arouse 'em; I razz 'em!"

    His phrases were likely to smolder and scald,
    And act like a blister to bluster;
    By the name of "buffoon" he was commonly called,
    Though possibly "jester" were juster.

    We recently met; he was clouded in gloom;
    His spirit was battered, embittered.
    He asked me to chisel these words on his tomb:
    "The universe tottered; I tittered."

    MORRIS BISHOP, "Epitaph for a Funny Fellow,"
    *A Bowl of Bishop.**

D. Nasal Consonants

11.01 The nasal consonants—/m/, as in *map,* /n/, as in *nap,* and /ŋ/, as in *sing*—are distinguished by being the only English sounds for which air must be emitted through the nasal passages. Most speakers have little difficulty articulating the /m/ and /n/ sounds, whereas the /ŋ/ sound frequently is accompanied by errors in pronunciation. This matter will be discussed in Section **11.04** to follow.

SHORT SENTENCES

11.02 The following sentences contain many /m/ and /n/ sounds. Pay particular attention to their articulation when they occur in conjunction with other consonants such as /d/ and /s/ at the ends of words.

1. He repeated the action hundreds of times.
2. Children like to play games on Sunday afternoons.
3. I saw the event clearly in my mind's eye.
4. It was the congressman's maiden speech.
5. Fran bought a pair of book ends for her living room.
6. The orchestra is scheduled to play two Haydn symphonies.
7. She had a charming dimple on her chin.
8. The little kitten runs with a slight limp.
9. Henry Hudson and his men were fond of playing ninepins.
10. James was quite smitten with her charms.
11. Everyone insisted that Janice shouldn't be so indiscreet.
12. I jumped when I heard the telephone ring.
13. The bannister was painted green.
14. These blossoms certainly brighten the room.
15. Clarence was fond of making very candid comments.
16. I'm going downtown around nine o'clock.
17. It seemed to be too heavy a burden to bear alone.
18. There was a beach umbrella left standing in the sand.
19. These sentences have many nasal sounds.

LONGER SELECTIONS

11.03 The following selections should be read aloud with special attention paid to the /m/ and /n/ sounds:

1. When a merry maiden marries,
   Sorrow goes and pleasure tarries;
   Every sound becomes a song,
   All is right and nothing wrong!
   From to-day and ever after
   Let your tears be tears of laughter.
   Every sigh that finds a vent
   Be a sigh of sweet content.
   When you marry merry maiden,
   Then the air with love be laden;
   Every flower is a rose,
      Every goose becomes a swan,
   Every kind of trouble goes
      Where the last year's snows have gone;

Sunlight takes the place of shade
When you marry merry maid!

W. S. GILBERT, *The Gondoliers*, I.

2. The sandy cat by the Farmer's chair
Mews at his knee for dainty fare;
Old Rover in his moss-greened house
Mumbles a bone, and barks at a mouse.
In the dewy field the cattle lie
Chewing the cud 'neath a fading sky.
Dobbin at manger pulls his hay:
Gone is another summer's day.

WALTER DE LA MARE, "Summer Evening." *

3. Try we life-long, we can never
    Straighten out life's tangled skein,
Why should we, in vain endeavour,
    Guess and guess and guess again?
Life's a pudding full of plums
Care's a canker that benumbs.
Wherefore waste our elocution
On impossible solution?
Life's a pleasant institution,
Let us take it as it comes!

W. S. GILBERT, "The Tangled Skein," *The Bab Ballads*.

4. It was many and many a year ago,
    In a kingdom by the sea,
That a maiden there lived whom you may know
    By the name of Annabel Lee;—
And this maiden she lived with no other thought
    Than to love and be loved by me.

EDGAR ALLAN POE, *Annabel Lee*.

5. The music of midsummer-madness
    Shall sting him with many a bite,
Till, in rapture of rollicking sadness,
    He shall groan with a gloomy delight:
He shall swathe him, like mists of the morning,
    In platitudes luscious and limp,
Such as deck, with a deathless adorning,
    The Song of the Shrimp!

LEWIS CARROLL, *Sylvie and Bruno*.

* Extract has been granted by The Literary Trustees of Walter de la Mare and The Society of Authors as their representative.

6. I never take a nap after dinner but when I have had a bad night, and then the nap takes me.

    JAMES BOSWELL, *Life of Samuel Johnson,* Vol. I.

7. O Memory, thou fond deceiver!
    Still importunate and vain;
To former joys recurring ever,
    And turning all the past to pain;

    Thou, like the world, th' oppress'd oppressing,
        Thy smiles increase the wretch's woe,
    And he who wants each other blessing
        In thee must ever find a foe.

    OLIVER GOLDSMITH, "Memory."

8.   Well! Maria was married yesterday. Don't we manage well? The original day was not once put off: lawyers and milliners were all ready canonically . . .

    Maria was in a white silver gown, with a hat very much pulled over her face; what one could see of it was handsomer than ever . . . I had liked to have demolished the solemnity of the ceremony by laughing.

    HORACE WALPOLE, "Letter to George Montague, Esq.,"
    Selected Letters of Horace Walpole.

9. When the moon is on the wave,
    And the glow-worm in the grass,
And the meteor on the grave,
    And the wisp on the morass;
When the falling stars are shooting,
And the answer'd owls are hooting,
And the silent leaves are still
In the shadow of the hill,
Shall my soul be upon thine,
With a power and with a sign.

    LORD BYRON, *Manfred,* I, i.

10.   Every man is sufficiently discontented with some circumstance of his present state, to suffer his imagination to range more or less in quest of future happiness, and to fix upon some point of time, in which, by the removal of the inconvenience which now perplexes him, or acquisition of the advantage which he at present wants, he shall find the condition of his life very much improved.

    SAMUEL JOHNSON, *The Rambler,* April 3, 1750.

11. With solace and gladness,
    Much mirth and no madness,
    All good and no badness;
    So joyously,
    So maidenly,
    So womanly,
    Her demeaning
    In every thing,
    Far, far passing
    That I can indite,
    Or suffice to write
    Of merry Margaret
        As midsummer flower
    Gentle as falcon
        Or hawk of the tower.
                JOHN SKELTON, "Mistress Margaret Hussey."

12. I think I could turn and live with animals, they're so placid
        and self-contain'd,
    I stand and look at them long and long.

    They do not sweat and whine about their condition,
    They do not lie awake in the dark and weep for their sins,
    They do not make me sick discussing their duty to God,
    Not one is dissatisfied, not one is demented with the mania of
        owning things,
    Not one kneels to another, nor to his kind that lived thousands
        of years ago,
    Not one is respectable or unhappy over the whole earth.
                WALT WHITMAN, "Song of Myself," Stanza 32.

13. Nuns fret not at their convent's narrow room,
        And hermits are contented with their cells;
    And students with their pensive citadels;
    Maids at the wheel, the weaver at his loom,
    Sit blithe and happy; bees that soar for bloom,
        High as the highest peak of Furness fells,
        Will murmur by the hour in foxglove bells:
    In truth the prison unto which we doom
    Ourselves no prison is: and hence for me,
        In sundry moods, 'twas pastime to be bound
        Within the sonnet's scanty plot of ground;
    Pleased if some souls (for such there needs must be)

Who have felt the weight of too much liberty,
    Should find brief solace there, as I have found.
                            WILLIAM WORDSWORTH, *The Sonnet* (1).

14. When the lamp is shattered,
        The light in the dust lies dead,
    When the cloud is scattered,
        The rainbow's glory is shed;

    When the lute is broken,
        Sweet tones are remembered not;
    When the lips have spoken,
        Loved accents are soon forgot.
                            PERCY BYSSHE SHELLEY, "Lines."

PRONUNCIATION OF /ng/

11.04 Rules for the pronunciation of words spelled with *ng* follow:

1. The spelling *-ng* represents /ŋ/ in all words in which the *ng* is final (as in *sing*). No /g/ is ever sounded in these words, whether the next word in the phrase begins with a vowel or a consonant. This rule also applies to the group of words ending with *-ngue* (as in *tongue*).

Examples: *bring, ring it, running away, hang up, swing low, tongue is, meringue*

2. The spelling *-ng* may represent /ŋ/ in words made by adding a suffix to words ending in *-ng* or *-ngue*.

Examples: *singer, ring, coat hanger, kingly, slangy, longing, strongly, haranguing*
Exception: When the ending *-er* or *-est* is added to any one of the three adjectives *long, strong,* and *young*, the *ng* is pronounced as /ŋg/.

3. The spelling *-ng-* represents /ŋg/ in all words in which it is followed by sounds that do not constitute a suffix.

Examples: *linger, finger, anger, hunger, angle, singular, language, distinguish, single*
Note: *length, strength, lengthen,* and *strengthen* are pronounced with /ŋkθ/ or /ŋθ/. The pronunciation of these words with /n/ is avoided by educated speakers.

The following phrases and sentences provide practice material for the pronunciation of words containing *ng* spellings:

1. She's training to be a singer.
2. Put the clothes into the wringer.
3. His youngest brother was banging on a drum.
4. He broke his finger by catching a ball in the wrong manner.
5. She's leaving Atlanta on the twelfth.
6. Hang up your hat.
7. Are you going on a winter vacation this year?
8. His mother tongue is English.
9. They were singing as they marched along.
10. They're clearing a path through the jungle.
11. Here's a hanger for your coat.
12. We were dying of hunger.
13. The plane was climbing at a steep angle.
14. He's the youngest man who has ever been appointed to the post.
15. There was a long line of men waiting at the door.
16. He didn't have the strength to walk the length of the room.

Use the following phrases in sentences of your own choosing:

anything else	thing of no importance	summing up
hang on	trying often	as long as
younger	spring up	stronger than
singing it	wrong answer	strengthen
rung of the ladder	reclining on	buying up
king of England	finding out	singer is

LONGER SELECTIONS

11.05 The following selections will provide more extensive practice on the pronunciation of words with *ng* spellings:

1. We're called *gondolieri*,
   But that's a vagary,
   It's quite honorary
      The trade that we ply.

For gallantry noted
Since we were short-coated
To beauty devoted
    Are Marco and I;

When morning is breaking,
Our couches forsaking,
To greet their awaking
    With carols we come.
At summer day's nooning,
When weary lagooning,
Our mandolins tuning,
    We lazily thrum.

When vespers are ringing,
To hope ever clinging,
With songs of our singing
    A vigil we keep,
When daylight is fading,
Enwrapt in night's shading,
With soft serenading
    We sing them to sleep.

W. S. GILBERT, *The Gondoliers*, I.

2.   My father has such a skirmishing, cutting kind of slashing
way with him, in his disputations, thrusting and ripping, and
giving every one a stroke to remember him by in his turn—
that if there were twenty people in company—in less than half
an hour he was sure to have every one of 'em against him.
    LAURENCE STERNE, *The Life and Opinions of Tristram
Shandy*, Book VIII, Chapter 34.

3. There was a rustling that seemed like a bustling
    Of merry crowds justling at pitching and hustling;
    Small feet were pattering, wooden shoes clattering,
    Little hands clapping, and little tongues chattering,
    And like fowls in a farm-yard when barley is scattering,
    Out came children running.
                ROBERT BROWNING, *The Pied Piper of Hamlin*.

4. Now the bright morning Star, Day's harbinger,
    Comes dancing from the East, and leads with her
    The Flowry *May*, who from her green lap throws
    The yellow Cowslip, and the pale Primrose.
    Hail, bounteous *May* that dost inspire
    Mirth and youth, and warm desire,

Woods and Groves, are of thy dressing,
Hill and Dale, dost boast thy blessing.
Thus we salute thee with your yearly Song,
And welcome thee, and wish thee long.

JOHN MILTON, "On May Morning."

5. Sing a song of sixpence
    A pocket full of rye;
Four and twenty blackbirds,
    Baked in a pie.
When the pie was opened,
    The birds began to sing;
Was not that a dainty dish,
    To set before the king?

The king was in the counting-house,
    Counting out his money;
The queen was in the parlor,
    Eating bread and honey.
The maid was in the garden,
    Hanging out the clothes,
When down came a blackbird
    And pecked off her nose.

ANONYMOUS.

6. Look not thou on beauty's charming;
    Sit thou still while kings are arming;
    Taste not when the wine-cup glistens;
    Speak not when the people listens;
    Stop thine ear against the singer;
    From the red gold keep thy finger;
    Vacant heart and hand, and eye,
    Easy live and quiet die.

SIR WALTER SCOTT, *The Bride of Lammermoor.*

7. Will no one tell me what she sings?—
    Perhaps the plaintive numbers flow
For old unhappy far-off things
    And battles long ago:

WILLIAM WORDSWORTH, "The Solitary Reaper."

8. Baby, sleep a little longer,
    Till thy little limbs are stronger;

ALFRED, LORD TENNYSON, "Sea Dreams."

9. Good people all, of every sort,
     Give ear unto my song;
And if you find it wondrous short,
     It cannot hold you long.
       OLIVER GOLDSMITH, "Elegy on the Death of a Mad Dog."

10. My strength is as the strength of ten,
     Because my heart is pure.
          ALFRED, LORD TENNYSON, "Sir Galahad."

11. Dimply damsel, sweetly smiling,
All caressing, none beguiling,
Bud of beauty, fairly blowing,
Every charm to nature owing,
This and that new thing admiring,
Much of this and that inquiring,
Knowledge by degrees attaining,
Day by day some virtue gaining,
Ten years hence, when I leave chiming,
Beardless poets, fondly rhyming,
(Fescu'd * now, perhaps, in spelling)
On thy riper beauties dwelling,
Shall accuse each killing feature,
Of the cruel, charming, creature,
Whom I know complying, willing,
Tender, and averse to killing.
       AMBROSE PHILIPS, "To Miss Margaret Pulteney."

12. Ring out old shapes of foul disease;
     Ring out the narrowing lust of gold;
     Ring out the thousand wars of old,
Ring in the thousand years of peace.
       ALFRED, LORD TENNYSON, "In Memoriam."

13. Where-e'er you find "the cooling western breeze,"
In the next line, it "whispers through the trees:"
If crystal streams "with pleasing murmurs creep,"
The reader's threatened (not in vain) with "sleep:"
Then, at the last and only couplet fraught
With some unmeaning thing they call a thought,
A needless Alexandrine ends the song
That, like a wounded snake, drags its slow length along.
       ALEXANDER POPE, "An Essay on Criticism."

---

* Fescue: a small pointer (usually a straw) used to point out letters in teaching children to read or spell.

14. Look, how my ring encompasseth thy finger,
    Even so thy breast encloseth my poor heart.
    Wear both of them, for both of them are thine.
    > WILLIAM SHAKESPEARE, *Richard the Third,* II, ii.

15. So vile your grimace, and so croaking your speech,
    One scarcely can tell if you're laughing or crying;
    Were you fix'd on one's funeral sermon to preach,
    The bare apprehension would keep one from dying.
    > GOTTHOLD LESSING, "Epigram," *Humorous Poetry of the
    > English Language.*

FOR IMPROMPTU TALK

11.06 Relate an incident of interest in which you were involved last summer. As you talk, pay particular attention to the resonance of the nasal sounds, and to proper pronunciation of words spelled with *ng*.

E. Lateral Consonant

11.07 The English /l/ sound is called the lateral consonant because the sound is made with the tip of the tongue touching the upper gum ridge as the air is emitted laterally over the sides of the tongue. Be sure your tongue tip is not placed back on the hard palate.

SHORT SENTENCES

11.08 Here are practice sentences for the proper articulation of the /l/ sound:

1. I'll tell you what Bill told me.
2. Will you sell it for a dollar?
3. I called Mr. Nelson on the telephone.
4. Four bottles of milk were spoiled.
5. We rolled the ball down the hill.
6. We'll sail for Italy on April third.
7. There's a tall elm in the middle of the field.
8. They used twelve rolls of film.
9. Can you solve the puzzle?
10. The Nile Valley is very fertile.
11. Monday is a college holiday.
12. An Australian naval officer sold a painting of great value.
13. The art collection was valued at over a million dollars.

14. The blue tablecloth is soiled.
15. He fought in one of the last battles of the Civil War.
16. She failed the oral exam.
17. These are all I'll be able to use.
18. She knelt at the altar rail.

DISTINCTION BETWEEN /r/ and /l/

11.09 Practice making a distinction between the /r/ and /l/ consonants in the following pairs of words:

reap—leap	reek—leak	rug—lug
rim—limb	rake—lake	royal—loyal
rain—lane	rent—lent	roar—loll
roam—loam	ram—lamb	rap—lap
rook—look	rot—lot	rock—lock
room—loom	wrong—long	rout—lout
rid—lid	Ruhr—lure	right—light

11.10 The following selections provide more extensive practice material for /l/ sounds:

1. Tobacco, divine, rare, superexcellent Tobacco, which goes far beyond all their panaceas, potable gold, and philosopher's stones, a sovereign remedy to all diseases . . . but, as it is commonly abused by most men, which takes it as Tinkers do Ale, 'tis a plague, a mischief, a violent purger of goods, land, health, hellish, devilish, and damned Tobacco, the ruin and overthrow of body and soul.
   ROBERT BURTON, *The Anatomy of Melancholy.*

2. Let not Ambition mock their useful toil,
       Their homely joys, and destiny obscure;
   Nor Grandeur hear with a disdainful smile,
       The short and simple annals of the poor.
   THOMAS GRAY, *Elegy Written in a Country Churchyard.*

3. Ben Battle was a soldier bold,
       And used to war's alarms;
   But a cannon-ball took off his legs,
       So he laid down his arms!
   THOMAS HOOD, "Faithless Nelly Gray."

4. The notice, which you have been pleased to take of my labours, had it been early, had been kind; but it has been delayed till I am indifferent, and cannot enjoy it; till I am solitary, and cannot impart it; till I am known, and do not want it.
   SAMUEL JOHNSON, "A Letter to Lord Chesterfield," 1755.

5. Roll on, thou ball, roll on!
   Through pathless realms of Space
       Roll on!
   What though I'm in a sorry case?
   What though I cannot meet my bills?
   What though I suffer toothache's ills?
   What though I swallow countless pills?
       Never *you* mind!
       Roll on!

   Roll on, thou ball, roll on!
   Through seas of inky air
       Roll on!
   It's true I have no shirts to wear;
   It's true my butcher's bill is due;
   It's true my prospects all look blue—
   But don't let that unsettle you:
       Never *you* mind!
       Roll on!

                   [*It rolls on.*]
               W. S. GILBERT, "To the Terrestrial Globe,"
                               The Bab Ballads.

6.   The common people of Spain have an Oriental passion for
   story-telling, and are fond of the marvelous. They will gather
   round the doors of their cottages in summer evenings, or in the
   great cavernous chimney-corners of the Ventas * in the winter,
   and listen with insatiable delight to miraculous legends of
   saints, perilous adventures of travellers, and daring exploits
   of robbers and contrabandistas. The wild and solitary character of the country, the imperfect diffusion of knowledge, the
   scarceness of general topics of conversation, and the romantic
   adventurous life that every one leads in a land where travelling
   is yet in its primitive state, all contribute to cherish this love
   of oral narration, and to produce a strong infusion of the
   extravagant and incredible.
                       WASHINGTON IRVING, *The Alhambra.*

7. Bedecked in fashion trim,
       With every curl a-quiver;
   Or leaping, light of limb,
       O'er rivulet and river;

* Ventas: rural inns.

Or skipping o'er the lea
  On daffodil and daisy;
Or stretched beneath a tree,
  All languishing and lazy;
Whatever be her mood—
Be she demurely prude
Or languishingly lazy—
My lady drives me crazy!

> W. S. GILBERT, "My Lady," *The Bab Ballads.*

8. When icicles hang by the wall
     And Dick the shepherd blows his nail
   And Tom bears logs into the hall
     And milk comes frozen home in pail,
   When blood is nipp'd and ways be foul,
   Then nightly sings the staring owl,
     "tu-whit, tu-who!"

   A merry note,
   While greasy Joan doth keel the pot.

> WILLIAM SHAKESPEARE, *Love's Labor's Lost,* V, ii.

9. When I was a small boy at the beginning of the century I remember an old man who wore knee-breeches and worsted stockings, and who used to hobble about the street of our village with the help of a stick. He must have been getting on for eighty in the year 1807, earlier than which date I suppose I can hardly remember him, for I was born in 1802. A few white locks hung about his ears, his shoulders were bent and his knees feeble, but he was still hale, and was much respected in our little world of Paleham.

> SAMUEL BUTLER, *The Way of All Flesh,* Chapter 1.

10.   Simple geometry tells us that the volume of a sphere varies as the cube of its radius, while the surface of a sphere varies as the square of the radius. Therefore as a lump of uranium increases in size, its surface does not increase as rapidly as its volume or mass. In other words, the larger the lump is, the less surface it offers per unit mass. Since the loss is through the surface, and capture is by the mass, the larger the lump the greater is the chance of the released neutrons staying inside the mass to be captured by U-234 for fission purposes.

> SELIG HECHT, *Explaining the Atom.**

---

* From *Explaining the Atom* by Selig Hecht. Copyright 1947 by Selig Hecht. Reprinted by permission of The Viking Press, Inc.

For Impromptu Talk

11.11 Talk briefly about the type of speech practice you find most valuable. During your answer, pay particular attention to the formation of the /l/ sounds. Be certain that you are really articulating an /l/ sound with the tongue tip on the upper gum ridge when you say such words as *college*, *valuable*, and *all*.

F. The Glide Consonants

12.01 In speech, a glide is a transition of sounds caused by the change in position of the articulators in the mouth. The glide consonants are /w/, /j/, and /r/. The /w/ sound is represented by the letter *w* (or *wh*); the /j/ sound usually by *y*, as in *yes* and *you* (although the same sound occurs in the word *onion* and in *Australia*); and the /r/ by words in which the letter *r* begins the word or is found between two vowels.

Exercises for /w/

12.02 The /w/ sound is a voiced bilabial glide, and the /ʍ/ is its voiceless bilabial counterpart. In the /w/, the sound is clearly voiced; the /ʍ/ has an initial voicelessness with an approximation of an /h/ followed by a slight degree of voicing. (Occasionally the /ʍ/ sound is represented phonetically by /hw/.) Speakers of two generations ago considered the substitution of /w/ for /ʍ/ incorrect. In the Middle West and the South, the distinction is still kept. For practice material on distinguishing these two sounds, turn back to Section **9.19**.

Sentences for Practice

12.03 Sentences for practice on the /w/ sounds follow:

1. Put the belt strap around your waist.
2. Whatever you want is on the shelf.
3. Anywhere you go, you will hear wrens.
4. To wash off the wax, use whatever you have at hand.

5. People who suffer from asthma wheeze when they have an attack.
6. Have you ever tried to whitewash a whale?
7. A whiff of tobacco smoke told Winifred that her little brother was under the sofa.
8. Why won't you whisper it to me?
9. When you marry, you marry for weal or woe.
10. Which one of the white horses will you ride?

LONGER SELECTIONS

12.04 Here is a group of selections for additional practice on the /w/ sound:

1. Welcome, maids of honour!
    You do bring
    In the spring,
And wait upon her.

She has virgins many,
    Fresh and fair;
    Yet you are
More sweet than any.

ROBERT HERRICK, "To Violets."

2. To a man the disappointment of love may occasion some bitter pangs; it wounds some feelings of tenderness—it blasts some prospects of felicity; but he is an active being—he may dissipate his thoughts in the whirl of varied occupation, or may plunge into the tide of pleasure; or, if the scene of disappointment be too full of painful associations, he can shift his abode at will, and, taking as it were the wings of the morning, can "fly to the uttermost parts of the earth, and be at rest."
WASHINGTON IRVING, "The Broken Heart,"
The Sketch Book.

3. Sweet western wind, whose luck it is,
    Made rival with the air,
To give Perenna's lip a kiss,
    And fan her wanton hair:

Bring me but one, I'll promise thee,
    Instead of common showers,
Thy wings shall be embalm'd by me,
    And all beset with flowers,
ROBERT HERRICK, "To the Western Wind."

4. 'T is a woodland enchanted,
   Where wonderful chances
       Have sway;
   Luck flies from the cold one
   But leaps to the bold one
       Half-way;
   Why should I be daunted?
       JAMES RUSSELL LOWELL, "The Fountain of Youth."

5. Once upon Iceland's solitary strand
   A poet wandered with his book and pen,
   Seeking some final word, some sweet Amen,
   Wherewith to close the volume in his hand.
       HENRY WADSWORTH LONGFELLOW, "The Broken Oar."

EXERCISES FOR /j/

12.05 The /j/ glide is variously represented in spelling, as the *y* in *yeast, i* in *million, u* (with /u/) in *music,* and *e* in *Europe.*
Practice saying the following sentences:

1. Yoke your wagon to a star.
2. Yelling is apt to abuse the voice.
3. Europe is not yet politically united.
4. My junior year seems just like yesterday.
5. Amuse yourself by playing in your own backyard.
6. Yarn of the right hue is difficult to find.
7. Pure beauty is to be found at the Grand Canyon.
8. Every year, millions of eyes look at the familiar face of Santa Claus.
9. Sometimes the Muses make me yawn with tedium.
10. Few have the ambition to be merely a loyal minion.
11. I plan to be a lawyer, but I know it is an arduous task.
12. The yield of yellow corn has been valuable this year.
13. One needs rich soil to grow onions.
14. Not all the people of the United States like yams.

LONGER SELECTIONS

12.06 Additional practice sentences for the /j/ sound follow:

1. Yield, ye youths! ye yeomen yield your yell!
       ANONYMOUS, "The Siege of Belgrade."

2. The genius of the Platonists is intoxicating to the student, yet
    how few particulars of it can I detach from all their books.
    RALPH WALDO EMERSON, "Nominalist and Realist," *Es-
    says,* Second Series.

3. Yet the hearts must childlike be
      Where such heavenly guests abide;
    Unto children, in their glee,
      All the year is Christmas-tide!
    LEWIS CARROLL, "Christmas-Greetings."

4. Though beauty be the mark of praise,
      And yours of whom I sing be such
      As not the world can praise too much,
    Yet 'tis your virtue not I raise.
    BEN JONSON, "An Elegy."

5. The chain I gave was fair to view,
      The lute I added sweet in sound;
    The heart that offered both was true,
      And ill deserved the fate it found.
    LORD BYRON, "The Chain I Gave."

For additional practice material on the /j/ sound, turn to
Sections **16.09, 16.10,** and **16.11.**

THE GLIDE /r/: EXPLANATION

12.07   In pronouncing the following words, compare the
speech sounds represented by the letter *r* in *red, very, cared,
earn, car,* and *father.* In some instances, it will be clearly a
consonant (as in *red*); in others, it will take on the characteristics of a vowel; and, in some words, it will not be sounded
at all by some speakers. It can, therefore, be a consonant or
a semivowel.

If the letter *r* comes before a vowel, it is a consonant. To
form it, the tongue is raised near the alveoli or upper gum
ridge. The tip of the tongue turns toward the hard palate.
In *red,* the tongue flaps forward toward the position for the
vowel; in *very,* the same thing happens, since the *r* is initial
in the syllable. In *cared,* the *r,* in the speech of many persons,
becomes a vowel with "*r* coloring" (for this "coloring," the
tongue tip is usually turned back slightly after the articula-

tion of the preceding vowel); much the same thing is true of the *r* in *earn, car,* and *father.* After a vowel, the sounding of an *r* is optional. However, when the final *r* in a word is followed by a vowel beginning the next word, the *r* is usually pronounced.

SENTENCES

12.08 In reading aloud the following sentences, try to determine what differences you make in the articulation of the various *r* sounds.

1. Put the car in the garage.
2. There is a damaged car down the street.
3. Father told me to do it.
4. Father is right.

DIALECTAL VARIATIONS OF /r/

12.09 The pronunciation of the *r* varies according to geographical area in the United States. In eastern New England and in many parts of the South, the *r* is not sounded after a vowel. Two practices with the sound /r/ should be avoided: the intrusive /r/, usually inserted between a word ending with a vowel and a word beginning with a vowel, as in "lawr office" for *law office,* and "idear of it," for *idea of it;* and the substitution of /w/ for /r/. In the latter deviation, speakers round their lips in making the position for the /r/ glide, producing, for example, "wed" for *red,* and "woast" for *roast.*

EXERCISES FOR PREVOCALIC /r/

12.10 In the following exercises, make sure you have a firm prevocalic /r/.

1. Richard ran around the race track.
2. Are you repaid?
3. The car is ready.
4. Write the story sometime this year.
5. They live very near Astoria.
6. Their rabbit is already too big for his box.
7. Carry this around to the back door.

8. A bigger bird in the hand is worth a dozen small ones in the rafters.
9. Roger Brown was a teacher in our study room.
10. Father rested before he went to church.
11. Wrap your coat around you.
12. Troy was not destroyed in a hurry.
13. Three raisins a day won't keep any doctor away.
14. Ride up to the filling station, and order four new tires.
15. Make yourself responsible for the routing from here to there.
16. Reproduce with accuracy the dialect of the easterners.
17. "America" for most people from other countries means both North and South America.
18. Growers of grain suffer if there is a lack of rainfall.
19. I like the song about the partridge in the pear tree.
20. There is no real royal road to learning.

INTRUSIVE /r/

12.11 Be careful not to insert an /r/ when it doesn't belong in the following sentences:

1. The idea isn't very sound.
2. The dog's paw is hurt.
3. The sofa is broken.
4. Australia and New Zealand are islands in the Pacific Ocean.
5. The Shah of Persia had visited America often.
6. Emma and Mary were there yesterday.
7. Utah is a western state.
8. George Bernard Shaw was the author of *Pygmalion*.
9. The rat was gnawing at the rope.
10. A comma isn't always necessary.
11. Panama is in the torrid zone.
12. He ate a raw egg.
13. The cawing of the crows is annoying.
14. The law of the land still holds.
15. Omaha, Nebraska, and Sioux City, Iowa, are in the same time zone.
16. It ought to thaw in the morning.
17. He put it on the drawing board.
18. He kept sawing the board.
19. Wichita is in Kansas.
20. That's not the only straw in the wind.

SENTENCES TO CONTRAST /w/ AND /r/

12.12 Here is a series of practice sentences during the reading of which make a clear distinction between the /r/ and the /w/:

1. The rest of the mourners did not weep.
2. Wait right here.
3. Progress and wealth do not necessarily go hand in hand.
4. The bride wore red.
5. You run a risk whenever you buy sight unseen.
6. Buy whenever the price is right.
7. What a brawl the freshmen had!
8. She rode high, wide, and handsome around the ring.
9. Whoever runs around in those weeds is sure to risk getting poison ivy poisoning.
10. The wrens are getting ready to nest right over our window.

LONGER SELECTIONS

12.13 The following selections of prose and poetry will provide additional practice on the /r/ glide:

1. But if the while I think on thee, dear friend,
   All losses are restored and sorrows end.
   WILLIAM SHAKESPEARE, Sonnet XXX.

2. "Gwacious Heavens!" said his Lordship, "I thought evewebody had seen the new mail cart; it is the neatest, pwettiest, gwacefullest thing that ever was upon wheels—painted wed, with a cweam piebald."
   "With a real box for the letters, and all complete," said the Honorable Mr. Crushton.
   "And a little seat in front, with an iwon wail, for the dwiver," added his Lordship. "I dwove it over to Bwistol the other morning in a cwimson coat, with two servants widing a quarter of a mile behind; and cwucify me if the people didn't wush out of their cottages, and awest my pwogwess, to know if I wasn't the post. Glorwious, glorwious!"
   CHARLES DICKENS, *Pickwick Papers*, Chapter 34.

3. I saw young Harry with his beaver on,
   His cuisses on his thighs, gallantly arm'd,
   Rise from the ground like feathered Mercury,
   WILLIAM SHAKESPEARE, *Henry the Fourth, Part I*, IV, i.

4. Sir, I had rather be right than President.
> HENRY CLAY to Senator W. C. Preston, 1839.

5.   Here's the rule for bargains—"Do other men, for they would do you," That's the true business precept. All others are counterfeit.
> CHARLES DICKENS, *Martin Chuzzlewit*, Chapter 11.

6. Upon Saint Crispin's Day
Fought was this noble fray,
Which fame did not delay,
    To England to carry.

O when shall English men
With such acts fill a pen,
Or England breed again
    Such a King Harry?
> MICHAEL DRAYTON, "Ballad of Agincourt."

7. Our country! In her intercourse with foreign nations, may she always be in the right; but our country, right or wrong.
> STEPHEN DECATUR, a toast, 1816.

8.   When a gentleman sent his son to Socrates that he might be informed of his genius and disposition, Socrates, after he had looked at the youth some time said, "Speak my boy, that I may see thee." Diogenes used to say that he always wondered why people were so exact as never to buy a pot of earthenware but they would try it by the sound or ringing of it, but when they bought a man, they thought it only sufficient to look at him.
> *The Universal Spectator*, No. 485, January 21, 1738.

9. He stood as erect as that tent-prop, both arms stretched out
    wide
On the great cross-support in the center, that goes to each
    side;
He relaxed not a muscle, but hung there as, caught in his
    pangs
And waiting his change, the king-serpent all heavily hangs,
Far away from his kind, in the pine, till deliverance come
With the springtime—so agonized Saul, drear and stark, blind
    and dumb.
> ROBERT BROWNING, *Saul*, IV.

10. From you, Ianthe, little troubles pass
      Like little ripples down a sunny river;
    Your pleasures spring like daisies in the grass,
      Cut down, and up again as blithe as ever.
                                WALTER SAVAGE LANDOR, "Ianthe."

11. Love is a sickness full of woes,
      All remedies refusing;
    A plant that with most cutting grows,
      Most barren with best using,
          Why so?
                         SAMUEL DANIEL, "Love Is a Sickness."

12. The robin and the bluebird, piping loud,
      Filled all the blossoming orchards with their glee;
    The sparrows chirped as if they still were proud
      Their race in Holy Writ should mentioned be;
    And hungry crows, assembled in a crowd,
      Clamored their piteous prayer incessantly;
    Knowing who hears the ravens cry, and said:
    "Give us, O Lord, this day, our daily bread!"
             HENRY WADSWORTH LONGFELLOW, "The Poet's Tale."

III. EXERCISES ON THE VOWELS

A. The Front Vowels

DISTINCTION BETWEEN /i/ AND /ɪ/

13.01 The front vowels are made with the highest point of the front part of the tongue (the part just behind the tip and blade of the tongue) raised to the required height toward the roof of the mouth.

For the /i/ sound, as in *eat, scene,* and *knee,* the tongue is raised almost to the gum ridge of the roof of the mouth. The /i/ is the highest and most fronted and tensed of the vowels. The /ɪ/ sound, as in *it* and *bit,* is made with the highest point of the front part of the tongue somewhat lower and less tense than for /i/.

SENTENCES FOR PRACTICE

13.02 In the following sentences, be sure you make a clear distinction between the /i/ and /ɪ/ sounds:

1. She did indeed say that he was a greedy pig.
2. The children are studying reading and arithmetic.
3. If he's here, I'll see him.
4. I was ill last week and couldn't go to the tea.
5. Give the kitten to Irene.
6. The ship is on an even keel.
7. It seems to be a reasonable story.
8. Listen to the buzzing of the bees.
9. The meat is full of gristle.
10. I'll speak to him this evening.
11. They climbed a steep hill.
12. Steel is made from pig iron.
13. He's sleeping in the inner room.
14. Their leader lives in Geneva, Switzerland.
15. It's a very weak mixture.
16. Dick believes he'll be picked for the team.
17. Bill stayed three weeks in the Virginia hills.
18. Jean seems to have hidden it in the sleeve of her dress.
19. He's been picking beans for dinner.
20. There's a great deal of dill in the pickles.

LONGER SELECTIONS

13.03 Here are some selections of prose and poetry for additional practice on these sounds:

1. Go, lovely rose—
   Tell her that wastes her time and me,
   That now she knows,
   When I resemble her to thee,
   How sweet and fair she seems to be.

   EDMUND WALLER, "Go, Lovely Rose."

2. How safe is it to live in a big metropolis? The answer is not so obvious as it might appear. To a reader of newspaper headlines, a city must seem the most perilous spot on earth, for all kinds of spectacular mishaps occur there. Walls collapse, cornices fall, pedestrians get mugged, water mains break, power fails, and cars plunge into crowded sidewalks.

To a mathematician, on the other hand, cities probably seem a safer place than most, for during a typical year millions of people are involved and relatively few are harmed.

WILLIAM K. ZINSSER, *The City Dwellers.**

3. He thought he saw a Kangaroo
  That worked a coffee-mill:
He looked again, and found it was
  A vegetable-pill.
"Were I to swallow this," he said,
  "I should be very ill!"

    LEWIS CARROLL, "The Gardener's Song."

4. The amount of women in London who flirt with their own husbands is perfectly scandalous. It looks so bad. It is simply washing one's clean linen in public.

   OSCAR WILDE, *The Importance of Being Earnest,* I.

5. Come, Sleep, O Sleep, the certain knot of peace,
  The baiting-place of wit, the balm of woe,
The poor man's wealth, the prisoner's release,
  The indifferent judge between the high and low!

    SIR PHILIP SIDNEY, "Astrophel and Stella."

6. The question of the mental health of the artist has engaged the attention of our culture since the beginning of the Romantic Movement. Before that time it was commonly said that the poet was "mad," but this was only a manner of speaking, a way of saying that the mind of the poet worked in a different fashion from the mind of the philosopher; it had no real reference to the mental hygiene of the man who was the poet. But in the early nineteenth century, with the development of a more elaborate psychology and a stricter and more literal view of mental and emotional normality, the statement was more strictly and literally intended.

   LIONEL TRILLING, *The Liberal Imagination.*†

7. The seed ye sow, another reaps;
The wealth ye find, another keeps;
The robes ye weave, another wears;
The arms ye forge, another bears.

  PERCY BYSSHE SHELLEY, "Song to the Men of England."

* From *The City Dwellers* by William K. Zinsser, published by Harper & Row.
 † From *The Liberal Imagination* by Lionel Trilling, published by The Viking Press, Inc.

8. There are certain things—as, a spider, a ghost,
   The income-tax, gout, an umbrella for three—
   That I hate, but the thing that I hate the most
   Is a thing they call the Sea.
                                 LEWIS CARROLL, "A Sea Dirge."

9. The Italians have voices like peacocks; the Spanish
   Smell, I fancy, of garlic; the Swedish and Danish
   Have something too Runic, too rough and unshod, in
   Their accent for mouths not descended from Odin;
   German gives me a cold in the head, sets me wheezing
   And coughing; and Russian is nothing but sneezing;
                                 ROBERT, LORD LYTTON, "Lucile."

10. They are slaves who fear to speak
    For the fallen and the weak;
    They are slaves who will not choose
    Hatred, scoffing, and abuse,
    Rather than in silence shrink
    From the truth they needs must think;
    They are slaves who dare not be
    In the right with two or three.
                                 JAMES RUSSELL LOWELL, "Stanzas on Freedom."

DISTINCTION BETWEEN /ɛ/ AND /ɪ/

13.04   The /ɛ/ sound, as in *any, then,* and *friend,* is made with the highest point of the front part of the tongue slightly lower than it is for /ɪ/. Use care that you do not substitute an /ɪ/ or /e/ sound where the /ɛ/ sound should be used.

SHORT SENTENCES FOR PRACTICE

13.05   Read aloud the following sentences:

1. Henry was born in Tennessee.
2. He wrote with a ten-cent ball-point pen.
3. Ben put the trash in the coal bin.
4. Jim bought a costly gem for his fiancée.
5. Dennis won a prize last Wednesday.
6. Since he can't knock any sense into the boy's head, it's best to send him to bed.
7. It was a pleasure to see a good production of *Measure for Measure.*
8. He may end by having to beg on the streets.

9. Many men attempted to secure the treasure.
10. It was a terrible strain to be merry while there was gloom everywhere.
11. He hid his head under the bedclothes.
12. America has many scenic treasures.
13. The emphasis in reading a sentence aloud should fall on the thought-carrying words.
14. Peg Woffington was an English actress of the eighteenth century.
15. The Indians wore elaborate headdresses.
16. She says she sent flowers in plenty of time for Henry's birthday.
17. He could smell that the egg wasn't very fresh.
18. Care should be taken in trying to mend an antique dress.
19. Old-fashioned thrillers were sometimes called "penny dreadfuls."
20. Kenneth bought a box of ten-cent cigars.

Longer Selections

13.06 Here is additional practice material for the /ɛ/ sound:

1. Jenny kiss'd me when we met,
       Jumping from the chair she sat in;
   Time, you thief, who love to get
       Sweets into your list, put that in!
   Say I am weary, say I am sad,
       Say that health and wealth have miss'd me,
   Say I am growing old, but add,
       Jenny kiss'd me.

Leigh Hunt, "Jenny Kiss'd Me."

2. Keep the faculty of effort alive in you by a little gratuitous exercise every day. That is, be systematically ascetic or heroic in little unnecessary points, do every day or two something for no other reason than that you would rather not do it, so that when the hour of dire need draws nigh, it may find you not unnerved and untrained to stand the test.

William James, *Psychology*.

3. When I am dead, my dearest,
       Sing no sad songs for me;
   Plant thou no roses at my head,
       Nor shady cypress tree:

Be the green grass above me
  With showers and dewdrops wet;
And if thou wilt, remember,
  And if thou wilt, forget.

CHRISTINA ROSSETTI, "Song."

4.   On the first day of January nothing happens except to the calendar. The date marks no astronomical event and corresponds to no change in the seasons, either here or anywhere else. The ancient Jews, Egyptians, and Greeks—all of whom put the beginning of the new year in March instead—were following a sound instinct, and so were the Englishmen who for so long stubbornly refused to change their old custom. Perhaps the world was not actually created for the first time in March of 4004 B.C. (as Archbishop Ussher demonstrated to his own and many people's satisfaction), but March is when it is annually created anew, and that is when the calendar of the soil begins.

JOSEPH WOOD KRUTCH, *The Twelve Seasons.* *

5.   The blessèd damozel lean'd out
  From the gold bar of Heaven;
Her eyes were deeper than the depth
  Of waters still'd at even;
She had three lillies in her hand,
  And the stars in her hair were seven.

DANTE GABRIEL ROSSETTI, "The Blessèd Damozel."

FOR IMPROMPTU TALK

13.07   Do you agree with the point of view expressed by William James in the selection from his *Psychology* in the preceding section? State the reasons for your agreement or disagreement. At the same time be aware of the accuracy and resonance of your vowel sounds.

THE VOWEL /æ/

13.08   The /æ/ sound, as in *absolute, bat,* and *man,* is made with the highest point of the front part of the tongue a little lower and more drawn back than for the /ɛ/ sound.

---

* From *The Twelve Seasons* by Joseph Wood Krutch. Copyright © 1949 by Joseph Wood Krutch, published by William Sloane Associates, Publishers.

Care must be taken that the /æ/ sound is not nasalized. The soft palate should be stretched upward in its articulation, making for an open throat.*

SENTENCES FOR PRACTICE

13.09

1. They passed the bandstand on their way to the dance.
2. Sam had a bad time trying to understand the problem.
3. Manx was an ancient language of Britain.
4. Frank became angry at the pranks of the children.
5. The man added the figures incorrectly.
6. Please pass me the plate of sandwiches.
7. They can't seem to analyze the facts.
8. The anxious crowd clamored for the candidate.
9. Thatcher fell into the trap.
10. The men were massed in battle formation.
11. I'll catch the last bus.
12. The accident badly damaged Ann's ankle.
13. His answers on the examination were not very accurate.
14. I asked him for a match.
15. The cloud was no bigger than a man's hand.
16. The wire contact was not adequate.
17. There's sand in the back of the car.
18. Fran said that she had had many happy times in Canada.
19. That man always wears a black hat.
20. He sang the operatic aria in the grand manner.

13.10 Be sure that you make a distinction between the vowel sounds in the following pairs of words:

ken–can	relish–radish	dense–dance
men–man	ketch–catch	lens–lance
den–Dan	expend–expand	bend–band
pen–pan	bench–branch	gem–jam

* Some words that most Americans pronounce with the /æ/ vowel are pronounced with a vowel halfway between /æ/ and /ɑ/ by most southern British speakers and by many people in eastern New England and in the South. These words, not numerous, include those in which the letter *a* is followed by an /f/ sound, as in *half* and *laugh*, or by an /s/ sound, as in *class* or *pass*, or by an /m/ or /n/ plus a consonant, as in *sample, dance,* and *can't*. You are advised to follow the usage of the educated speakers in your locality.

13.11 Students whose first language is not English are cautioned to distinguish well between the /ɑ/ and the /æ/ sound in the following pairs of words:

bond—band	palm—Pam	Don—Dan
cot—cat	sot—sat	shock—shack
fond—fanned	cob—cab	knotty—natty
hock—hack	knock—knack	block—black
stock—stack	lock—lack	jockey—Jackie

LONGER SELECTIONS

13.12

1. Here's to the maiden of bashful fifteen;
    Here's to the widow of fifty;
   Here's to the flaunting extravagant queen,
    And here's to the housewife that's thrifty.
   Let the toast pass,
   Drink to the lass,
   I'll warrant she'll prove an excuse for the glass.

   RICHARD BRINSLEY SHERIDAN, *The School for Scandal,* III, iii.

2.   Professor Blackie of Edinburgh, being indisposed one day, caused to be posted on the door of his lecture room the following notice: "Professor Blackie will not meet his classes today."
       A student who was a bit of a wag erased the "c" in "classes." The Professor, hearing of it sent a messenger with instructions to erase the "l."

   ANONYMOUS, "What's in a Letter?" *Modern Eloquence,* Vol. XII.

3. When God at first made man,
    Having a glass of blessings standing by—
   Let us (said he) pour on him all we can;
    Let the world's riches, which dispersed lie,
   Contract into a span.

   GEORGE HERBERT, "The Pulley."

4. If you wish in this world to advance,
   Your merits you're bound to enhance,
    You must stir it and stump it,
    And blow your own trumpet,
   Or, trust me, you haven't a chance.

   W. S. GILBERT, *Ruddigore,* I.

5.   To the traveller imbued with a feeling for the historical and poetical, so inseparably intertwined in the annals of romantic Spain, the Alhambra is as much an object of devotion as is the Caaba * to all true Moslems. How many legends and traditions, true and fabulous—how many songs and ballads, Arabian and Spanish, of love and war and chivalry, are associated with this Oriental pile! It was the royal abode of the Moorish kings, where, surrounded with the splendors and refinements of Asiatic luxury, they held dominion over what they vaunted as a terrestial paradise, and made their last stand for empire in Spain.

WASHINGTON IRVING, *The Alhambra.*

6. I've been cast adrift on a raft of melancholy.
    The night-wind passed me, like a sail across
    A blind man's eye. There it is,
    The interminable tumbling of the great grey
    Main of moonlight, washing over
    The little oyster-shell of this month of April:
    Among the raven-quills of the shadows
    And on the white pillows of men asleep:
    The night's a pale pastureland of peace,
    And sometimes condones the world, incorrigibly.

CHRISTOPHER FRY, *The Lady's Not for Burning,* III.†

7. Know then thyself, presume not God to scan;
    The proper study of Mankind is Man.

ALEXANDER POPE, "An Essay on Man."

8. "Will you walk a little faster?" said a whiting to a snail,
    "There's a porpoise close behind us, and he's treading on my tail,
    See how eagerly the lobsters and the turtles all advance!
    They are waiting on the shingle—will you come and join the dance?"

LEWIS CARROLL, *Alice's Adventures in Wonderland.*

9. His brow is wet with honest sweat,
        He earns whate'er he can,
    And looks the whole world in the face,
        For he owes not any man.

HENRY WADSWORTH LONGFELLOW, "The Village
Blacksmith."

* Caaba: Islamic shrine at Mecca.
† Published by the Oxford University Press.

10. . . . he who has mastered any law in his private thoughts, is
master to that extent of all men whose language he speaks,
and of all into whose language his own can be translated.
RALPH WALDO EMERSON, "The American Scholar."

11. True ease in writing comes from art, not chance,
As those move easiest who have learn'd to dance.
'Tis not enough no harshness give offence,
The sound must seem an Echo to the sense:
ALEXANDER POPE, "An Essay on Criticism."

12. In Xanadu did Kubla Khan
A stately pleasure-dome decree:
Where Alph, the sacred river ran
Through caverns measureless to man
Down to a sunless sea.
SAMUEL TAYLOR COLERIDGE, "Kubla Khan."

B. The Back Vowels

DISTINCTION BETWEEN /ɑ/ AND /ɔ/

14.01 The back vowels (/ɑ/, /ɔ/, /o/, /ʊ/, /u/) are
made with the highest point of the tongue curve raised in
varying degrees toward the roof of the mouth. The /ɑ/
sound, as in *are, far, father,* and *palm,* is made with the highest point on the back of the tongue low and in a relaxed state.
This sound is sometimes called the "Italian *a.*" Usually, no
great difficulties are involved in its formation. However, care
must be taken that a distinction is made between the vowels
in *cord* and *card.*

Pronounce the following pairs of words, making a distinction between vowels in the first and second of them:

bar–bore	car–caw	far–for
mar–more	tar–tore	garden–Gordon
hard–hoard	stark–stork	arson–Orson
parch–porch	barn–born	shah–Shaw
Don–dawn	Otto–auto	cot–caught

SENTENCES FOR PRACTICE

14.02

1. The band marched through Central Park.
2. Don't argue with your father.

3. The farmers drove in to market.
4. He's a sergeant in the army reserve corps.
5. She beats the carpets in the backyard.
6. A cargo ship has just arrived from Argentina.
7. The highest card he held was the king of hearts.
8. Are you going to Arthur's party?
9. She went to the bargain counter of the largest department store in town.
10. They went through an archway into a large park.
11. Martha was very calm about being charged with arson.
12. Are you going to drive the car into the garage?
13. We went farther and farther into the forest.
14. The stars sparkled in the autumn sky.
15. It's hard to find a place to park on Charles Street.
16. The Mardi Gras is a carnival held in New Orleans.
17. They ate rhubarb from the family's garden.
18. You'll find Carl at the barber's.
19. Harlan had tickets for a concert at Carnegie Hall.
20. Her husband's sarcasm started an argument.

LONGER SELECTIONS

14.03

1. Unlearn'd, he knew no schoolman's subtle art.
   No language, but the language of the heart.
                    ALEXANDER POPE, "An Essay on Criticism."

2. The Queen of Hearts
   She made some tarts,
       All on a summer's day;
   The Knave of Hearts
   He stole the tarts,
       And took them clean away.

                                        ANONYMOUS.

3. Sabina has a thousand charms
       To captivate my heart;
   Her lovely eyes are Cupid's arms,
       And every look a dart:
   But when the beauteous idiot speaks,
       She cures me of my pain;
   Her tongue the servile fetters breaks
       And frees her slave again.
                    ANONYMOUS, "Amphion Anglicus."

4.   . . . There are members of Parliament so unhappy with the spoken word that if waylaid, *en route* to the House, an important speech in their pocket—they would, at the cry 'Your Typescript or your Trousers' (if hesitantly), part with the latter. A taxi and a tailor could save *that* situation: the other loss, nothing. Again, there are those sad persons we see on newsreels: with next to nothing to say, and no hope of saying it without the paper, from which they lift reluctant eyes an anxious moment, for would-be human glances.

A. P. Rossiter, *Our Living Language.**

5.   Of all the girls that are so smart
  There's none like pretty Sally;
She is the darling of my heart,
  And she lives in my alley.
There is no lady in the land
  Is half so sweet as Sally;
She is the darling of my heart
  And she lives in our alley.

Henry Carey, "Sally in Our Alley."

Distinction Between /ɔ/ and /ɑ/

14.04   The /ɔ/ sound, as in *caught, walk, tall,* and *war,* is made with the high point of the back of the tongue somewhat higher and the lips more rounded than for the /ɑ/ sound. Although there is considerable regional variation in the articulation of this vowel, take care neither to retract the tongue nor to round the lips so much that it sounds like an /o/.

Make a distinction between the vowel sounds in the following pairs of words:

flaw—flow	saw—sew	bossed—boast
gnaw—know	bought—boat	chalk—choke
jaw—Joe	caught—coat	cost—coast
law—low	naught—note	Paul—poll
raw—row	quart—quote	tall—toll
malt—moult	pawn—pone	awning—owning

* From *Our Living Language* by A. P. Rossiter, published by Longmans, Green & Co. Ltd.

14.05

1. I called him on the phone at four o'clock.
2. He wrote on the sidewalk with a piece of chalk.
3. He stole three bases in the ball game.
4. I thought I'd go on vacation in August.
5. They all voted for Mr. Dawson.
6. He's caught an awfully bad cold.
7. The lawyer thought it was a matter for the courts.
8. The snow had melted, and the ground had thawed.
9. She taught drawing in elementary school.
10. The boys ordered a malted milk and some corn muffins.
11. He hauled the car off the road.
12. They sold the yawl and bought a motorboat.
13. George Bernard Shaw is the author of many long plays.
14. Get me some gauze and some warm water.
15. The police officer helped staunch the flow of blood.
16. Claude ordered four quarts of distilled water.
17. I don't like to hear the cawing of crows at dawn.
18. Paul lost his coat yesterday morning.
19. He bought an old saxophone in a pawnshop.
20. She caught herself just as she was beginning to fall from the wall.

LONGER SELECTIONS

14.06

1. I remember the bulwarks by the shore,
     And the fort upon the hill;
   The sunrise gun, with its hollow roar,
   The drum beat repeated o'er and o'er,
     And the bugle wild and shrill.
   And the music of that old song
     Throbs in my memory still:
     "A boy's will is the wind's will,
   And the thoughts of youth are long, long thoughts."
         HENRY WADSWORTH LONGFELLOW, "My Lost Youth."

2. The Walrus and the Carpenter
     Were walking close at hand;

They wept like anything to see
  Such quantities of sand
"If this were only cleared away,"
  They said, "it would be grand!"
LEWIS CARROLL, Through the Looking Glass.

3.   Life was never a May-game for men: in all times the lot of the dumb millions born to toil was defaced with manifold sufferings, injustices, heavy burdens, avoidable and unavoidable; not play at all, but hard work that made the sinews sore, and the heart sore.
THOMAS CARLYLE, Past and Present.

4. There is a pleasure in the pathless woods,
    There is a rapture on the lonely shore,
 There is society, where none intrudes,
    By the deep Sea, and music in its roar;
    I love not man the less, but Nature more.
LORD BYRON, Childe Harold's Pilgrimage,
Canto IV, Stanza 178.

5. I dreamt I dwelt in marble halls,
   And each damp thing that creeps and crawls
   Went wobble-wobble on the walls.
LEWIS CARROLL, "The Palace of Humbug."

6. He gave Sir Knight the end of cord,
   To lead the captive of his sword
   In triumph, whilst the steeds he caught,
   And them to further service brought,
   The Squire, in state, rode on before,
   And on his nut-brown whinyard * bore
   The trophy-Fiddle and the case,
   Leaning on shoulder like a mace.
SAMUEL BUTLER, Hudibras, Part I, Canto II.

7. Helen, thy beauty is to me
    Like those Nicean barks of yore,
 That gently, o'er a perfumed sea,
    The weary, way-worn wanderer bore
    To his own native shore.
EDGAR ALLAN POE, "To Helen."

* Whinyard: a short sword.

8. The splendor falls on castle walls
   And snowy summits old in story;
   The long light shakes across the lakes,
   And the wild cataract leaps in glory.
   ALFRED, LORD TENNYSON, *The Princess,* Part III.

9. We arrived at Louisville on the fourth night, and gladly availed ourselves of its excellent hotel. Next day we went on in the Ben Franklin, a beautiful mail steamboat, and reached Cincinnati shortly after midnight. Being by this time nearly tired of sleeping upon shelves, we had remained awake to go ashore straightway; and groping a passage across the dark decks of other boats, and among labyrinths of engine-machinery and leaking casks of molasses, we reached the streets, knocked up the porter at the hotel where we stayed before, and were, to our great joy, safely housed soon afterwards.
   CHARLES DICKENS, *American Notes* (1842).

10. Ringed with the azure world, he stands.
    The wrinkled sea beneath him crawls;
    He watches from his mountain walls,
    And like a thunderbolt he falls.
    ALFRED, LORD TENNYSON, "The Eagle."

DISTINCTION BETWEEN /ʊ/ AND /u/

14.07 The vowel /ʊ/, as in *look, would,* and *full,* is made with the highest point of the back of the tongue high in the mouth and the lips rounded. The /u/ vowel, as in *ooze, move, room,* and *Ruth,* is made with the tongue still higher, the lips protruded and rounded, and the articulators more tense than for the /ʊ/ sound. Speakers whose first language is not English often encounter difficulty in making a distinction between these vowels.

14.08 In reading aloud the following pairs of words, be certain you use the /ʊ/ vowel in the first of each pair and the /u/ vowel in the second of the pair:

book—boot	foot—food	stood—stoop
took—tool	rook—rule	brook—broom
could—cool	wood—woo	should—shooed
look—Luke	wool—womb	pull—pool

14.09 The following words are pronounced with either of these two vowels (/ʊ/ or /u/). Check that your pronunciation is in accord with educated usage in your locality: *coop, broom, groom, roof, root, soot, hoop, room, hoof, Cooper, rooster, whooping* (as in *whooping cough*).

SENTENCES FOR PRACTICE

14.10

1. They pushed him into the pool.
2. Can you prove that the book is yours?
3. The room was already full.
4. She sat on a low footstool.
5. There's going to be a full moon tonight.
6. I saw it on the bulletin board at school.
7. Ruth has just had a tooth pulled.
8. The woman looked in the cookbook for a recipe for roast goose.
9. He stood first in the group.
10. They shook the sand out of their shoes.
11. I bought a spool of thread and some wool at the store.
12. He bought a set of wood-carving tools.
13. Sugar is an important food.
14. He relaxed on a cushion on the roof.
15. The duty on the worsted material amounted to $2.40.
16. Mr. Fuller has a good room overlooking the river.
17. Who would like a glass of grapefruit juice?
18. She didn't like the look of the prune pudding.
19. I've got some good news for you.
20. The poodle looked around the room for some food.

LONGER SELECTIONS

14.11

1. Come live with me, and be my love,
   And we will some new pleasures prove
   Of golden sands, and crystal brooks,
   With silken lines, and silver hooks.

   JOHN DONNE, "The Bait."

2.   Sheridan once said of some speech in his acute, sarcastic way, that "it contained a great deal both of what was new and what was true: but that unfortunately what was new was not true, and what was true was not new."
   WILLIAM HAZLITT, "On Paradox and Common-Place,"
   Table Talk.

3. We are little airy creatures,
   All of different voice and features;
   One of us in glass is set,
   One of us you'll find in jet.
   T'other you may see in tin,
   And the fourth a box within.
   If the fifth you should pursue,
   It can never fly from you.

   JONATHAN SWIFT, "On the Vowels."

4.   Some books are to be tasted, others to be swallowed, and
   some few to be chewed and digested:

   FRANCIS BACON, "Of Studies."

5. There was a young lady named Rood,
   Who was such an absolute prude
      That she pulled down the blind
      When changing her mind,
   Lest curious eyes should intrude.

   ANONYMOUS (from *The Silver Treasury of Light Verse,*
   by OSCAR WILLIAMS).

6.   Times grew worse and worse with Rip Van Winkle as years
   of matrimony rolled on; a tart temper never mellows with age,
   and a sharp tongue is the only edged tool that grows keener
   with constant use.

   WASHINGTON IRVING, *Rip Van Winkle.*

7. Oh for a seat in some poetic nook,
   Just hid with trees and sparkling with a brook,
   Where through the quivering boughs the sunbeams shoot
   Their arrowy diamonds upon flowers and fruit,
   While stealing airs come fuming o'er the stream,
   And lull the fancy to a waking dream!

   LEIGH HUNT, "Politics and Poetics."

8. Was ever woman in this humour woo'd?
   Was ever woman in this humour won?

   WILLIAM SHAKESPEARE, *Richard the Third,* I, ii.

9. I never saw a moor,
      I never saw the sea;
   Yet know I how the heather looks,
      And what a wave must be.

   EMILY DICKINSON, "I Never Saw a Moor." *

* From *The Complete Poems of Emily Dickinson,* published by Little,
Brown & Co.

C. The Central Vowels

THE VOWEL IN *Sir*

15.01   The stressed vowel in the words *early, hurt,* and *occur* is pronounced with or without "*r* coloration." The sound uttered by those speakers who "drop their *r*'s" is represented by the symbol /ɜ/. The sound is articulated with the highest point of the tongue raised in the center of the mouth in the direction of the hard palate. W. S. Gilbert, in *The Bab Ballads,* suggests this pronunciation by rhyming *girl* with *gull.* If, however, "*r* coloration" is used with /ɜ/, it is accomplished by turning back the tip of the tongue and raising the middle part of it. The resultant vowel is represented by the symbol /ɝ/. This latter pronunciation is heard more frequently throughout the United States than the "*r*-less" pronunciation. If it is used, be careful that the tongue tip is not too greatly retracted. If this occurs, there is tension and harshness of tone.

SENTENCES FOR PRACTICE

15.02

1. The committee decided to adjourn to adjoining rooms.
2. Boyd saw two birds in a small nest.
3. The situation is certainly not perfect.
4. He was transferred to the New Jersey office.
5. The girl was accused of murder in the first degree.
6. Herbert is very earnest about his work.
7. She lost her purse on Myrtle Avenue.
8. The early bird catches the worm.
9. Bertha taught a class in German.
10. Colonel Boyd was sent to Berlin.
11. The doctor urged her to lose thirty pounds.
12. It was a worldwide news service.
13. All the words in the list were verbs.
14. The storm became worse and worse.
15. He was ordered to pull over to the curb.
16. His poise deserves much praise.
17. It was a matter of "first come, first served."
18. The shirt must have been washed in dirty water.

19. He should be urged to return to work.
20. She wore a Persian lamb fur coat.

LONGER SELECTIONS

15.03

1. Good-nature and good-sense must ever join;
   To err is human, to forgive divine.
   ALEXANDER POPE, "An Essay on Criticism."

2. We've a first-class assortment of magic;
       And for raising a posthumous shade
   With effects that are comic or tragic,
       There's no cheaper house in the trade.
   Love-philtre—we've quantities of it;
       And for knowledge if anyone burns,
   We keep an extremely small prophet, a prophet
       Who brings us unbounded returns:
   W. S. GILBERT, The Sorcerer, I.

3.   To make a new friend at all, in fact, is difficult in the compartmental city, as any urban boy or girl hoping to fall in love will testify. The road to romance is, paradoxically, one of the city's most elusive trails. In theory the odds of meeting a life partner should increase with the size of the metropolis—every boy is sure that the girl of his dreams has been drawn to the big city by the same dreams that drew him there. She is right around the corner, waiting for him as eagerly as he is waiting for her. But *where* is she? And how can he find her?
   WILLIAM K. ZINSSER, The City Dwellers.*

4. Beside yon straggling fence that skirts the way,
   With blossom'd furze unprofitably gay,
   There, in his noisy mansion, skill'd to rule,
   The village master taught his little school;
   A man severe he was, and stern to view,
   I knew him well, and every truant knew:
   OLIVER GOLDSMITH, The Deserted Village.

5. What of a hasty word?
   Is the fleshly heart not stirred
       By a worm's pin-prick
       Where its roots are quick?

* From *The City Dwellers* by William K. Zinsser, published by Harper & Row.

See the eye, by a fly's foot blurred—
Ear, when a straw is heard
Scratch the brain's coat of curd!
>> ROBERT BROWNING, "A Lover's Quarrel," Stanza XVI.

6. The greatest error ever erred
Is a nice girl with a naughty word.
>> OGDEN NASH, "Oh Shucks, Ma'am, I Mean Excuse Me,"
>> *Verses from 1929 On.*

DISTINCTION BETWEEN /ʌ/ AND /ɑ/

15.04 The vowel sound in *sun, month,* and *rough* is represented by the symbol /ʌ/ and is always found in stressed syllables. It is usually made with the highest point of the middle part of the tongue in a lowered central position, the lips unrounded, and the jaw relaxed. Non-native speakers of English frequently confuse this vowel with the /ɑ/ sound, as in *calm.* The latter is usually a longer sound, made with a wider mouth opening.

In reading aloud the following pairs of words, be certain you make a distinction between the first of each pair (with an /ʌ/ vowel) and the second of each pair (with an /ɑ/ vowel).

bun–bond	cup–cop	won–wan
sum–psalm	suck–sock	fund–fond
cud–cod	luck–lock	run–Ron
rub–rob	come–calm	dun–Don
gut–got	nub–nob	cub–cob

SENTENCES FOR PRACTICE

15.05

1. He has just been made a judge of the Supreme Court.
2. Subways are not always very comfortable.
3. Get something to cover the rough part of the chair.
4. That's another reason for contributing to the fund.
5. This bus is much too crowded.
6. The cut caused much loss of blood.
7. Lunch will be served at one o'clock.
8. Monday will be the first day of the month.
9. She spent a vast sum of money on her country place.
10. Uncle Henry got caught in the rush.

11. The robber stumbled over the large rubber plant in the hall.
12. Something should be done to cut the cost of play production.
13. The girl came running to me with a bunch of lovely flowers in her hands.
14. John loves to putter around the house.
15. She mumbled something about being all thumbs as she tried to cut the dress pattern.
16. There is abundant evidence that he won't run for office next year.
17. The young writer was advised to cut some of the redundancies from his writing.
18. The jungle stretches for hundreds of miles.
19. There are few comforts in the life of a frontiersman.
20. He jumped at the firing of the gun.

LONGER SELECTIONS

15.06

1. For Freedom's battle once begun,
   Bequeathed by bleeding Sire to Son,
   Though baffled oft is ever won.

   LORD BYRON, *The Giaour.*

2. He thought he saw a Banker's Clerk
       Descending from the bus:
   He looked again, and found it was
       A Hippopotamus:
   "If this should stay to dine," he said,
       "There won't be much for us!"

   LEWIS CARROLL, "The Gardener's Song."

3. Much has been given us, and much will rightfully be expected from us. We have duties to others and duties to ourselves; and we can shirk neither. We have become a great nation, forced by the fact of its greatness into relations with other nations of the earth, and we must behave as beseems a people with such responsibilities. Toward all other nations, large and small, our attitude must be one of cordial and sincere friendship. We must show not only in our words, but in our deeds, that we are earnestly desirous of securing their good will by acting toward them in a spirit of just and generous recognition of all their rights.

   THEODORE ROOSEVELT, *Inaugural Address,* March 4, 1905.

4. Let not the dark thee cumber;
   What though the moon does slumber?
      The stars of the night
      Will lend thee their light,
   Like tapers clear without number.
                    ROBERT HERRICK, "The Night-Piece: To Julia."

FOR IMPROMPTU TALK

15.07 Talk about a fact or concept of special interest that you have learned in one of your classes in recent weeks. As you talk, be aware of working for good articulation and voice production.

UNSTRESSED VOWELS REPRESENTED BY /ə/

15.08 Vowels occur in stressed and unstressed syllables. In stressed syllables, each vowel has its symbol for representation. In unstressed syllables, vowels have a different sound and are represented, usually, by the symbol /ə/, called the *schwa.* The schwa may represent the pronunciation of *a, e, i, o,* or *u,* if the syllable in which any of these vowels occurs is unstressed. Some illustrations of unstressed vowels follow: the *a* in *about,* the *e* in the first syllable of *celestial,* the *i* in *giraffe,* the *o* in *observance,* and the *u* in *circus.*

The /ə/ is used to represent the vowel in monosyllables that have reduced stress in a phrase or sentence. A few of these words are *an, the, a, of, but, for, or, can,* and *was.* Whenever these words are not stressed, the schwa vowel is used. For example:

twice an hour	for example
two a day	wood or coal
half of a cup	I can go
all but Helen	he was playing

The schwa is sometimes called the *neutral vowel,* because it represents so many vowels in unstressed form.* The schwa is articulated in the central area of the mouth.

Proper emphasis and pleasing rhythm in speaking or reading aloud are much more easily obtained if vowels in normally

---

* At times /ɪ/, as in *granted* /græntɪd/, and /ʊ/, as in *today* /tʊdeɪ/, appear in unstressed syllables.

unaccented syllables are unstressed. Speech becomes very stilted, and meaning is impaired, if every syllable in every word is stressed.

UNSTRESSED WORDS

15.09 It is necessary to remember that most vowels in articles, conjunctions, pronouns, and prepositions are unstressed because these words do not usually carry the weight of meaning in the sentence. Many verbal auxiliaries also have unstressed vowels. In the following exercise, note that, although all the words listed on the left can be pronounced with stressed vowels for reasons of emphasis (for example, "They *are* rather good, after all."), they are usually pronounced with unstressed vowels. Read the phrases and sentences aloud, putting stress on the thought-bearing words.

EXAMPLES OF UNSTRESSED FORMS

15.10

a and *an:*   Take a chance. It's a new one. They're three for a dollar. He pays twenty dollars a month. He's an old man. She was wearing an evening dress.

and: War and Peace. Time and tide. Bread and butter. Live and let live. Body and soul. Pen and pencil. New York and New Jersey.

at: I'll see you at eleven o'clock. We saw them at the opera. He spoke at the meeting.

are: Men are mortal. Those are the ones I want. Some of them are pretty good. My arms are tired. Here are the boys.

as: It's just as good. He was as tall as his brother. It's over twice as much.

but: I saw all but two of them. I've got everything but the money. I'm going, but I don't want to.

can: I can go on Monday. You can do it easily. Do you know if she can come?

could: Who could it be? They could go on Monday. I wish I could find it.

do: How do you know? How do they know? Do you like it?

does:	How does it work? When does he come? Why does she cry?
for:	I'll meet you for lunch. He spoke for an hour. They're here for a week.
from:	He's back from Europe. They work from nine to five. They brought it from France.
had:	He had already gone. If he had done so, things would have been different.
has:	He has already gone. John has returned. It has happened.
have:	I might have done it. I ought to have thought of it. I should have remembered it.
he:	I know he does. What will he think of us? Does he know it yet?
her:	Give it to her. We must tell her soon. They told her the bad news.
him:	I saw him today. Have you ever met him? Give him the ball. They've known him for a long time.
his:	He must do his share. Bill took his hat. I knew his cousins.
must:	I must hurry. Henry must do his own work. They must spend less money.
of:	The break of day. The high cost of living. I'll walk to the top of the hill. He's a member of the company. What do you think of it?
or:	Two or three are not bad. Say either yes or no.
shall:	How shall I do it? What shall we say to them? I shall be glad to go.
should:	Why should they worry? I think you should go now.
some:	Will you have some candy? I want some more. Give me some larger ones. He needs some money.
that:	He said that he couldn't. I know that he did. These are the books that I bought. She wrote that she was ill.
them:	We met them at the restaurant. Give it to them. I bought them a present. Will you read them a story?
to:	They're ready to go. I went to the movies. He spoke to Fred. Come to dinner on Thursday.
us:	She sat between us. He advised us to go. Take us with you. Will you save us three seats?

was: It was all I could do. She was very tired. What was the right answer? Time was flying.

were: They were there. Who were the students? We were exhausted. You were not there yesterday.

would: What would they want for it? Who would object to it?

you and *your:* Take all you want. Did you get your hat? Take your time. I saw your mother yesterday.

LONGER SELECTIONS

15.11 In the practice selections that follow, pay particular attention to the rhythm of your speaking. Read the vowel of an unaccented syllable as an unstressed vowel. The stressed vowels in the first two of the following selections are underlined. The remaining vowels in those selections, therefore, are either unstressed or silent.

1. Read not to contradict and confute, nor to believe and take for granted, nor to find talk and discourse, but to weigh and consider.

FRANCIS BACON, "Of Studies."

2. In the depths of college shades, or in his lonely chamber, the poor student shrunk from observation. He found shelter among books, which insult not; and studies, that ask not questions of a youth's finances. He was lord of his library, and seldom cared for looking out beyond his domains. The healing influence of studious pursuits was upon him, to soothe and to abstract.

CHARLES LAMB, "Poor Relations."

3. A tuna battle may last from ten minutes to several hours, depending on the skill of the angler and the size and strength of the individual fish. Two sportsmen in a launch off Ogunquit one season hooked a tuna estimated to weigh about 1000 pounds, and the ensuing struggle lasted throughout many hours of a day and a night, the fish towing the launch about 50 miles out to sea and back. Almost on the spot where he had taken the hook, the tuna swished his saw-like tail and cut the line for freedom.

"Maine: A Guide to Down East," * *American Guide Series.*

* Published by the Houghton Mifflin Co.

4. Werther had a love for Charlotte
   Such as words could never utter;
Would you know how first he met her?
   She was cutting bread and butter.

  Charlotte was a moral lady,
    And a moral man was Werther,
  And for all the wealth of Indies,
    Would do nothing for to hurt her.

  So he sighed and pined and ogled,
    And his passion boil'd and bubbled,
  Till he blew his silly brains out,
    And no more by it was troubled.

  Charlotte, having seen his body
    Borne before her on a shutter,
  Like a well conducted person,
    Went on cutting bread and butter.
      WILLIAM MAKEPEACE THACKERAY, "Sorrows of Werther."

5. Swift as a shadow, short as any dream,
Brief as the lightning in the collied night,
That, in a spleen, unfolds both heaven and earth,
And ere a man hath power to say "Behold!"
The jaws of darkness do devour it up:
So quick bright things come to confusion.
    WILLIAM SHAKESPEARE, *A Midsummer Night's Dream*, I, i.

6.   In a London park on Monday, a paradise of birdsong and roses, every prospect pleased and only man was vile, offending eye and ear. As peace lay heavy and even the distant hum of traffic thinned to silence, there entered on the pleasance a stout party in sun-glasses, from whose inner pocket issued at full throttle Brahms in E Minor. On the far side of the scene there entered simultaneously a mountainous woman in tight trousers emitting boogie at full belt. As these two unlovely examples of the human race approached each other, cacophony grew to a hideous climax, declined, and ultimately subsided. "O for a muse of fire, or a death ray," said a man on the bench close by, "to fuse them and shrivel their transistors to a cinder!" The birds resumed their song.
    Manchester Guardian Weekly, June 8, 1961.

7. And like a dying lady, lean and pale,
   Who totters forth, wrapped in a gauzy veil,
   Out of her chamber, led by the insane
   And feeble wanderings of her fading brain,
   The moon rose up in the murky east,
   A white and shapeless mass.

   PERCY BYSSHE SHELLEY, "The Waning Moon."

8.   On board this steamboat, there were two young gentlemen, with shirt collars reversed as usual, and armed with
   very big walking-sticks; who planted two seats in the middle
   of the deck, at a distance of some four paces apart; took out
   their tobacco-boxes; and sat down opposite each other to chew.
   In less than a quarter of an hour's time, these hopeful youths
   had shed about them on the clean boards, a copious shower
   of yellow rain; clearing, by that means, a kind of magic circle,
   within whose limits no intruders dared to come, and which
   they never failed to refresh before a spot was dry. This being
   before breakfast, rather disposed me, I confess, to nausea,
   but looking attentively at one of the expectorators, I plainly
   saw that he was young in chewing and felt inwardly uneasy
   himself.

   CHARLES DICKENS, *American Notes* (1842).

9. To-morrow, and to-morrow, and to-morrow,
   Creeps in this petty pace from day to day,
   To the last syllable of recorded time;
   And all our yesterdays have lighted fools
   The way to dusty death.

   WILLIAM SHAKESPEARE, *Macbeth*, V, v.

10. *Shepherd:* Echo, I ween, will in the wood reply,
    And quaintly answer questions: shall I try?
    Echo: Try.
    Shepherd: What must we do our passion to express?
    Echo: Press.
    How shall I please her, who ne'er loved before?
                    Before.
    What most moves women when we them address?
                    A dress.
    Say, what can keep her chaste whom I adore?
                    A door.
    If music softens rocks, love tunes my lyre.
                    Liar.

Then teach me, Echo, how shall I come by her?
Buy her.
When bought, no question I shall be her dear?
Her deer.
But deer have horns: how must I keep her under?
Keep her under.
But what can glad me when she's laid on bier?
Beer. . . .
What must I do when women will be cross?
Be cross.
Lord, what is she that can so turn and wind?
Wind.
If she be wind, what stills her when she blows?
Blows. . . .
Is there no way to moderate her anger.
Hang her.
Thanks, gentle Echo! right thy answers tell
What woman is and how to guard her well.
Guard her well.

JONATHAN SWIFT, "A Gentle Echo on Woman
(in the Doric Manner)."

11.   Our place of destination in the first instance is Columbus.
It is distant about a hundred and twenty miles from Cincinnati, but there is a macadamised road (rare blessing!) the
whole way, and the rate of travelling upon it is six miles an
hour.

CHARLES DICKENS, *American Notes* (1842).

IV. EXERCISES ON THE DIPHTHONGS

DIPHTHONGS: EXPLANATION

16.01 A diphthong is a sequence of two vowel sounds
connected through a gliding process within a single syllable.
They are classified in several ways. For the purpose of these
exercises, they have been separated into *full, partial,* and
centering, or *murmur,* diphthongs. The *full diphthongs* are
represented by the sounds in *eye* /aɪ/, *out* /aʊt/, *few* /fɪu/,
and *boy* /bɔɪ/. In these diphthongs, the sound of the second
element is essential to the full understanding of the word.
Partial diphthongs occur in open syllables such as *know*

/noʊ/ and *they* /ðeɪ/. Some listeners do not hear the second element of these diphthongs even when it is made, because of the lack of stress; however, the second element in these diphthongs is not essential to the understanding of the word. *Centering,* or *murmur, diphthongs* occur with the appearance of *r,* as in *hare* /hɛɚ/, *pour* /poɚ/, *fear* /fɪɚ/, and *poor* /pʊɚ/. (Notice the contrast between *pour* and *poor.*)

A. The Full Diphthongs /aɪ/, /aʊ/, and /ɔɪ/

The Diphthong /aɪ/

16.02 The diphthong /aɪ/ occurs in the words *ice, kind,* and *buy.* Do not drop the tongue position at the end of this diphthong so that, for example, *mind* sounds like "moind" and *file* like "foil." The usage in some areas of this country is to change the first element in the diphthong to a lower vowel under the influence of a nasal or the lateral consonant /l/. Avoid "mahnd" for *mind* and "fahl" for *file.*

Sentences for Practice

16.03

1. He's flying to Ohio.
2. You'll find them in five sizes.
3. I'll meet you in the sweet by-and-by.
4. It's high time they arrived.
5. Why is she crying?
6. They arrived last night.
7. You'll find that old Mr. Bryan is a miser.
8. Ireland is called the Emerald Isle.
9. They saw a bright light over the horizon.
10. We advised him to retire.
11. Do you want your sandwich on white or rye?
12. The gas station is three miles from Elmira.
13. These are crimes punished by fines and imprisonment.
14. Ballplayers sign on the dotted line.
15. His childhood was spent in Iowa.
16. Idaho and Wyoming are western states.
17. In the United States, one drives to the right.

18. Neither Ida nor I knows how to fix tires.
19. The grapes are ripening on the vines.
20. The zoo was well stocked with lions and tigers.

LONGER SELECTIONS

16.04

1. Cherry-ripe, ripe, ripe, I cry,
    Full and fair ones; come and buy.
    If so be you ask me where
    They do grow, I answer: There
    Where my Julia's lips do smile;
    There's the land, or cherry-isle,
    Whose plantations fully show
    All the year where cherries grow.
    ROBERT HERRICK, "Cherry-Ripe."

2. Sweet day, so cool, so calm, so bright!
        The bridal of the earth and sky—
    The dew shall weep thy fall tonight;
        For thou must die.
    GEORGE HERBERT, "Virtue."

3. Some say the world will end in fire,
        Some say in ice.
    From what I've tasted of desire
    I hold with those who favor fire.
        But if it had to perish twice,
    I think I know enough of hate
        To say that for destruction, ice
    Is also great
        And would suffice.
    ROBERT FROST, "Fire and Ice." *

4. He that loves a rosy cheek,
        Or a coral lip admires,
    Or from star-like eyes doth seek
        Fuel to maintain his fires:
    As old Time makes these decay,
    So his flames must waste away.

---

* From *Complete Poems of Robert Frost.* Copyright 1923 by Holt, Rinehart & Winston, Inc. Copyright renewed 1951 by Robert Frost. Reprinted by permission of Holt, Rinehart & Winston, Inc.

But a smooth and steadfast mind,
  Gentle thoughts and calm desires,
Hearts with equal love combined,
  Kindle never-dying fires.
Where these are not, I despise
  Lovely cheeks or lips or eyes.
THOMAS CAREW, "The Unfading Beauty."

5. Good-bye, proud world! I'm going home:
    Thou art not my friend, and I'm not thine.
  Long through the weary crowds I roam;
    A river-ark on the ocean brine,
  Long I've been tossed like the driven foam;
  But now, proud world! I'm going home.
  Good-bye to Flattery's fawning face;
  To Grandeur with his wise grimace;
  To upstart Wealth's averted eye;
  To supple Office, low and high;
  To crowded halls, to court and street;
  To frozen hearts and hasting feet;
  To those who go, and those who come;
  Good-bye, proud world! I'm going home.
ELIZABETH BARRETT BROWNING, "Good-bye."

THE DIPHTHONG /aʊ/

16.05 The diphthong /aʊ/ in *owl, house, cow,* and *sound* is usually represented in spelling by *ou,* as in *out,* or *ow,* as in *now.* This diphthong is frequently nasalized if preceded or followed by a nasal consonant. It is sometimes not distinguished sufficiently from the single vowel /ɑ/ or from variations of /o/. Guard against these deviations from acceptable pronunciation in the sentences to follow.

SENTENCES FOR PRACTICE

16.06

1. It took me an hour to clean the counter.
2. The wind howled around the building.
3. It weighs two pounds and eight ounces.
4. Did you take the downtown subway?
5. The man went around to the back of the house.
6. There is often difficulty between town and gown.

7. She's traveling down South.
8. Mr. Powell counted his money.
9. It was a cloudy day.
10. He was surrounded by a crowd of people.
11. Mr. Brown is out to lunch.
12. They roused him out of a sound sleep.
13. Now I began to doubt all the evidence I had heard.
14. I'd like to close out the bank account.
15. He tried to speak but was shouted down.
16. The ball went out of bounds on the last down.
17. An ounce of prevention is worth a pound of cure.
18. Mr. Townsend will vouch for him.
19. The clown rode around the circus ring.
20. He found a brown envelope lying on the ground.

LONGER SELECTIONS

16.07

1. I hate the drum's discordant sound,
   Parading round, and round, and round:
   To me it talks of ravaged plains,
   And burning towns, and ruined swains,
   And mangled limbs, and dying groans,
   And widow's tears, and orphan's moans;
   And all that Misery's hand bestows
   To fill the catalogue of human woes.
   >JOHN SCOTT, "I Hate the Drum's Discordant Sound."

2. It was interesting, when I dressed before daylight, to peep out of the window, where my candles were reflected in the black panes like two beacons, and, finding all beyond still enshrouded in the indistinctness of last night, to watch how it turned out when the day came on. As the prospect gradually revealed itself, and disclosed the scene over which the wind had wandered in the dark, like a memory over my life, I had a pleasure in discovering the unknown objects that had been around me in my sleep.
   >CHARLES DICKENS, *Bleak House*, Chapter 8.

3. In all my wanderings round this world of care,
   In all my griefs—and God has given my share—
   I still had hopes, my latest hours to crown
   Amidst these humble bowers to lay me down;
   >OLIVER GOLDSMITH, *The Deserted Village.*

4. It was a robber's daughter, and her name was Alice Brown,
   Her father was the terror of a small Italian town;
   Her mother was a foolish, weak, but amiable old thing;
   But it isn't of her parents that I'm going for to sing.
   W. S. GILBERT, "Gentle Alice Brown," *The Bab Ballads.*

5.   "Now! Now!" cried the Queen. "Faster! Faster!" And
   they went so fast that at last they seemed to skim through the
   air, hardly touching the ground with their feet, till suddenly,
   just as Alice was getting quite exhausted, they stopped, and
   she found herself sitting on the ground, breathless and giddy.
   LEWIS CARROLL, *Through the Looking Glass.*

6. An ankle is a marvel
     When first the buds are brown,
   And not a lass but knows it
     From Stowe to Gloucester town.
   And not a girl goes walking
     Along the Cotswold lanes
   But knows men's eyes in April
     Are quicker than their brains.
   JOHN DRINKWATER, "Cotswold Love," *Poems 1908–1919.*

7. Fr[iend] . . . I think your friends are out, and would be in.
   P[ope]   If merely to come in, Sir, they go out,
             The way they take is strangely round about.
   Fr[iend] They too may be corrupted, you'll allow?
   P[ope]   I only call those knaves who are so now.
   ALEXANDER POPE, "Dialogue II," *Epilogue to the Satires.*

8. Under green apple-boughs
   That never a storm will rouse,
   My lady hath her house
     Between two bowers;
   In either of the twain
   Red roses full of rain;
   She hath for bondswomen
     All kinds of flowers.
   ALGERNON SWINBURNE, "Madonna Mia," *Laus Veneris.*

9.   The first step is to remind ourselves that, bad as our times
   are, in the long run, knowledge is power, still moral power,
   that human beings are still human; that free societies manage
   somehow to survive and to revive.
   IRWIN EDMAN, in a panel discussion on "America's Town
                     Meeting of the Air," February 6, 1951.*

* Courtesy of Town Hall, a Division of New York University.

10. As some day it may happen that a victim must be found,
    I've got a little list—I've got a little list
Of society offenders who might well be underground,
    And who never would be missed—who never would be
    missed!

                       W. S. GILBERT, *The Mikado,* I.

11. I'm up and down, and round about,
    Yet all the world can't find me out;
    Though hundreds have employ'd their leisure,
    They never yet could find my measure.
    I'm found almost in every garden,
    Nay, in the compass of a farthing.
    There's neither chariot, coach, nor mill,
    Can move an inch except I will.

                       JONATHAN SWIFT, "On a Circle."

THE DIPHTHONG /ɔɪ/

16.08   The diphthong /ɔɪ/, as in *toy* and *boil,* is a Johnny-come-lately sound in English. The speakers of the eighteenth century rhymed *mind* and *join,* using the /aɪ/ sound for both of them. Care should be taken that it does not become a single vowel as, for example, *call* /kɔl/, for *coil* /kɔɪl/ or *ball* /bɔl/, for *boil* /bɔɪl/.

SENTENCES FOR PRACTICE

16.09

1. We had an enjoyable time.
2. Iodine is believed to prevent goiter.
3. It was covered with tinfoil.
4. She bought a loin of pork.
5. It's an alloy of tin and copper.
6. Can you point him out to me?
7. The coin stuck in the machine.
8. Oysters are in season in September.
9. John is in the basement looking at the oil burner.
10. The soil is not very rich near Oyster Bay.
11. Many people use ointment to soothe attacks of poison ivy.
12. The boys were told not to loiter around the drugstore.

13. The noise from the air compressors turned out to be very annoying.
14. She was criticised for being utterly devoid of poise.
15. The committee agreed to split up and adjourn to adjoining rooms.
16. A visit to a toy store just before Christmas is usually very enjoyable.
17. His appointment to the post seemed unavoidable.
18. Aldous Huxley was the author of *Point Counterpoint.*
19. His head was anointed with oil.
20. The salesman used a very oily voice, which considerably annoyed me.

LONGER SELECTIONS

16.10

1. For just experience tells, in every soil,
   That those who think must govern those that toil.
   OLIVER GOLDSMITH, *The Traveler.*

2. When I was a beggarly boy
      And lived in a cellar damp,
   I had not a friend nor a toy,
      But I had Aladdin's lamp.
   JAMES RUSSELL LOWELL, *Aladdin.*

3. And ev'n while fashion's brightest arts decoy,
   The heart distrusting asks, if this be joy.
   OLIVER GOLDSMITH, *The Deserted Village.*

4. Softly sweet, in Lydian measures,
   Soon he sooth'd his soul to pleasures.
   War, he sung, his toil and trouble;
   Honour but an empty bubble;
      Never ending, still beginning,
   Fighting still, and still destroying.
      If all the world be worth thy winning,
   Think, oh think it worth enjoying:
   JOHN DRYDEN, "Alexander's Feast."

5. We are boys
   That fear no noise
   Where the thundering cannons roar.
   OLIVER GOLDSMITH, *She Stoops To Conquer,* II.

6. Ah, what can ail thee, wretched wight,
      Alone and palely loitering;
   The sedge is wither'd from the lake,
      And no birds sing.
           JOHN KEATS, "La Belle Dame Sans Merci," Stanza 1.

THE DIPHTHONG /ju/ OR /ɪu/

16.11 The diphthong /ju/ is a combination of a glide, /j/, plus the vowel, /u/. Sometimes it is represented as /ɪu/. Where /ju/ is initial in the word, it is usually a full diphthong (*youth, use, union, Yukon, yule, unit,* etc.). Following initial consonants that do not use the forward part of the tongue (/p/, /b/, /k/, /f/, /v/, /m/, /h/), the full diphthong is heard (*pure, pupil, beauty, bureau, cue, Cuba, few, feudal, funeral, view, amuse, mutual, human, hew*). Following /s/, /z/, /θ/, or /ð/, the first element, /j/, is frequently lost in pronunciation: *assume, resume, enthusiasm, thews,* etc. Articulation of the /j/ is optional after /d/, /t/, or /n/, as in *duty, tune,* or *news.*

SENTENCES FOR PRACTICE

16.12

1. Few people will tell you the honest truth.
2. A huge derrick was stationed on New Avenue.
3. It is futile to light a candle to view a landscape.
4. A subway in London is called a tube.
5. Not all news is good news; you have to read it with a judicial eye.
6. To make pewter shine takes a lot of human energy.
7. Some Americans chew gum for amusement.
8. The Duke took a front pew and refused to move.
9. Beauty is a jewel to be worn with honor and respect.
10. On Tuesday, we will salute the new president.
11. The issue is a matter of interpretation of the constitution.
12. There were numerous clews to the missing steward.

LONGER SELECTIONS

16.13

1. "Beauty is truth, truth beauty,—that is all
   Ye know on earth, and all ye need to know."
           JOHN KEATS, "Ode on a Grecian Urn."

2. . . . I also desire to encourage and foster an appreciation of the advantages which I implicitly believe will result from the union of the English-speaking peoples throughout the world and to encourage in the students from the United States of North America who will benefit from the American Scholarships . . . an attachment to the country from which they have sprung but without I hope withdrawing them or their sympathies from the land of their adoption or birth.

From *The Last Will and Testament of Cecil John Rhodes.*

3. Just now, however, culture change has assumed in both its variants a rapidity and magnitude unprecedented in human history. The technical inventions, the developments of industrial enterprise and of financial and mercantile organization have speeded up evolution in the Western world, giving it a far-reaching mastery of the material environment. Mechanical progress, however, has not been parallelled by a corresponding control of social conditions and spiritual culture. The Western control is divided by war and by danger of new wars; by an acute strife in political principle and by the inability in most countries to cope with some of the most urgent economic difficulties.

Bronislaw Malinowski, *The Dynamics of Culture Change.**

B. The Centering Diphthongs

The Diphthongs Ending in Schwa

17.01 The *centering diphthongs* are all those ending in the neutral vowel, schwa /ə/. In some parts of the United States, the last element is identifiable as an *r*, but, in other parts of the country, there is no "*r* coloration" of the vowel. Pronunciation of *dear, air, door,* and *poor* is acceptable with or without the suggestion of an *r*. In pronouncing these centering diphthongs spelled with an *r*, follow the practice of your area of the country. If you try putting *r* sounds in or taking them out in opposition to your own usage, you will be certain to compound an error. The following list of words illustrates the various types of centering diphthongs:

/ɪə/ beer, dear, fear, gear, jeer, mere, near, peer, rear, seer, tear, veer, we're, clear, spear, sneer

* From *The Dynamics of Culture Change* by Bronislaw Malinowski, published by the Yale University Press.

/ɛə/ air, bear, care, chair, dare, fair, hair, lair, pair, pear, rare, scare, share, stair, wear

/oə/ boar, core, door, fore, lore, more, pour, sore, tore, wore, or

/ɔə/ floor, store, snore, score

/ʊə/ boor, cure, endure, lure, poor, sewer, tour, bluer, fewer, doer, skewer, newer.

Sentences for Practice

17.02

1. The rear floor has fewer stairs.
2. The poor man could scarcely pour the water from the glass.
3. Bluer flowers are sought by every grower.
4. She wore her fair hair most becomingly.
5. The core curriculum is sometimes a newer name for reading, writing, and arithmetic.
6. He bought a pair of rare antiques.
7. Corn grows best when the temperature soars.
8. We're paying half-fare for the children.
9. The shares of the stock are near a high point.
10. He is the doer of at least a pair of rare good deeds.
11. He tore open the letter only to find a mere advertisement.
12. The Boer War cost England dearly.
13. Where are the robes for the peers?
14. The wooer and his lass are poor viewers of the landscape.
15. The bear dragged the poor tiny animal to his lair.
16. I wouldn't dare offer a cure for boredom.
17. There was more occasion for jeers than there was for tears in the play's performance.
18. He wore your coat and tore it climbing over the fence.
19. The horns of a deer are called antlers.
20. Take care that you don't trip over the chair.

Longer Selections

17.03

1. Shall I, wasting in despair,
   Die because a woman's fair?
   Or make pale my cheeks with care,
   'Cause another's rosy are?

   George Wither, "The Author's Resolution."

2. Loose his beard, and hoary hair
   Stream'd like a meteor, to the troubled air.
   THOMAS GRAY, The Bard, II, i.

3. No! let me taste the whole of it, fare like my peers,
      The heroes of old,
   Bear the brunt, in a minute pay glad life's arrears,
      Of pain, darkness and cold.
   ROBERT BROWNING, "Prospice."

4. 'Tis neither here nor there.
   WILLIAM SHAKESPEARE, Othello, IV, iii.

5.   A larger group of spell-bound spectators stand in mute wonder at the performance of a snake-charmer from the Souss. He pours forth a wild whirl of hoarse, frienzied words on the power of Allah, the greatness of the Prophet, the ways of holy saints, and the dire influences of afrits, demons, ogres, and djenoun.
   C. E. ANDREWS, Old Morocco and the Forbidden Atlas.

C. The Partial Diphthongs

THE DIPHTHONGS /eɪ/ AND /oʊ/

18.01 The /eɪ/, as in *cake*, and the /oʊ/, as in *note*, are termed *partial diphthongs*. These diphthongs occur in syllables in which the progress of diphthongization is checked or arrested by a following sound. In *cake*, for example, the consonant /k/ and, in *note*, the consonant /t/ check complete diphthongization. However, in the words *say* and *go*, the diphthongs have no such consonant and will, in consequence, have the full diphthong sounds.

Remember to speak these vowels naturally, that is, do not try for any artificiality in pronouncing them. If you have always made full diphthongs of them, continue to do so; if they have been shortened in your speech from childhood, continue to use the shortened forms. Among students whose first language is not English, there is a tendency to keep these vowels quite short. Remember, however, that, where the /o/ or the /e/ concludes the word, as in *no* and *say*, the diphthong is usually formed /noʊ/ and /seɪ/.

Sentences for Practice

18.02

1. I hope you ate enough at dinner.
2. Notepaper is found in most hotels.
3. Counterfeiters make fake paper money.
4. Cloak and dagger stories keep one awake.
5. Bake the cake slowly.
6. Make a note of our date on Saturday.
7. The President makes a "State of the Union" address each year.
8. Wait here until I get my coat.
9. A fencer uses a rapier to make a fake pass at his opponent.
10. We are not a nation of natives but are all a few generations removed from another country.
11. Many Irish came to America as a result of the failure of a potato crop.
12. One has to have the courage to say no to beggars.
13. Jane was first to notice a break in the ice floe.
14. Don't go to the tropics in late May.
15. We'll send a crate of tomatoes to the motel.
16. You take the high road, and I'll take the low one.
17. It's wise to go below deck in a storm at sea.
18. The crow sat in a tree on the edge of a lake.
19. This is an age to try men's souls.
20. That Broadway show is all the rage at the moment.

Longer Selections

18.03

1. D'ye ken John Peel with his coat so gay?
   D'ye ken John Peel at the break of day?

   > J. W. Graves, "John Peel."

2. Rough winds do shake the darling buds of May
   And summer's lease hath all too short a date.

   > William Shakespeare, Sonnet XVIII.

3. An old man broken with the storms of state,
   Is come to lay his weary bones among ye;

   > William Shakespeare, *Henry the Eighth*, III, ii.

4. . . . the Mikado's food was cooked every day in new pots and served up in new dishes; both pots and dishes were of common clay, in order that they might be broken or laid aside after they had been used. They were generally broken, for it was believed that if any one else ate his food out of these sacred dishes, his mouth and throat would become swollen and inflamed.

Sir James Frazer, *The Golden Bough.**

5. The nature of primitive Christianity is accordingly most apparent today in regions where faith is most nearly universal and unconscious. The great majority of the peasants of southern Europe and Latin America are still *pagani,* whose fatalism, passive brotherliness, and superstition antedate Christianity by thousands of years.

Herbert F. Muller, *The Uses of the Past.*†

* Published by The Macmillan Co.
† Published by Oxford University Press.

Chapter 3

American English: Standards and Variations in Pronunciation and Intonation

I. AMERICAN ENGLISH VS. BRITISH ENGLISH

EXPLANATION

19.01   One might ask the question "Why *American* English—isn't all English the same?" The answer is that it is not. Indeed, even within the British Isles, the spoken language differs greatly from one part of England, Scotland, or Wales to another.

In making distinctions among varieties of English, it is not the intent of the authors to set up preferences. That the English language spoken in the former colonies differs from that of the motherland is quite natural. The geographical separation alone would account for much of the difference. The divergences between British and American English grew wider in the eighteenth and nineteenth centuries, when the United States was developing as a nation and its people, including enormous numbers of non-English-speaking immigrants, were spreading across the continent. During this period, American English developed independently, with somewhat different vowel sounds, and a method of spelling divergent from that prescribed by Samuel Johnson. Our own Noah Webster set forth some of these differences, which we, the speakers of American English, have inherited.

Although there are great dialectal differences within it, British English is generally understood to refer to the speech of the south of England. British-English pronunciation can be contrasted with that of American English in tongue placement for the vowels, degree of muscular tension during articulation, degree of sharpness of articulation of the consonants, and phrase and sentence intonation. There are also differences in stress between these two major branches of the language. The British, for example, frequently use a single stress on words of more than two syllables, obscuring the other vowels in words such as *library, dictionary, category,* and *secretary.* These stress differences easily identify the British speaker.

II. STANDARDS AND VARIATIONS IN AMERICAN–ENGLISH PRONUNCIATIONS

A. Spellings

SPELLINGS AND SOUNDS

20.01 The spelling of English is the bane not only of native speakers of English but also of all foreigners who wish to learn the language. English spelling has not been built on a system by which one letter of the alphabet represents one and only one sound. The letter *i,* for example, represents the sound /i/ in *machine,* the /aɪ/ in *fine,* the /ɪ/ in *bit,* the /ɝ/ in *sir,* and the /ɚ/ in *tapir.* The sound /aɪ/ is to be found in *eye, aye, my, nice, high, lies,* and *sleight*—all representing different spellings. Among the consonants, the *ch* is /tʃ/ in *child,* /ʃ/ in *machine,* and /k/ in *Christmas.* The letter *s* also varies in pronunciation. It is /s/ in *son,* /z/ in *easy,* /ʃ/ in *sure,* and /ʒ/ in *decision.*

B. Pronunciation

RULES FOR PRONUNCIATION

21.01 Rules for the pronunciation of English words are numerous, complicated, and filled with exceptions to cover special instances. In learning to master English pronunciation, have a good American dictionary always at hand. Learn the significance of the diacritic marks used in the dictionary to indicate pronunciation. The key to them usually appears on the inside cover, and the directions for pronunciation are usually found in the fine print of the Introduction. In some dictionaries, they also appear at the bottom of the pages. Notice also the marks of syllabic stress; these marks differ in the various dictionaries.

Whenever you consult the dictionary for any information on spelling, meaning, synonyms, etc., note the pronunciations of the word in question. Check them with your own usage. Give second looks to pronunciation indications, to be sure you have read them correctly the first time. Diacritic marks represent subtle variations and are sometimes difficult to distinguish because of the small type.

DICTIONARY ENTRIES ON PRONUNCIATION

21.02　The entry of a certain pronunciation in a dictionary is not based on an arbitrary decision made by a small group of specialists interested in reform. It represents a considered judgment made on the basis of pronunciations used by many educated speakers from all parts of the country.

Read carefully the explanatory material on levels of usage after the listing of pronunciations. Frequently, such terms as "substandard," "dialectal," "informal," and "usage divided" will be found. The order in which the pronunciations occur in the listing is determined by various factors: (1) a statistically greater frequency for the first recorded pronunciation, (2) a system of indicating dialectal differences between the major speech areas of the United States, or (3) a pronunciation preferred by the majority of the editors.

VARIATIONS IN PRONUNCIATION

21.03　The pronunciation of certain words varies considerably from one part of the English-speaking world to another. Even within the United States, considerable divergences occur in the pronunciation of the same word. As a general rule, it is your obligation to use the patterns of pronunciation most often heard from the educated speakers of your community. Become aware of the usage of your teachers and of responsible representatives of your cultural area. The pronunciations of *missile, schedule,* and *lieutenant* in the southern British dialect would be absurd in the speech of someone from Columbus, Ohio; and, while American films have made the American dialects very familiar to most Britishers, our pronunciations of these words would sound like an affectation from a British speaker.

In the United States, the major dialects are (1) *southern,* heard in the old South and as far north as the Mason-Dixon line, west to Arkansas, and down through much of Texas; (2) *eastern,* heard along the northeastern seaboard and inland to the Pennsylvania–New Jersey border (the New York City area must be considered separately, as a sort of speech island); (3) *midwestern,* or *western* (sometimes called *General American*), encompassing a vast area of the Middle and Far West.

Most of the dialectal differences in American-English pronunciation center around the insertion or omission of sounds, particularly the postvocalic *r,* as in *near* and *arm;* the vowel sounds such as those that occur in *path* and *aunt, forest* and *orange;* the failure to complete the diphthong /aɪ/; or differences in the pattern of intonation.

Difficulties of Pronunciation: Examples

21.04 The representation of pronunciation of the words in the following list indicates the process by which mispronunciation occurs:

1. Omission of one or more consonants, as in /ˈrɛkənaɪz/ for /ˈrɛkəgnaɪz/ and /lɪs/ for /lɪsts/
2. Omission of an entire syllable, as in /pəˈtɪklɚ/ for /pəˈtɪkjulɚ/
3. Words with consonant clusters that are not articulated: /æst/ for /æskt/ and /fɪfs/ for /fɪfθs/
4. Substitution of one sound for another, as in /ˈɔrgɪ/ for /ˈɔrdʒɪ/, /ˈpɪtʃɚ/ for /ˈpɪktʃɚ/
5. Misplaced stress, as in /ɪmˈpaɪəs/ for /ˈɪmpɪəs/, /ɪnkəmˈpɛrəbl/ for /ɪnˈkɑmpərəbl/, and /mɪsˈtʃivəs/ for /ˈmɪstʃɪvəs/

6. Sounds that have been juxtaposed (*metathesis*) or sounds put in reversed order, as in /'kælvərɪ/ for /'kævəlrɪ/, /'hɑrpɪskɔrd/ for /'hɑrpsɪkɔrd/
7. The addition of a sound to a word, as in /æθə'lɛtɪk/ for /æθ'lɛtɪk/ and /'grivɪəs/ for /'grivəs/
8. In overprecise speech, sounds that are frequently added, as in /'ɛvərɪ/ for /'ɛvrɪ/ and /'krɪstməs/ for /'krɪsməs/

Summary on Pronunciation

21.05 Here are some general rules to follow for acceptable pronunciations:

1. Use the pronunciation favored by the educated speakers of your region.

2. Consult the dictionary to get precise, authoritative information. Get an American dictionary published within the last ten years, if possible. Pronunciation changes occur slowly, but they do occur.

3. Read diacritic markings in the dictionary carefully. Make certain you understand and are able to translate into sounds each symbol. Consult the key to pronunciation.

4. Read carefully the remarks in parentheses in the dictionary indicating pronunciation variation, such as "archaic," "obsolete," and "nonstandard."

5. Keep in mind that some pronunciations are more formal than others and that, occasionally, a pronunciation acceptable in casual conversation at the lunch table would sound out of place from the assembly platform.

6. Cultivate the habit of referring to the dictionary for guidance in pronunciation. Remember that not all the pronunciations listed there are equally acceptable in speaking. Learn to make the distinctions and, if necessary, to reject a pronunciation there indicated that might be inappropriate to your use. (See Sections **25.01–25.03** on assimilation.)

C. Words Frequently Mispronounced

Pronunciation Practice

22.01 The words in the following list are frequently mispronounced. It is well, therefore, never to be complacent about your own pronunciation of them without verifying the pronunciation with a reputable American dictionary. Learn something about the derivations and meanings of these words too. Use them in sentences of your own.

abyss	electoral	mirage
accede	epitome	mischievous
accompanist	equipage	municipal
acumen	err	naïve
admirable	eschew	niche
adumbration	exigency	obsequious
adversary	façade	onerous
aegis	film	orchestra
ague	flaccid	parliament
alias	forecastle	percolate
amphitheater	formidable	perspiration
arctic	gauge	picture
arraign	gesture	piquant
asthma	grievous	pique
assuage	grimace	poem
athletic	harbinger	portentous
bade	height	positively
balmy	heinous	precedent
beatific	hiatus	preferable
blatant	hundred	preventive
burial	ignominy	pronunciation
cache	imbroglio	quay
capricious	impious	quiescent
cavalry	impotent	recognize
chameleon	inchoate	relevant
champion	inclement	repartee
chimera	incognito	respite
chiropodist	incomparable	ribald
clientele	incongruous	rouge
columnist	indict	ruin
combatant	indissolubly	ruthless
comely	irrelevant	sagacious
comparable	irremediable	satiety
comptroller	irreparable	schism
condolence	irrevocable	scion
consumate (adj.)	isthmus	scourge
corps	larynx	secretary
coterie	length	short-lived
coup	machination	sinuous
covert	malingerer	strength
culinary	mausoleum	subtle
demoniacal	mauve	succinct
disingenuous	memorable	suite

superfluous	vehement	wizen
theater	vehicle	worsted
thyme	via	writhe
tremendous	victuals	zealous
tumult	visage	zoology
vagary	viscount	

Words with More than One Acceptable Pronunciation

22.02   The words in the following list have more than one acceptable pronunciation listed in most dictionaries. What is your pronunciation of them? Check with the dictionary as to whether or not your pronunciation is listed there.

abdomen	contemplative	indisputable
abject	conversant	inexplicable
absolutely	coupon	infantile
absorb	dais	inhospitable
absurd	data	inquiry
academician	decadence	isolate
acclimate	decorative	kiln
address (n.)	despicable	leisure
adept	detail	literati
adult	detour	mercantile
advertisement	diphthongize	nomenclature
aerial	discern	obligatory
allies	dour	ordeal
almond	eczema	pecan
alternate	ensign	peremptory
amateur	epoch	precedence
amenable	evidently	provost
apparatus	exemplary	ration
association	exquisite	refutable
basilica	extraordinary	requiem
bouquet	financial	research
brooch	forehead	resource
brusque	garage	respiratory
buoy	garrulous	romance
Caribbean	gibberish	route
cerebral	gladiolus	sacrilegious
chastisement	greasy	sadism
chauffeur	harass	soviet
chivalric	herculean	status
cigarette	Himalayas	tomato
clangor	homage	usage
clique	hospitable	valet
coadjutor	implacable	waistcoat

Words with Frequently Misplaced Stress

22.03   In pronouncing the following words, take care to place the primary and secondary stresses on the proper syllables. Have a dictionary at hand to check definitions and pronunciations of which you are not certain.

anthropogeny	idiosyncrasy	magnanimity
argumentative	impracticable	misanthropy
asphyxiation	incalculable	misogyny
authenticity	incommensurably	negligible
authoritatively	incongruity	onomatopoetic
bibliographical	incorrigible	palpably
caricature	indefatigability	particularly
chrysalis	indefatigable	peculiarity
chrysanthemum	indisputably	perspicacity
conscientious	indomitable	philological
definiteness	inestimable	practicable
deprecatory	inexorable	questionable
deteriorate	inexorably	recrudescence
diminution	inexpiable	regularly
disinterestedness	inexplicably	rhetorician
disparate	inextricable	statistical
eccentricities	inimical	statistician
ecumenical	inimitable	statistics
efficacy	intelligibility	superfluous
etymological	interpretative	supernumerary
explicable	inviolable	synthesis
femininity	irrelevantly	tentatively
formidable	irreparably	ubiquitous
hypochondriac	irrevocable	unanimity

Pronunciation of Place Names

22.04   Place names and proper names do not always follow the laws of pronunciation. Frequently, the pronunciation is peculiar to the place itself. Egypt, Pennsylvania, is not pronounced in the expected fashion but is, rather, "Eggwipe." It is, therefore, advisable to check on pronunciation of place names of which you are unsure.

Albuquerque, N.M.	Baton Rouge, La.	Chautauqua, N.Y.
Alcatraz Prison	Boise, Idaho	Cheyenne, Wyo.
Amherst College	Bryn Mawr, Pa.	Des Moines, Iowa
Arkansas	Butte, Mont.	Faneuil Hall, Boston, Mass.
Barnard College	Cairo, Ill.	

Havre de Grace, Md.
Hawaii
Holyoke, Mass.
Housatonic River,
  Conn.
Houston St., N.Y.C.
Houston, Tex.
La Jolla, Calif.
Las Vegas, Nev.
Los Angeles, Calif.
Louisville, Ky.
Mojave Desert

Monticello, Va.
New Orleans, La.
Notre Dame Uni-
  versity
Oneida County,
  N.Y.
Poughkeepsie, N.Y.
Reading, Pa.
Rio Grande
St. Louis, Mo.
San Jose, Calif.

Sault Ste. Marie,
  Mich.
Schenectady, N.Y.
Schuylkill River, Pa.
Spokane, Wash.
Terre Haute, Ind.
Thames River, Conn.
Tucson, Ariz.
Wichita, Kan.
Wilkes-Barre, Pa.
Worcester, Mass.
Ypsilanti, Mich.

FOREIGN PLACE AND PROPER NAMES

22.05   Every educated person today is a citizen of the world and needs to have a wide acquaintance with foreign cultures and geography as well as with foreign political and economic trends. How accurate is your pronunciation of foreign places names? Test your skill with the following well-known names. Check each one with your dictionary to determine how proficient you are.

Aegean Sea
Agincourt, France
Aix-la-Chapelle, France
Azores
Bahamas
Balmoral Castle, Scotland
Barbados
Bayreuth, Germany
Beirut or Beyrouth, Lebanon
Buenos Aires, Argentina
Cannes, France
Capri, Italy
Champs-Elysées, Paris
Chartres Cathedral
Curaçao, West Indies
Dijon, France
Edinburgh, Scotland
Eire
Genoa, Italy
Guadeloupe, West Indies
Haifa, Israel
Harwich, England
Inverness, Scotland
Leicester, England

Limoges, France
Lyons, France
Madagascar
Madeira
Magdalen College, Oxford,
  England
Marseilles, France
Monaco
Montevideo, Uruguay
New Delhi, India
Newfoundland
Port Said, Egypt
Quai d'Orsay, Paris
Rio de Janeiro, Brazil
Salzburg, Austria
Saudi Arabia
South Viet Nam
Thailand
Thames River, England
Tintagel, England
Trafalgar Square, London
Versailles, France
Warwick, England

PRONUNCIATION OF PROPER NAMES

22.06   The following list of proper names includes those of some of the greatest figures in Western culture. Check your pronunciation of these names with the pronunciation recorded in the dictionary.

Aeschylus	Donne	Pericles
Aristophanes	Dostoevsky	Petrarch
Aristotle	El Greco	Praxiteles
Bach	Freud	Proust
Beethoven	Gaugin	Ptolemy
Bizet	Gide	Puccini
Boethius	Goethe	Rabelais
Botticelli	Hadyn	Raphael
Catullus	Handel	Rodin
Cervantes	La Rochefoucauld	Schopenhauer
Chopin	Manet	Stendhal
Cicero	Matisse	Synge
Corneille	Maupassant	Thucydides
Dante	Montaigne	Turgenev
Debussy	Mozart	Van Gogh
Degas	Ovid	Wagner
Descartes	Pasteur	Yeats

PRONUNCIATION OF PROPER NAMES FROM LITERATURE

22.07   Characters from literature often bear names that present problems in pronunciation. Identify the names of the following figures, and know how their names are pronounced. Some of them have two possible pronunciations.

Adonais	Jaques (in *As You*	The Pleiades
Aeneas	*Like It*)	Prometheus
Alcestis	Dr. Jekyll	Psyche
Ali Baba	Don Jose	Don Quixote
Amphitryon	Don Juan (of	Salambo
Andromache	Byron's poem)	Salome
Antigone	Laocoön	Scheherazade
Aphrodite	Manon Lescaut	Siegfried
Beelzebub	Lohengrin	Tannhäuser
Madame Bovary	Lysistrata	Telemachus
Clytemnestra	Oedipus	Termagant
Cymbeline	Sancho Panza	Terpsichore
Dionysius	Pegasus	Valkyrie
Eros	Penelope	Yseult
The Eumenides	Persephone	

LATIN WORDS AND PHRASES FREQUENTLY USED IN AMERICAN ENGLISH

22.08 Here are some Latin words and expressions frequently used in both British and American English. Acquaint yourself with their meanings and their pronunciation in American English.

a fortiori	de facto	modus vivendi
a posteriori	de jure	ne plus ultra
a priori	deus ex machina	nota bene
ad hoc	dramatis personae	per diem
ad hominem	ex cathedra	per se
ad infinitum	ex libris	prima facie
alma mater	ex officio	pro rata
alter ego	exempli gratia (e.g.)	reductio ad
alumna	habeas corpus	absurdum
alumnae	homo sapiens	requiescat in pace
alumnus	lapis lazuli	sine die
anno Domini	Magna Charta	sine qua non
ante bellum	magna cum laude	summa cum laude
bona fide	magnum opus	viva voce
carpe diem	modus operandi	vox populi
causus belli		

FRENCH WORDS AND PHRASES IN COMMON USE IN AMERICAN ENGLISH

22.09 Hundreds of English words are derived from French, and the pronunciation of the vast majority of these words has gradually been Anglicized over the years. Some words and expressions, however, retain their French pronunciation in English. Although they are widely used in both Britain and the United States, they have not really taken out final citizenship papers in either country, so to speak. Test yourself on the list below. Do you pronounce these expressions acceptably? Can you use them in meaningful sentences?

agent provocateur	cause celèbre	coup d'oeil
au courant	coup de grâce	croix de guerre
au revoir	coup de main	déshabillé
bon vivant	coup de théâtre	double-entendre
carte blanche	coup d'état	en route

entente cordiale	laissez faire	pièce de résistance
faux pas	maître d'hôtel	pince-nez
hors d'oeuvres	noblesse oblige	raison d'être
idée fixe	nouveau riche	sang-froid
je ne sais quoi	papier maché	table d'hôte
joie de vivre	petits fours	tour de force

SENTENCES FOR PRACTICE IN PRONUNCIATION

22.10

1. There were hundreds of vehicles on the road.
2. Alexander Pope wrote, "To err is human, to forgive divine."
3. I didn't recognize the minister behind the pulpit. His height was impressive, and he looked athletic, but his expression was rather dour.
4. It's preferable to let the coffee percolate a few minutes. It guarantees a better flavor.
5. The mischievous child upset a pile of books in the library.
6. He noticed a tremendous deficit in the municipal accounts.
7. A hiccough is not comparable to a cough.
8. He stared at the Sanitation Corps worker in impotent rage.
9. The acoustics of the new concert hall were lamentable.
10. He was indicted as a wartime malingerer.
11. The electoral college is not employed in mayoralty elections.
12. A piquant sauce is a culinary achievement.
13. A column of air vibrated at the larynx produces the sounds of speech.
14. Members of Parliament usually don't make grievous errors in pronunciation.
15. There are usually many cases of diphtheria in February.
16. She grimaced wryly at the obvious machinations of the charlatan.
17. Many infamous Nazis were convicted of heinous and bestial crimes.
18. Chameleons are not found in the Arctic.
19. The maniacal fury of the dance resembles an orgy.
20. Comptrollers often deal with the minutiae of finance.
21. Can you gauge the distance between Des Moines, Iowa, and Los Angeles?

22. The poem evoked some of the grandeur of medieval times.
23. The picture mounted in the niche in the wall brought poignant memories to the owner.
24. The prelate mounted the dais and astonished us by making a series of impious statements.
25. She is entitled to a respite from her travail.
26. The rear echelon of the army tank corps suffered grievously in the campaign.
27. The cavalry consisted of horse-drawn vehicles and horse-mounted soldiers.
28. The prestige of the speaker suffered because of his poor pronunciation.
29. The evidence presented by the consul was considered both irrelevant and refutable.
30. The wizened old man denied the charge with vehemence.
31. The aspirant was remarkably calm as he acclimated himself to the exigencies of the situation.
32. Although the orchestra played the new work in incomparable fashion, ribald laughter could be heard from one of the balconies.
33. The schism resulted in a new party in Parliament.
34. The average anesthetist has studied zoology.
35. The aging viscount didn't have the strength to walk the length of the room.
36. The girl looked very chic in her worsted suit.
37. The vagary of the princess turned out to be disastrous.
38. He sent a note of condolence to his hostess on the lamentable affair.
39. The debutante wore an exquisite dress of mauve chiffon.
40. Eschew the extraneous, and be succinct in your writing.

D. Sight Readings for Pronunciation

Exercise for Sight Reading

23.01

1.
     What You Do Not Learn from TV

The average TV viewer is unable to distinguish between a kayak and a kyack, a gripe from the grippe, a chiropractor from a chiropodist, or an aspirin from an aspirant, but he knows a reportorial documentary from a rosaceous *zeitgeist* on xenophobia and a parricide that might have been caused by a human parasite. The phlegmatic viewer, pious or impious, is nourished on a flaccid pabulum of inane comedies or esoteric symbolistic concoctions.

He is likely to see an orrery apparently put together by some navvy or a nuthatch that shows him the achievements 10 of science and how a vortiginous planet reaches its syzygy in a synodical orbit. He views the astronaut with his viaticum readying himself for ultima Thule from a terrigenous or autochthonous rocket.

The visual reproduction is a record of quixotic events in this non-Ptolemaic system, but entertainers have a predilection, by precedent, to precede a picture with long-winded, phrenetic explanations for the myopic viewer. Whenever there is a presidential, gubernatorial, or mayoralty election, the viewer has to choose between a fustian persiflage and an 20 exhilarating solfeggio of praise and blame, or watch a scion of a political party sound an orotund tocsin indicating that, for his opponents, the scythe of senile Father Time awaits.

ADDITIONAL SIGHT READINGS

23.02

1.   The Duchess

As the fortissimo cacophony of the orchestra died down, one heard the phthistic coughing of the Dowager Duchess of Landport sitting in the august, royal box in the Golden Tier. Then the audience burst into applause. When the maestro reappeared, they applauded a fortiori with a swelling buoyancy of sound. The Dowager Duchess continued harassing the arytenoid cartilage of the glottis. In time, Her Grace rose and withdrew from the box, like a cirrus cloud of diaphanous gossamer. And for her, the concert was over.

2.   The Victualer

As "Victualer to Her Majesty," S. Snaggs and Sons brought saline scallops daily to the palace to be eaten with hasenpfeffer on lambent zucchini. Mr. Snaggs had caught the sovereign's sovran appetite by providing old vintage Yquem for her ague. Now he was providing yoghurt and vulpine steaks to transmogrify the sovereign weight to that of a hautboy so that there would be no subcartilaginous mass to add avoirdupois.

3.   The Alchemist

In the hexagonal crypt used now as a lapidary, the alchemist set to work on the schism of turning out a philosopher's stone by which all things could be transformed into gold. By machinations throughout the mammalian world, the savant had brought together the rocks and paraphernalia to impress the dupes of the kingdom. An anthracite fire glowed under a huge retort and gave off acrid fumes. A lampion fluttered while the sage, given to jactation, harangued the incognizant spirits in the fetid air.

4.   The Whaler
     Tobias Snigglesworth walked down Thames Street in New London, Connecticut, under the glowering sky black with rain clouds scudding across the horizon and fitfully showing a yellow moon. Out in the Thames River, whaling vessels, gallants furled, genuflected to the waves of a high wind. There they waited crews, horrid and idiomorphic, and victuals salted and dried readying for the long voyage to the South Pacific waters for whale and oil. The salience of the Thames waters seeped into his lungs and made his lupine hunger for whales and green water all the more keen 10 and cutting. Tobias Snigglesworth on land was nothing; on *The Mermaid* he was a satrap who knew no Magna Charta. He worked for hardheaded commissioners and got part of the oil; and his men worked for him and a little of the oleic acid left over from a voyage. Overhead the syzygy of the moon bade good for the voyage and for Tobias Snigglesworth.

5.   The Talker
     A predilection for semasiology and hagiarchy made Judson Goldblutter unpopular. He always interrogated speakers by "What do you mean by that?" and was always arguing with neophytes that only holy men should rule. He muttered hendecasyllabic, ingenuous apothegms that he did not comprehend. Tritheism was his forte, with an occasional fluxion toward polytheism, if necessary. Verbiage he loved and verbatim quotations he descanted. This stopped with a surgeon's fleam, or lancet, caused another fluxion of blood, not words, and silence fell upon him.   10

6.   The Letter
     The copiousness of the English language perhaps was never more apparent than the following character, by a lady, of her own husband:—
     "He is," says she, "an abhorred, barbarous, capricious, detestable, envious, fastidious, hard-hearted, illiberal, ill-natured, jealous, keen, loathesome, malevolent, nauseous, obstinate, passionate, quarrelsome, raging, saucy, tantalising, uncomfortable, vexatious, abominable, bitter, captious, disagreeable, execrable, fierce, grating, gross, hasty, malicious,

nefarious, obstreperous, peevish, restless, savage, tart, un- 10
pleasant, violent, waspish, worrying, acrimonious, blustering,
careless, discontented, fretful, growling, hateful, inattentive,
malignant, noisy, odious, perverse, rigid, severe, teasing, un-
suitable, angry, boisterous, choleric, disgusting, gruff, hector-
ing, incorrigible, mischievous, negligent, offensive, pettish,
roaring, sharp, sluggish, snapping, snarling, sneaking, sour,
testy, tiresome, tormenting, touchy, arrogant, austere, awk-
ward, boorish, brawling, brutal, bullying, churlish, clam-
orous, crabbed, cross, currish, dismal, dull, dry, drowsy,
grumbling, horrid, huffish, insolent, intractable, irascible, 20
ireful, morose, murmuring, opinionated, oppressive, outra-
geous, overbearing, petulant, plaguy, rough, rude, rugged,
spiteful, splenetic, stern, stubborn, stupid, sulky, sullen,
surly, suspicious, treacherous, troublesome, turbulent, tyran-
nical, virulent, wrangling, yelping dog-in-a-manger."

MARK LEMON, *The Jest Book.*

III. SOUND CHANGES IN THE FLOW OF SPEECH

A. Assimilations

ASSIMILATION: EXPLANATION

24.01 In every utterance, one sound exerts an influence
on a neighboring sound. A position taken by the articulators
modifies, in some small way, the position of the articulators
for an adjacent sound. If an unvoiced sound is surrounded
by voiced sounds, it often changes to a voiced sound. The
reverse is also true. The change that results from this influence is called *assimilation*. It is the tendency in speech, as
in many aspects of life, to assimilate, or "to become similar
to," the surroundings.

For examples of the change that occurs in assimilation,
look at the words *anchor, bank, congress, ink,* and *pancake.*
The spelling of each of these words is with the letter *n.* However, the sound produced is not /n/ but /ŋ/, because of the
influence of the /k/ or /g/ sound that follows it. The tongue
modifies its position toward that of the anticipated sound,
that is, from /n/ to /ŋ/.

Assimilations occur in phrases as well as in individual words. *He used to* when assimilated becomes /hi just tu/; the *-ed* in *used* changes to a /t/ because of the influence of the /t/ following in *to*. In much the same way *I have to* assimilates to /ai hæf tu/, the /v/ of *have* changing to /f/ because of the /t/ that follows in *to*.

LIMITS OF ASSIMILATION

24.02 In assimilation, one or more consonants or vowels may be dropped from a combination of sounds in order to ease articulation. However, this type of assimilation can become almost gibberish when carelessly used. When, for example, we hear "djeet?" out of context, we may not realize that it is the question "Have you eaten?" Such pronunciations are not part of standard speech. Are you guilty of using any of the following slovenly pronunciations?

"wanna" for *want to*	"dyuno" for *do you know*
"lemme" for *let me*	"shunuf" for *sure enough*
"shunt" for *shouldn't*	"gimme" for *give me*
"wunt" for *wouldn't*	"frinstans" for *for instance*

KINDS OF ASSIMILATION

24.03 *Anticipatory* assimilations are those wherein the change is anticipated in either the voicing of a consonant or a shift in articulatory position. Examples are:

Change in Voicing	*Change in Articulatory Position*
1. husband	concord
2. cupboard	handkerchief
3. Israel	anxious
4. mouths	horse show
5. gosling	sit down

Forward assimilations are just the reverse of anticipatory ones. Here, the sound change occurs *after* the influencing sound.

Change in Voicing	*Change in Articulatory Position*
1. cads	open
2. walked	deepen
3. wives	old Yale
4. robes	would you

Reciprocal assimilations are those that result from the influence of two sounds on one another to produce a third sound in their place. For example, *picture* (which you may have heard as "pitcher") is pronounced correctly with the reciprocal assimilation of /t/ plus /ʃ/, or /tʃ/, and becomes /ˈpɪktʃʊɚ/ rather than /ˈpɪktjʊɚ/. Reciprocal assimilations occur in the following words:

altercation	national
amateur	nature
dispersion	tincture
education	transient
gesture	usual
gradual	virtue
mobilization	visual

Exercises in Assimilation

24.04 In the following words and phrases, convenient assimilations occur. Speak them naturally, and identify the kind of assimilation, if you can.

1. whetted	11. cup and saucer
2. blackguard	12. Concord
3. pumpkin	13. wristband
4. clapboard	14. literature
5. widths	15. I can go
6. Magdalene College, Oxford	16. Townshend
7. let me see it	17. Cholmondeley
8. Tucson, Ariz.	18. cap and bells
9. waistcoat	19. boatswain
10. Worcester, Mass.	20. Waltham, Mass.

Short Selections Containing Assimilations

24.05

1. But a broomstick, perhaps, you will say, is an emblem of a tree standing on its head; and pray what is man, but a topsy-turvy creature, his animal faculties perpetually mounted on his rational, his head where his heels should be, groveling on the earth! and yet, with all his faults, he sets up to be a universal reformer and corrector of abuses, a remover of grievances, rakes into every slut's corner of Nature, bringing hidden corruption to the light, and raises a mighty dust where there was none before.

    Jonathan Swift, *A Meditation upon a Broomstick.*

2. *Alice.* I do not like this being out so late. Master
Franklin, where did you leave my husband?
Franklin. Believe me I saw him not since morning.
Fear you not, he'll come anon; meantime
You may do well to bid his guests sit down.
Alice. Ay, so they shall; Master Bradshaw, sit you there;
I pray you, be content, I'll have my will.
Master Mosbie, sit you in my husband's seat.
ANONYMOUS, *Arden of Feversham*, V, i.

3.   The most profound and capacious minds of Rome and
Greece were never able to reach the idea, at once so general
and so simple, of the common likeness of men and of the common birthright of each to freedom; they tried to prove that
slavery was in the order of nature and that it would always exist.
ALEXIS DE TOCQUEVILLE, *Democracy in America.*

4.   Socrates used to say that if you asked a man how many little
sheep he owned he readily answered exactly how many; but
if one asked him how many friends he had acquired, he could
not number them because he put such a low value on them.
DIOGENES LAERTIUS, "Socrates," *Lives of Eminent
Philosophers*, II, 30.

5.   There is, however, one direction in which the Naturalism
of the Gothic workmen is peculiarly manifested; and this direction is even more characteristic of the school than the
Naturalism itself; I mean their peculiar fondness for the forms
of Vegetation. In rendering the various circumstances of daily
life, Egyptian and Ninevite sculpture is as frank and as diffuse
as the Gothic. From the highest pomps of state or triumphs of
battle to the most trivial domestic arts and amusements, all is
taken advantage of to fill the field of granite with perpetual
interest of a crowded drama; . . .
JOHN RUSKIN, "The Nature of Gothic," *The Stones of
Venice*, Section LXVIII.

6.   The word "Renaissance," signifying re-birth, was originally
applied to this movement and period [the last stage of medieval
civilization] by men who incorrectly regarded the preceding
medieval period as a dark age when there was no civilization.
They believed that with the revival of the classics civilization
again began to appear in Italy for the first time since the passing of ancient culture. They disregarded or were unaware of
the fact that many features of modern civilization, such as the
modern languages and the European universities and the study
of natural science, had already started in the twelfth and thir-

teenth centuries, and that many features of classical culture, such as Aristotle and other Greek learning, Roman law, and city life had also already been revived at that time.

LYNN THORNDIKE, *The History of Medieval Europe.**

7. At the round earth's imagin'd corners, blow
       Your trumpets, Angels, and arise, arise
    From death, you numberless infinities
       Of souls, and to your scattered bodies go

JOHN DONNE, *Holy Sonnets,* VII.

B. Metathesis and Haplology

METATHESIS: EXPLANATION

25.01 *Metathesis* means the "changing of place," that is, the transposition of letters, sounds, or syllables within a word. It is as common in print as it is in speech. A general error of this kind appears when *Falstaff* is printed *Fastolph.* The word *ask* has often been metathesized to *axe.*

Some of the following transpositions are frequently heard:

"calvery" for *cavalry*
"revelent" for *relevant*
"prespiration" for *perspiration*
"hunderd" for *hundred*
"childern" for *children*

An apparent metathesis occurs in the spelling *centre, theatre, ochre,* and *metre,* but these are old, established spellings imported from the French.

PRECAUTIONS

25.02 Metathesis is a common occurrence in careless speech; one must, in consequence, be acquainted with the correct arrangement of sounds so that the transposition of them will be immediately corrected. It is easy to catch the

* From *The History of Medieval Europe* by Lynn Thorndike, published by the Houghton Mifflin Co.

error, if the word is written, but the sharpening of one's hearing is necessary to catch a metathesis in the flow of speech.

Haplology: Explanation

25.03 *Haplology* is the omission of one or more similar sounds or syllables in a word. Excessive speed of speech may, in some instances, be the cause of this omission; but a far more frequent source of the error is careless, loose articulation and a lack of pride in one's speech. For example, one writer reports that his young daughter says "Helowis" when she intends to say *Hello Lois*. Almost every speaker makes such common errors occasionally, and he is forgiven if they are few in number.

Words that are common offenders are *probably* and *police*. Under the influence of the process of haplology, they break down to "probly" and "pleece," and *naturally* has been so cut into that it often becomes "natch." You might well examine your speech for a tendency to omit sounds in this fashion. How many times have you heard "Misipi" for *Mississippi* or "clyde" for *collide* and made no point to avoid them in your own speech? In order to bring this type of error to your consciousness, the following story is written in what has been labeled *Slurvian* to indicate the slurring of sounds and syllables. There has been no effort to copy the speech of any known person or any regional dialect; here is a sort of tape recording of speech such as you or anyone whose ear has not been sharpened to catch errors might fall into.

Specimen Containing Common Errors in Pronunciation

25.04   A Potty for Ferners

Wenn I finished shopping, Larns, the grosryman ast, "Thassal?" and I 'plied, "Gesso, but I'll pwobly be back Sady mornin for more grosrys and chalklate candy, 'cause we're giving a cookout for some talian visters." "Howd jew come kwainted?" he ast. "Thru U.N.," I ansurd, "cause they'd like to have ferners see house we do things in murka." "Are they commonists?" he ast gen. "No," I said, "they are mostly famin people who have lived from cultivating the soil. They think we murkans eat alla time in cafterias, and I wanted to show them difrent." I put alla things in the car 10 and drove home whered put the preshibls in the frigair and the candy n other things on the back porch where theydall keep cool.

Florns Chalmodestan (Chomson, she calls it) who came from Portlan, Argon, and I youst to know each other in eye school; well, she came over to talk about the potty and brought her young son, Harl, with her. Harl's a nice boy, but he just shunt be around when there's an opportinuty to get into troubl. At leas he does mos of the time. So we tole him to run-n-play which ee did.   20

Florns, Elner Tynemouth (called Tinmuth), and I were givn this potty, but Elner had gone to Nargansit sos we hadda dowit ourselves. Florns, before Elner left, shasta if she proved this rangement: cocktails, matojuice, hottogs, corn-n-cob, salit, eyescream, and coffee. And Elner proved it.

We talked it all over gen and memrized the list of names of the guests: Ernst Celloti, Bors Pillotov, Dorthy Caroli, Mars Slami, Als Vesuv, and Sanda Romano. We wanted to know the names sos we wunt be dollar than we seemed. We shunt let on we was afraid of fern names. Many people 30 had said we shunt dowit, but I said to myself, "Arm gonna duwot, and it's gonna be a frustrate potty, too, with lotsa things that people lack to eat."

Wenn Florns and I finished our plans, Harl ran in with his face covrd with chalklate and said his stummik hurt. Florns took him home wheree was sick. They hadda get a doctor. And for me and my husband, Grame, we hadda give the potty all by oursels. Elner dint get home because of a cole, and Harl was too sick for Florns and her husband, Sinclr, to come. But I hadda go to Larns for more chalklate 40 candy Sady morning.

C. Shifts in Stress Influencing Pronunciation

Stress in American-English Pronunciation

26.01 In English, both British and American, words of more than one syllable possess one or more stresses or accents. In words of several stressed syllables, one of the stresses is usually *primary* or greater, and the others *secondary*. Sometimes the syllables are evenly stressed and become *spondees*, for example, as in *pancake* or *bookcase*.

In the word *about*, there is a primary accent, or stress, on the second syllable; and, in *after*, a primary stress occurs on the first syllable. Notice the syllabic stresses in *accordingly* and *photographical*. English is particularly puzzling when words are spelled alike (*'address* vs. *ad'dress*) but stressed differently and, in consequence, have different meanings.

SHIFT IN STRESS BETWEEN NOUNS AND VERBS

26.02   Most speakers stress the first syllable of the following words when they use them as nouns but put the stress on the second syllable when they use them as verbs: *abstract, contrast, convert, converse, convict, finance, import, insult, produce, protest, record, rebel.* These are but a few such instances. You will undoubtedly be able to bring to mind a number of others.

SHIFT IN STRESS IN DIALECTAL AREAS

26.03   The stress of words often shifts from region to region, so it is well to know the pattern of speech of your own region and not to run strongly counter to it. A shift from the accepted pattern of stress can cause difficulty in understanding.

SHIFT IN STRESS IN CONTEXTS

26.04   Words are related to the context of a phrase, a sentence, or a paragraph. These elements have a rhythm of their own as well as a grammatical structure. Do you find that the stress of some of the following words changes as the sentence changes?

1. This is a small sixteen.
   This is a small sixteen dress.
2. You'll find him somewhere.
   You'll find him somewhere else.
3. The room is air-conditioned.
   It is an air-conditioned room.
4. Shoot for the bull's-eye.
   Shoot for the bull's-eye center.

You will discover that there is a slight but nevertheless noticeable shift in stress as the sentence changes. These

slight changes will not be recorded in the dictionary but your
ear should detect them.

Exercises in Shifts in Stress

26.05   The following sentences are so devised that the
speaker will stress the words naturally as he goes along without frequent use of the dictionary. You might "listen back"
on what you have said to try to discover a reason for your
change of stress from one syllable to another.

1. Providence will not provide for the improvident.
2. It is demonstrable that one can demonstrate the improvement in public health.
3. The impious are to the pious as the sacrilegious are to the
   religious.
4. An elegy is not a eulogy, but it should be elegiac.
5. The Communists do not hold the tenet that everything is
   communal.
6. You cannot compare the incomparable.
7. No incident is incidental.
8. A pianist without a piano is a musician without his music.
9. The contents of the container made him discontented.
10. A Dane from Denmark is the hero of an English play
    whose heroine, also Danish, looks more the part than the
    black-clothed hero.
11. Preparatory for the monsoon, an advertisement appeared
    in the Bombay papers for the sale of cheap Venetian
    gondolas.
12. An expert is paid for his expert knowledge.
13. The culpability of a culprit means his liability to blame.
14. He listened to a recording which, for sales, had made a
    record for the recorder.
15. He alleged that his allegiance was to a foreign ally.
16. No one whose character is firmly fixed would characterize
    himself as without a philosophy.
17. Give me no gratuitous gratitude nor gratulatory gratula-
    tion.
18. The weather forecast was forecasted in Washington be-
    fore it ever reached headquarters.
19. The former marquis had given the marquise a marquise
    diamond which the marquise wore as she sat under the
    marquee made of marquisette.

D. Passages for Recording and Testing

NEED FOR READING AT SIGHT

27.01   Anyone interested in improving his speech needs to be alert to all aspects of speaking: reading aloud, public speaking, discussion. In addition, he needs to have interest in the use of the voice (articulation, voice quality, projection, and so forth). One of the best methods of providing an indication as to how well one does in these activities is through a recording on tape or on discs. The following selections are given here to be used primarily as material for recording, but they may also be used as additional reading exercises.

READING FOR TESTING

27.02   Everyone is under more or less of a strain in front of a microphone, knowing that it can be a very harsh judge. Few people are altogether satisfied with any recording; it may be unsatisfactory for a number of reasons: the acoustics of the room in which the recording was made; the imperfections of the recording machine; the tensions of the speaker at the time; the unsuitability of the material; the nature of the audience, if there is one; distracting noise; and so forth. These directions may be helpful in recording:

1. Be as natural as you can under the circumstances.
2. Take the time to find out how far you should be from the microphone. Incorrect microphone placement can cause considerable distortion of voice.
3. Don't touch the microphone during the time of recording. It causes explosion-like sounds on the recording.
4. Avoid any artificiality of manner, such as overprecise articulation, a snail's pace in reading, or the use of pronunciation not usually heard in your geographical area.
5. Use a good firm voice and breathe easily during the pauses at the ends of units of meaning in your utterance.
6. Keep foremost in mind the sense of the material you are reading, and try to interest your listener in what you are saying.

MATERIAL FOR RECORDING

27.03 Most of the material presented in the following selections has been devised with certain sounds and combinations of sounds in mind. This material has been carefully constructed for a specific purpose—to provide the instructor and student with a reliable sampling of the student's speech. If you are puzzled by the pronunciation of some of the words, do your best with them in the reading and remember to look up those pronunciations of which you are uncertain in a dictionary later.

1.   Arthur the Rat
Once there was a young rat named Arthur who never could make up his mind. Whenever the other rats asked him if he would come out with them, he wouldn't say "Yes" or "No" either. He would always shirk making a choice.
One day his Aunt Helen said to him, "Now look here, no one is going to care for you if you carry on like this. You have no more mind than a blade of grass."

2.   The Hurt Oyster
For some months now, all the oysters in Long Island Sound have been threatened with extermination by being eaten by starfish. The oyster beds are fast disappearing, and the Fish and Wildlife Service of the Department of the Interior has been working arduously to rid the waters of the starfish and has had to go so far as to move the oyster beds to other parts of the Sound. A third of the oysters now have to be thrown back into the water because they have been partly consumed.

3.   Baggage and Weight
On a first-class transatlantic air flight, the traveler is permitted to carry sixty-six pounds of baggage without extra cost. In the tourist class, the passenger is restricted to a load of luggage of forty-four pounds. An extra charge is asked for greater weight up to a specified limit. These charges are often considerable. Some people protest; some demand reimbursement; some have never read the material on baggage and weight sent to them by the passenger lines.

4.   Masked Ball
At a masked ball last Saturday night, there were to be seen the expected number of witches, acrobats, ballet dancers, princes and princesses, potentates, coachmen, and

a few apes and monkeys. The prize, however, went to a most superbly dressed, brushed, and shined policeman. When he was asked why he had dressed so well and becomingly, he replied, "You see, I'm paid to dress this way so that I can watch you people to see that you don't steal anything."

5. ## Weather or Not

We talk about the weather; we talk against the weatherman and all his tribe, but we don't do anything about the weather. But don't we? We sent Tiros I into space, and it sent back pictures of the weather of the world until a short while ago when a short circuit stopped transmission of signals. Then we sent up Tiros II, and it still sends messages and pictures of the weather over the entire earth. There are daily firings of rockets from several stations between Florida and California. These operations cost millions of dollars. We are, therefore, doing something about 10 the weather even when we complain that it rains too much or not enough or it's too hot or too cold. We are paying for what we are not getting.

6. ## The Babylonians

The dress of the Babylonians is a linen tunic reaching to the feet, and above it another tunic made in wool, besides which they have a short white cloak thrown round them, and shoes of a peculiar fashion, not unlike those worn by the Boeotians. They have long hair, wear turbans on their heads, and anoint their whole bodies with perfumes, every one carries a seal, and a walking stick, carved at the top into the form of an apple, a rose, a lily, an eagle, or something similar; for it is not their habit to use a stick without an ornament. 10

The History of Herodotus, translated by
GEORGE RAWLINSON.

7. ## Take Your Choice

Once there was an uncivil civil servant in the post office whose main duty was to carry messages, to clean floors, to guard the mail as it was taken from the trucks, and to get coffee for the others when needed. He was around everywhere because his business took him there. People would ask him all kinds of questions such as "How much is the air mail to Madagascar?" or "How many pounds can I send to Australia?" He would groan back, "Ask the man at the window." Invariably came another question: "Which window?" And his constant reply would be "Take your 10 choice; they all charge the same."

8. Church and Field

A churchmouse once met a fieldmouse by chance. Each greeted the other cordially as mice are wont to do, and the churchmouse said (rather loftily), "I haven't seen you at service for a long time." "No," replied the fieldmouse (rather humbly), "I have been working hard trying to earn enough money to rent a pew in your church." "You don't need any money for that," generously spoke the churchmouse. "The people who pay the rent for them are never there, so you will always have a front seat. Just see me next Sunday." 10

9. Concord Hymn

By the rude bridge that arched the flood,
    Their flag to April's breeze unfurled,
Here once the embattled farmers stood,
    And fired the shot heard round the world.

The foe long since in silence slept;
    Alike the conqueror silent sleeps;
And Time the ruined bridge has swept
    Down the dark stream which seaward creeps.

On this green bank, by this soft stream,
    We set to-day a votive stone;
The memory may their deed redeem,
    When, like our sires, our sons are gone.

Spirit, that made those heroes dare
    To die, and leave their children free,
Bid Time and Nature gently spare
    The shaft we raise to them and thee.

                    RALPH WALDO EMERSON, *Concord Hymn.*

10. Forget, Forgive

Wrath-kindled gentlemen, be rul'd by me;
Let's purge this choler without letting blood.
This we prescribe, though no physician;
Deep malice makes too deep incision.
Forget, forgive; conclude and be agreed;
Our doctors say this is no month to bleed.
Good uncle, let this end where it began;
We'll calm the Duke of Norfolk, you your son.

              WILLIAM SHAKESPEARE, *Richard the Second,* I, i.

11.   I'll Come Down Alone
Sir Thomas More. Oh, is this the place?
                    I promise ye, it is a goodly scaffolde:
                    In sooth, I am come about a headless
                        errand,
                    For I have not much to say, now I am here.
                    Well, let's ascend, a God's name:
                    In troth, methinks, your stair is somewhat
                        weak.
                    I prethee, honest friend, lend me thy hand
                    To help me up; as for my coming down,
                    Let me alone, I'll look to that myself.
                        ANONYMOUS, *Sir Thomas More*, V, iv.

12.   The Inspired Singer
        Of Israel's sweetest singer now I sing,
        His holy style and happy victories;
        Whose Muse was dipt in that inspiring dew
        Arch-angels stilled from the breath of Jove,
        Decking her temples with the glorious flowers
        Heavens rain'd on tops of Sion and Mount Sinai.
        Upon the bosom of his ivory lute
        The cherubins and angels laid their breasts;
        And, when his consecrated fingers struck
        The golden wires of his ravishing harp,   10
        He gave alarm to the host of heaven,
        That, wing'd with lightening, brake the clouds, and cast
        Their crystal armour at his conquering feet.
            GEORGE PEELE, "Prologue," *David and Bethsabe.*

13.   Bird Song
        What ornithologist has not heard the notes from the
    syrinx of his favorite bird in the vicinage of its lair. Some-
    times the sound may be unisonous, but, nevertheless, the
    bird lover will stand awed in a chasm of the forest or in a
    niche in a quarry, quietly listening. Nor will he take
    umbrage if the bird remains silent, because he will be
    amply rewarded by tangential sounds like that from some
    Islamic muezzin on top of a siccative tower; or of some
    isolated instrument of an orchestra; or a blurred oil-barge
    whistle. Thus, while he waits, he can write the ontogeny of   10
    the bird he had heard so that he may, in solitude, as a
    supine reader, enjoy the experience all afresh.

14.   The Storm

The gunwale of the xebec, a three-masted ship with a
low bow and stern, was almost under white foam. The
glyph on the bow was spattered with green water and a
saline slipperiness. Far distant, one could discern the mys-
terious, occult Island of Isis where man longed to linger
and listen to singers of songs. Now, however, every former
malingering seaman was alert to the immediate danger,
and the ship was yare for the storm. As nones sounded,
the quasi-storm cloud broke apart and an ingot of bright
vermilion sun shone through the cumulus and cirrus clouds. 10
All cried, viva voce, the trochee "Salve!" and looked again
toward the Island of Isis.

15.   Cathedral Close

From the pulpit at the vespertine service, the parson,
with a deep tussis, the titulary dean of the cathedral,
preached one Whitsuntide. The nave, full of draughts,
housed but a few auditors, continuously uninspirable, un-
emotional, unmoved, cold, etc., no matter how potent the
preacher or the message. They continued to be as un-
altered as the lichen on the lich gate at the west entrance.
These parishioners wanted some leprechaun to arise from
the damp vapors of the crypt and metamorphose their
quiescence into fanaticism; such no parson yet had done.   10

16.   The Plague

The reptiles in the reptilian part of the zoo had been
suffering from an unknown virosis, and now the wildebeest,
or gnu, had died from some unisolated cause. The keepers
were giddy with rushing hither and thither. Now a parrot
had just died of psittacosis, a disease that man himself
could easily contract. Several persons had already been
counted as deceased from it. Everyone was in great travail,
the animals included, and human attempts to avoid phthisis
or something worse were frantically being made. Everyone
put on a mask, took weak tea, ate sparingly, and prayed. 10
Then, suddenly, all symptoms disappeared, and with them
went the masks, weak tea, and prayer.

17.   It Happened in Mexico, of All Places

"By jingo, you're a gringo, if I ever saw or heard one,"
said the pigmy in an enormous pyramidal straw hat.

"Perhaps I'm a quasi-gringo, or part gingko for all I
know. But I'll record here and now that I'm not a karoo.
And, moreover, I'm not used to standing in a queue to wait
for a predatory salesman to argue with me the price of
shagreen," I replied infuriated.

This colloquy took place in the purlieu of the market-place in Xochimilco, and I thought I really looked more like a native than a man from the U.S.A. on vacation. I [10] had tried to homogenize myself into looking like one of the people, but, even though my clothes and shoes were like theirs, I forgot, of course, not to carry three cameras around my neck. I guess I haven't the foggiest idea how to avoid being an old fogy. I'm just a bourgeois fathead, and I know it but don't care.

18.   Gentlemen in 1858!

If gentlemen are always finding fault with the ladies dresses why does not some lady retaliate and have something to say about gentlemen's whiskers. Would that we could get daguerreotypes of some of those that we daily meet! There is one that it requires a stretch of the imagination to fancy, a sky terrier in pantaloons. The likeness is perfect. And there is another, whom to compare with any species of dog would be an insult to that noble animal. As we look out of our office now we can see standing a knot of these creatures. Their make-up is wonderful. Each one has [10] on the new-fashioned pantaloons very small over the boot, and uncommonly large at the knee. We can see three pairs of eyes, and the top of the nose of each. All the rest is hair! hair! hair! There ought to be an asylum for these creatures, for they frighten children.

Godey's Lady's Book and Magazine, June, 1858.

19.   Knife and Ice

The Utica *Herald* says, Dr. Walcott of that city, acting under the suggestion of a French journal, has resorted to ice as a means of destroying pain in surgical operations. A few days since, he removed a very large tumor from a man's leg. He took a preparation of snow and common table salt, and applied it to the diseased part, which was almost immediately reduced to an insensible state. The removal of the tumor was accompanied by very little loss of blood, and little or no pain. The doctor's fingers were, however, slightly frozen in the operation. Dr. W. thinks [10] that this method of producing insensibility to pain is preferable to that of chloroform, inasmuch as it is not dangerous, and does not injure the blood.

Godey's Lady's Book and Magazine, February, 1858.

20.   The Computer Is Always Right

An irrational robot ruminated on the rationale of his own quixotic manufacture by innumerable scientists. He did his thinking by punching keys of a programed computer. Finally, an answer came out, giving a complicated formula. He fed this back into the computer for solving, and, in a few minutes, the work of five hundred scientists working for five hundred years appeared. The answer read "Zero."

IV. AMERICAN–ENGLISH INTONATION

A. Variations in Vocal Tone as Semantic Elements in Speech

Intonation: Explanation

28.01 Every speaker with a normal vocal apparatus utters each speech sound on one or more notes. Speech, like music, rises and falls in a vocal scale, although the notes are not discrete as they are in singing or in playing an instrument. This rising and falling in speech is called *intonation,* the patterns of variation of which are used to help convey meaning.

In your experience with animals, dogs in particular, have you ever tried to see what vocal tone without corresponding words will do? Speak commanding words with a low, gentle intonation, and the dog wags his tail. Speak gentle words in a commanding intonation, and he obeys the tone and not the words.

The notes of the human vocal scale may extend from very low to very high. Some actors have a range of as much as four octaves of a piano scale. However, the notes of the human speaking voice are usually not many—perhaps about four tones. In moments of excitement or deep depression, one uses especially high or low tones. The highness or lowness of these tones (or notes) differs from person to person and is determined by the length and width of the speaker's vocal cords, or bands. In general, women have shorter and narrower vocal cords than men and, consequently, have higher voices. The tones for women and men will be different on a musical scale, but the difference will be relative, existing within the four usual tones on the scale of conversation.

A simple numerical system is used to indicate the relative differences in intonation notes. The number (1) represents a low note (but not the lowest of which the speaker is capable); (2) is a note somewhat higher than (1); (3) is a note somewhat above the middle speaking register; and (4) is high on the scale (but not the highest note the speaker can reach).

INTONATION ESSENTIAL TO COMMUNICATION IN SPEECH

28.02 Assume that you have been invited to a dance. One of your friends asks you, "Are you going to the Alpha Beta dance?" and you reply, "Yes." But with what intonation do you make that reply? Would it always be the same?

How would you say *yes* if

1. You were anxious to go
2. You did not want to go
3. You were not sure whether or not you wanted to go
4. Your answer were a challenge to the questioner ("and you can't keep me from going")
5. You were puzzled as to why the question should be asked

By the intonation pattern you use in answering "yes," the listener will be able to infer what your attitude is in answering as you do. It is important, therefore, to be able to control the intonation of your statements, because the pattern you use may, in great part, give a meaning to your utterance that the words themselves do not convey. This fact is not taken into account at court trials, for example, when a reply is written in literal fashion whereas the intonation of it may indicate an opposite meaning from the literal.

PITCH LEVELS

28.03 As was indicated earlier, four levels of intonation are used in speaking. They include (1) the lowest level, (2) the normal level, (3) the level for stressed words or a sequence of words to be stressed, and (4) the highest level, used for special emphasis. Except in unusual instances, these levels run into one another so that the progression from one tone to another is almost imperceptible.

Since the various levels are connected, they form what is known as a *contour* or *pattern* or *shape* of the utterance. In the sentences to follow, the contour of each is given in the parentheses after it. The contour is the same for the first two sentences. It changes with the third to indicate that the speaker made special emphasis on the word *brilliant* to stress his belief.

I think I'll go Saturday. (231)
I'll take the red dress. (231)
She has a brilliant mind. (241)

EXERCISES IN MARKING SIMPLE CONTOURS

28.04 In your notebook or on a separate sheet of paper, mark the contours you use for the following utterances. Listen carefully for the distinctions among the various levels. If you hear a rising tone at the end of a sentence, indicate it by an arrow pointing upward (↑); if you hear a drop in pitch, use an arrow pointing downward (↓); if the pitch stays about the same, use a horizontal arrow (→).

1. Good morning, Bob.
2. Good morning. How are you?
3. Fine. And you?
4. Not so good.
5. What's the matter?
6. Oh, I can't go to the game Saturday.
7. Ah, come on.
8. No. I've got work to do.
9. Forget it.
10. I can't. I need the money.
11. Well, that's different. You getting paid? Need an assistant?
12. Sure. You want to work, too?
13. You bet. I need the money more than a game.

Let us examine a few of these utterances:

In item 1, the contour would be something like this:

2   3 1 1
Good morning, Bob. or (231→1↓)

In the reply, the contour might be

3   2   1   2   3
Good morning. How are you? or (321 ↓) (23 ↑)

Get someone from your class or a person who does not know about these details, and ask him or her to read these sentences for you. Discover what, if any, difference there is in the contours. Begin to listen to your friends and to strangers in order to catch their intonation contours, and attempt to note them. If you try to set down the utterance you hear in phonetic symbols as well as in intonation contours, you will have a good approximation of actual speech.

FURTHER EXERCISES IN BASIC INTONATIONS

28.05 Practice with the following sentence, to see what intonation you use to convey the meaning indicated by (a), (b), (c), etc.:

Santa Fe is a wonderful place.

..........................(a) Yes, indeed it is.

..........................(b) Yes, but it doesn't excite me.

..........................(c) It is only another stop on the highway as far as I am concerned.

..........................(d) As contrasted with Albuquerque, I agree with you.

..........................(e) Of course it is; I'm not saying it isn't.

..........................(f) I'm astonished you think so. I certainly don't think that way.

SELECTIONS FROM PLAYS FOR MARKING INTONATION

28.06

1. *Antony.* Friends, Romans, countrymen, lend me your ears!
   I come to bury Caesar, not to praise him.
   The evil that men do lives after them,
   The good is oft interred with their bones;
   So let it be with Caesar.

   WILLIAM SHAKESPEARE, *Julius Caesar*, III, ii.

2. *Banquo.* Thou hast it now: King, Cawdor, Glamis, all.
As the weird women promis'd, and, I fear,
Thou play'dst most foully for't: yet it was said
It should not stand in thy posterity;
But that myself should be the root and father
Of many kings.

WILLIAM SHAKESPEARE, *Macbeth,* III, i.

3. *Fawkner.* Tugg me not, I'm no bear. Sblood, if all
the dogs on Paris Garden hung at my tail,
I'd shake 'em off with this, that I'll appear
before no kind christened but my good Lord
Chancellor.

Sheriff. We'll christen you sirra. Bring him forward.

Sir Thomas More. How now! What tumults make you?

Fawkner. The azure heavens protect my noble Lord
Chancellor.

Sir Thomas More. What fellow is this?

Sheriff. A ruffian, my lord, that hath set half the city
in an uproar.

Fawkner. My lord—

Sheriff. There was a fray in Paternoster-row, and because they would not be parted, the street
was choked up with carts.

Fawkner. My noble lord, Paniar Allie's throat was
open.

ANONYMOUS, *Sir Thomas More,* III, ii.

B. Contours in American-English Intonation

USUAL CONTOURS

29.01 The most generally used contour in American
English is the pattern (231 ↓). This contour is used in sentences stating a truth or scientific finding, a request or command, and in asking a question that requires more than a *yes*
or *no* answer.

Statement of a truth: "10 and 10 and 2 are 22." (231 ↓)
Scientific statement: "The chemical formula for water is
H_2O." (231 ↓)
Request: "Please come on Thursday." (231 ↓)
Command: "Go get this immediately." (231 ↓)
Question asking for more than a yes or no answer: "What are
the good points of horseracing?" (231 ↓)

Another contour is used for the asking of questions requiring a *yes* or *no* answer. The intonation of the answer will be different if affirmative or negative, or equivocal. For example,

"Is it far to the Truman Library?" (232 23 ↑)
"No." (32 ↓) (It is not far.)
"No." (23 →) (Well, yes and no, perhaps.)
"Yes." (32 ↓) (It is far.)

Exercises on Contours

29.02 From the basic information above, work out the possible contours in the following exercises. Ask others to read them, and contrast your own intonation with theirs. Which contours seem to be the most natural and understandable?

1. For breakfast we had orange juice, coffee, and rolls.
2. Who knows where to find the volumes of Shakespeare?
3. . . . and that government of the people, by the people, for the people, shall not perish from the earth.

In the following exercises, adopt the intonation contour that is appropriate to the attitude suggested within the parentheses:

4. You need an encyclopedia. (Statement of fact.)
   You need an encyclopedia? (You, of all people?)
   You need an encyclopedia? (Do you, really?)
   You need an encyclopedia. (In spite of what you might think.)

5. I'm glad you came today. (Statement of fact.)
   I'm glad you came today. (But my sister isn't.)
   I'm glad you came today? (How did you get that idea?)
   I'm glad you came today. (I won't be here tomorrow.)

6. Where is the bookstore? (Simple question of direction.)
   Where is the bookstore? (I've looked everyplace, and I can't find it.)
   Where is the bookstore? (I found where I can buy everything except books!)

7. *Foodle.*   At length the enemy advances nigh,
   I hear them with my ear, and see them with my eye.

Grizzle.	Draw all your swords: for liberty we fight,
	And liberty the mustard is of life.
Tom Thumb.	Are you the man whom men famed Grizzle name?
Grizzle.	Are you the much more famed Tom Thumb?
Tom Thumb.	The same.
Grizzle.	Come on; our worth upon ourselves we'll prove;
	For liberty I fight.
Tom Thumb.	And I for love.

HENRY FIELDING, *Tom Thumb the Great*, III, ix.

8. *Mrs. Peachum.* Never was a man more out of the way in an argument than my husband! Why must our Polly, forsooth, differ from her sex, and love only her husband? And why must Polly's marriage, contrary to all observation, make her the less followed by other men? All men are thieves in love, and like a woman the better for being another's property.

JOHN GAY, *The Beggar's Opera*, I, v.

9. *Cato.* It must be so—Plato, thou reason'st well!—
Else whence this pleasing hope, this fond desire,
This longing after immortality?
Or whence this secret dread, and inward horror,
Of falling into naught? why shrinks the soul
Back on herself, and startles at destruction?
'Tis the divinity that stirs within us;
'Tis heaven itself, that points out an hereafter,
And intimates eternity to man.

JOSEPH ADDISON, *Cato*, V, i.

10. *Mrs. Malaprop.* You are very good, and very considerate, Captain.—I am sure I have done everything in my power since I exploded the affair! Long ago I laid my positive conjunction on her never to think on the fellow again;—I have since laid Sir Anthony's preposition before her;—but, I'm sorry to say, she seems resolved to decline every particle that I enjoin her.

RICHARD BRINSLEY SHERIDAN, *The Rivals*, III, iii.

11. Come, said my soul,
Such verses for my body let us write, (for we are one,)
That should I after death invisibly return,

Or, long, long hence, in other spheres,
There to some group of mates the chants resuming,
(Tallying earth's soil, trees, winds, tumultuous waves,)
Ever with pleas'd smile I may keep on,
Ever and ever yet the verses owning—as, first, I here and now,
Signing for soul and body, set to them my name.

WALT WHITMAN, prefatory poem to *Leaves of Grass.*

12.   Polite Conversation

"You have a son, I believe, [Mr. Toodles]?" said Mr. Dombey.

"Four of 'em, Sir. Four hims and a her. All alive!"

"Why, it's as much as you can afford to keep them!" said Mr. Dombey.

"O couldn't hardly afford but one thing in the world less, Sir."

"What is that?"

"To lose 'em, Sir."

"Can you read?" asked Mr. Dombey.

"Why, not partik'ler, Sir."

"Write?"

"With chalk, Sir?"

"With anything?"

"I could make shift to chalk a little bit, I think, if I was put to it," said Toodle after some reflection.

"And yet," said Mr. Dombey, "you are two or three-and-thirty, I suppose?"

"Thereabouts, I suppose, Sir," answered Toodle, after more reflection.

"Then why don't you learn?" asked Mr. Dombey.

"So I'm going to, Sir. One of my little boys is a going to learn me, when he's old enough, and been to school himself."

"Well!" said Mr. Dombey . . . "You heard what I said to your wife just now?"

"Polly heerd it," said Toodle. . . . "it's all right."

"As you appear to leave everything to her," said Mr. Dombey . . . "I suppose it is of no use saying anything to you."

"Not a bit," said Toodle. "Polly heerd it. *She's* awake, Sir."

"I won't detain you any longer then," returned Mr. Dombey, disappointed. "Where have you worked all your life?"

"Mostly underground, Sir, till I got married. I come to the level then. I'm going on one of these here railroads when they comes into full play."

CHARLES DICKENS, *Dombey and Son,* Chapter 2.

PART II

SELECTIONS FOR ORAL INTERPRETATION, ANALYSIS, AND DISCUSSION

DIVISION OF SELECTIONS: EXPLANATION

30.01 The materials of Part II constitute several divisions. Specific uses are suggested for the materials in each division, but the instructor and the student should feel free to use these materials in any way that fits their needs.

30.02 The purposes of the specific divisions are (1) assignments for practice in connection with particular sections of Part I, (2) individual readings for oral interpretation and analysis, (3) practice materials for laboratory and conference work, (4) subject matter for class discussion and speeches.

Chapter 4

Voice, Articulation, and Pronunciation Exercises

31.01 The first division contains reading selections, of greater length than those in Part I, that have been chosen expressly for work on articulation, pronunciation, and improvement in voice quality.

In reading aloud the following group of patter songs from the Gilbert and Sullivan operettas, be sure your articulation is precise and accurate without being overdone. You need also to strive for a sense of the lively rhythm necessary to read them effectively.

1.   Sweetening the Bitter Pill
I've wisdom from the East and from the West,
   That's subject to no academic rule;
You may find it in the jeering of a jest,
   Or distill it from the folly of a fool.
I can teach you with a quip, if I've a mind;
   I can trick you into learning with a laugh;
Oh, winnow all my folly, and you'll find
   A grain or two of truth among the chaff!

I can set a braggart quailing with a quip,
   The upstart I can wither with a whim;
He may wear a merry laugh upon his lip,
   But his laughter has an echo that is grim!
When they're offered to the world in merry guise,
   Unpleasant truths are swallowed with a will—
For he who'd make his fellow creatures wise
   Should always gild the philosophic pill!
             W. S. GILBERT, *The Yeomen of the Guard,* I.

2.   A Dealer in Magic and Spells

Oh! my name is John Wellington Wells,
I'm a dealer in magic and spells,
    In blessings and curses,
    And ever filled purses,
In prophecies, witches, and knells.
If you want a proud foe to "make tracks"—
If you'd melt a rich uncle in wax—
        You've but to look in
        On the resident Djinn,
Number seventy, Simmery Axe!

We've a first class assortment of magic;
    And for raising a posthumous shade,
With effects that are comic or tragic,
    There's no cheaper house in the trade.
Love-philtre, we've quantities of it!
    And for knowledge if any one burns,
We're keeping a very small prophet, a prophet
    Who brings us unbounded returns:

For he can prophesy
With a wink of his eye,
Peep with security
Into futurity
Sum up your history,
Clear up a mystery,
Humor proclivity
For a nativity—for a nativity;
With mirrors so magical,
Tetrapods tragical,
Bogies spectacular,
Answers oracular,
Facts astronomical,
Solemn or comical,
And if you want it, he
Makes a reduction on taking a quantity!
Oh! If anyone anything lacks,
He'll find it already in stacks,
    If he'll only look in
    On the resident Djinn,
Number seventy, Simmery Axe!

He can raise you hosts
Of ghosts,
And that without reflectors;
   And creepy things
   With wings,
And gaunt and grisly spectres.
   He can fill you crowds
   Of shrouds,
And horrify you vastly;
   He can rack your brains
   With chains,
And gibberings grim and ghastly!

Then, if you plan it, he
Changes organity
With an urbanity,
Full of Satanity,
Vexes humanity
With an inanity
Fatal to vanity,—
Driving your foes to the verge of insanity!
Barring tautology,
In demonology,
'Lectro-biology,
Mystic nosology,
Spirit philology,
High-class astrology,
Such is his knowledge, he
Isn't the man to require an apology!
Oh! My name is John Wellington Wells, (etc.)

                      W. S. GILBERT, *The Sorcerer*, I.

3.   A Model Major-General
I am the very model of a modern Major-General,
I've information vegetable, animal, and mineral,
I know the kings of England, and I quote the fights historical,
From Marathon to Waterloo, in order categorical;
I'm very well acquainted too with matters mathematical;
I understand equations, both the simple and quadratical;
About binomial theorem I'm teeming with a lot o'news—
With many cheerful facts about the square of the hypote-
     nuse; . . .
I'm very good at integral and differential calculus;

I know the scientific names of beings animalculous;
In short, in matters vegetable, animal, and mineral,
I am the very model of a modern Major-General.

W. S. GILBERT, *The Pirates of Penzance*, I.

4.   How To Achieve Popularity
If you give me your attention, I will tell you what I am:
I'm a genuine philanthropist—all other kinds are sham.
Each little fault of temper and each social defect
In my erring fellow-creatures I endeavour to correct.
To all their little weaknesses I open people's eyes;
And little plans to snub the self-sufficient I devise;
I love my fellow-creatures—I do all the good I can—
Yet everybody says I'm such a disagreeable man!
    And I can't think why!

To compliments inflated I've a withering reply;
And vanity I always do my best to mortify;
A charitable action I can skillfully dissect;
And interested motives I'm delighted to detect;
I know everybody's income and what everybody earns;
And I carefully compare it with the income tax returns;
But to benefit humanity however much I plan,
Yet everybody says I'm such a disagreeable man!
    And I can't think why!

I'm sure I'm no ascetic; I'm as pleasant as can be;
You'll always find me ready with a crushing repartee,
I've an irritating chuckle, I've a celebrated sneer,
I've an entertaining snigger, I've a fascinating leer.
To everybody's prejudice I know a thing or two;
I can tell a woman's age in half a minute—and I do.
But although I try to make myself as pleasant as I can,
Yet everybody says I am a disagreeable man!
    And I can't think why!

W. S. GILBERT, *Princess Ida*, I.

In reading aloud the following poem, pay particular attention that your final voiced consonants are well articulated:

5.   Winter Nights
Now winter nights enlarge
    The number of their hours,
And clouds their storms discharge
    Upon the airy towers.

Let now the chimneys blaze
    And cups o'erflow with wine;
Let well-tuned words amaze
    With harmony divine.

Now yellow waxen lights
    Shall wait on honey Love,
While youthful Revels, Masques, and Courtly sights
    Sleep's leaden spells remove.

This time doth well dispense
    With lovers' long discourse;
Much speech hath some defence,
    Though beauty no remorse.

All do not all things well;
    Some measures comely tread,
Some knotted Riddles tell;
    Some Poems smoothly read.

The Summer hath his joys,
    And Winter his delights;
Though Love and all his pleasures are but toys
    They shorten tedious nights.
                THOMAS CAMPION, *The Third Booke of Ayres,* XII.

Strive for an easy blending of sounds from the end of one word to the beginning of another within the same phrase in reading the poems to follow. You should also be aware of the need for precision in the articulation of consonants.

6.   On the Sea
    It keeps eternal whisperings around
        Desolate shores, and with its mighty swell
        Gluts twice ten thousand Caverns, till the spell
    Of Hecate leaves them their old shadowy sound.
    Often 'tis in such gentle temper found,
        That scarcely will the very smallest shell
        Be mov'd for days from whence it sometime fell,
    When last the winds of Heaven were unbound.
    Oh ye! who have your eye-balls vex'd and tir'd,
        Feast them upon the wideness of the Sea;

Oh ye! whose ears are dinn'd with uproar rude,
Or fed too much with cloying melody,—
Sit ye near some old Cavern's Mouth, and brood,
Until ye start, as if the sea-nymphs quir'd!

JOHN KEATS, *Literary Remains.*

7.   Mirth

'Tis mirth that fills the veins with blood,
More than wine, or sleep, or food;
Let each man keep his heart at ease;
No man dies of that disease.
He that would his body keep
From diseases, must not weep;
But whoever laughs and sings,
Never he his body brings
Into fevers, gouts, or rheums,
Or lingeringly his lungs consumes;
Or meets with aches in the bone,
Or catarrhs, or griping stone:
But contented lives for aye;
The more he laughs, the more he may.

BEAUMONT and FLETCHER, *The Knight of the
Burning Pestle*, II, vii.

8.   Delight in Disorder

A sweet disorder in the dress
Kindles in clothes a wantonness:
A lawn about the shoulders thrown
Into a fine distraction:
An erring lace, which here and there
Enthrals the crimson stomacher:
A cuff neglectful, and thereby
Ribbands to flow confusedly:
A winning wave, deserving note,
In the tempestuous petticoat:
A careless shoe-string, in whose tie
I see a wild civility:
Do more bewitch me than when art
Is too precise in every part.

ROBERT HERRICK, *Hesperides.*

9.   Love is a Sickness

Love is a sickness full of woes,
    All remedies refusing;

A plant that with most cutting grows,
   Most barren with using.
      Why so?
More we enjoy it, more it dies;
If not enjoy'd, it sighing cries—
      Heigh ho!

Love is a torment of the mind,
   A tempest everlasting;
And Jove hath made it of a kind
   Not well, nor full nor fasting.
      Why so?
More we enjoy it, more it dies;
If not enjoy'd, it sighing cries—
      Heigh ho!

SAMUEL DANIEL, *Hymen's Triumph*, I, v.

In reading aloud the following poem, be sure the consonant sounds have sharpness of definition to make the words
easily intelligible:

10.   Take Sky
      Now think of words. Take *sky*
      And ask yourself just why—
      Like sun, moon, star, and cloud—
      It sounds so well out loud,
      And pleases so the sight
      When printed black on white.
      Take syllable and thimble:
      The sound of them is nimble.
      Take balsam, fir, and pine:
      Your woodland smell and mine.
      Take kindle, blaze, and flicker—
      What lights the hearth fire quicker?
      Take bucket, spring, and dip
      Cold water to your lip.

      Three words we fear but form:
      Gale, twister, thunderstorm;
      Others that simply shake
      Are tremble, temblor, quake.
      But granite, stone, and rock:
      Too solid, they, to shock.

Put honey, bee, and flower
With sunny, shade, and shower;
Put wild with bird and wing,
Put bird with song and sing.
Aren't paddle, trail, and camp
The cabin and the lamp?
Now look at words of rest—
Sleep, quiet, calm, and blest;

At words we learn in youth—
Grace, skill, ambition, truth;
At words of lifelong need—
Faith, courage, strength, and deed;
Deep-rooted words that say
Love, hope, dream, yearn, and pray;
Light-hearted words—girl, boy,
Live, laugh, play, share, enjoy.

October, April, June—
Come late and gone too soon.
Remember, words are life:
Child, husband, mother, wife;
Remember, and I'm done:
Words taken one by one
Are poems as they stand—
Shore, beacon, harbor, land;
Brook, river, mountain, vale,
Crow, rabbit, otter, quail;
Oak, apple, water, snow,
Wind, weather, flood, and floe.
Like light across the lawn
Are morning, sea, and dawn;
Words of the green earth growing—
Seed, soil, and farmer sowing.
Like wind upon the mouth
Sad, summer, rain, and south.
Amen. Put not asunder
Man's first word: wonder . . . wonder . . .

DAVID MCCORD, *The New York Times Book
Review,* June 11, 1961.*

A strong sense of the rhythm of the following excerpt from Edward Lear's nonsense poem *The Jumblies* will be helpful in reading it aloud: *

11.   They went to sea in a Sieve, they did,
        In a Sieve they went to sea:
      In spite of all their friends could say,
      On a winter's morn, on a stormy day,
        In a Sieve they went to sea!
      And when the Sieve turned round and round,
      And every one cried, "You'll all be drowned!"
      They called aloud, "Our Sieve ain't big,
      But we don't care a button! we don't care a fig!
      In a Sieve we'll go to sea!"
      Far and few, far and few,
        Are the lands where the Jumblies live;
      Their heads are green, and their hands are blue,
        And they went to sea in a Sieve.

In reading aloud the following poem by Algernon Swinburne, direct your attention again to the articulation of consonants. Swinburne wrote this poem as a parody without real meaning in itself. Can you make it sound meaningful?

12.   A Parody
        From the depth of the dreamy decline of the dawn through a
          notable nimbus of nebulous moonshine,
        Pallid and pink as the palm of the flag-flower that flickers
          with fear of the flies as they float,
        Are the looks of our lovers that lustrously lean from a marvel
          of mystic miraculous moonshine,
        These that we feel in the blood of our blushes that thicken
          and threaten with throbs through the throat?
        Thicken and thrill as a theatre thronged at appeal of an
          actor's appalled agitation,
        Fainter with fear of the fires of the future than pale with the
          promise of pride in the past;
        Flushed with the famishing fulness of fever that reddens with
          radiance of rathe recreation,
        Gaunt as the ghastliest of glimpses that gleam through the
          gloom of the gloaming when ghosts go aghast?

* See material in Part I, Sections **9.10–9.12,** on /s/ sounds.

Nay, for the nick of the tick of the time is a tremulous touch
on the temples of terror,
Strained as the sinews yet strenuous with strife of the dead
who is dumb as the dust-heaps of death;
Surely no soul is it, sweet as the spasm of erotic emotional
exquisite error,
Bathed in the balms of beatified bliss, beatific itself by
beatitude's breath.
Surely no spirit or sense of a soul that was soft to the spirit
and soul of our senses
Sweetens the stress of surprising suspicion that sobs in the
semblance and sound of a sigh;
Only this oracle opens Olympian, in mystical moods and
triangular tenses,—
"Life is the lust of a lamp for the light that is dark till the
dawn of the day when we die."
Mild is the mirk and monotonous music of memory, melodi-
ously mute as it may be,
While the hope in the heart of a hero is bruised by the breach
of men's rapiers, resigned to the rod;
Made meek as a mother whose bosom-beats bound with the
bliss bringing bulk of a balm-breathing baby,
As they grope through the grave-yard of creeds, under skies
growing green at a groan for the grimness of God.
Blank is the book of his bounty beholden of old, and its binding
is blacker than bluer:
Out of blue into black is the scheme of the skies, and their
dews are the wine of the bloodshed of things:
Till the darkling desire of delight shall be free as a fawn that
is freed from the fangs that pursue her,
Till the heart-beats of hell shall be hushed by a hymn from
the hunt that has harried the kennel of kings.

ALGERNON SWINBURNE, "Nephelidia."

In reading the following excerpt from Gertrude Stein's
Four Saints in Three Acts, pay particular attention to the
rhythm of utterance. The selection also provides a practice
exercise for /æ/ and /l/ sounds.

13.   Pigeons on the grass alas.
         Pigeons on the grass alas.
         Short longer grass short longer longer shorter yellow grass
Pigeons large pigeons on the shorter longer yellow grass alas
pigeons on the grass.

If they were not pigeons what were they.

If they were not pigeons on the grass alas what were they.
He had heard of a third and he asked about it it was a magpie
in the sky. If a magpie in the sky on the sky can not cry if
the pigeon on the grass alas can alas and to pass the pigeon
on the grass alas and the magpie in the sky on the sky and to
try and to try alas on the grass alas the pigeon on the grass
the pigeon on the grass and alas. They might be very well
very well very well they might be they might be very well
they might be very well very well they might be.

Let Lucy Lily Lily Lucy Lucy let Lucy Lucy Lily Lily
Lily Lily Lily let Lily Lucy Lucy let Lily. Let Lucy Lily.

GERTRUDE STEIN, *Four Saints in Three Acts*, II, ii.*

See material in Part I, Section **13.08,** on /æ/ sounds, and
in Sections **11.07–11.10,** on /l/ sounds.

In reading the excerpts from famous speeches that follow, achieve a firm support for tone. Do not be afraid to use
sufficient voice to permit the tone to carry to a large audience.
(See material in Part I, Section **1.01,** on support of tone.)

14.   Prudence as a Policy
America, gentlemen say, is a noble object. It is an object
well worth fighting for. Certainly it is, if fighting a people be
the best way of gaining them. Gentlemen in this respect will
be led to their choice of means by their complexions and their
habits. Those who understand the military art will, of course,
have some predilection for it. Those who wield the thunder
of the state may have more confidence in the efficacy of arms.
But I confess, possibly for want of this knowledge, my opinion
is much more in favor of prudent management than of force;
considering force not as an odious, but a feeble instrument for
preserving a people so numerous, so active, so growing, so
spirited as this, in a profitable and subordinate connection
with us.

EDMUND BURKE, *Speech on Conciliation with America*, 1775.

15.   With Malice Toward None
With malice toward none, with charity for all, with firmness in the right, as God gives us to see the right, let us strive
on to finish the work we are in, to bind up the nation's
wounds, to care for him who shall have borne the battle, and
for his widow and orphans; to do all which may achieve and
cherish a just and lasting peace among ourselves and with all
nations.

ABRAHAM LINCOLN, *Second Inaugural Address*, 1865.

* From *Four Saints in Three Acts* by Gertrude Stein. Copyright 1934 by
Random House, Inc.

16.   Work, Work, Work

I preach to you, then, my countrymen, that our country
calls not for the life of ease, but for the life of strenuous endeavor. The twentieth century looms before us big with the
fate of many nations. If we stand idly by, if we seek merely
swollen, slothful ease, and ignoble peace, if we shrink from
the hard contests where men must win at hazard of their lives
and at the risk of all they hold dear, then the bolder and
stronger peoples will pass us by and will win for themselves
the domination of the world. Let us therefore boldly face the
life of strife, resolute to do our duty well and manfully; resolute to uphold righteousness by deed and by word; resolute
to be both honest and brave, to serve high ideals, yet to use
practical methods. Above all, let us shrink from no strife,
moral or physical, within or without the nation, provided that
we are certain that the strife is justified; for it is only through
strife, through hard and dangerous endeavor, that we shall
ultimately win the goal of true national greatness.

THEODORE ROOSEVELT, *The Strenuous Life*, 1899.

17.   A Day of National Consecration

I am certain that my fellow Americans expect that on my
induction into the Presidency I will address them with a
candor and a decision which the present situation of our nation impels. This is preëminently the time to speak the truth,
the whole truth, frankly and boldly. Nor need we shrink from
honestly facing conditions in our country today. This great
Nation will endure as it has endured, will revive and will
prosper. So, first of all, let me assert my firm belief that the
only thing we have to fear is fear itself—nameless, unreasoning, unjustified terror which paralyzes needed efforts to convert retreat into advance. In every dark hour of our national
life a leadership of frankness and vigor has met with that
understanding and support of the people themselves which is
essential to victory. I am convinced that you will again give
that support to leadership in these critical days.

FRANKLIN D. ROOSEVELT, *First Inaugural Address*, 1933.

18.   Churchill's Determination

We shall not flag nor fail. We shall go on to the end. We
shall fight in France and on the seas and oceans; we shall fight
with growing confidence and growing strength in the air.

We shall defend our island whatever the cost may be; we
shall fight on beaches, landing grounds, in fields, in streets and
on the hills. We shall never surrender and even if, which I
do not for the moment believe, this island or a large part of
it were subjected and starving, then our empire beyond the
seas, armed and guarded by the British fleet, will carry on the

struggle until in God's good time the New World, with all its power and might, sets forth to the liberation and rescue of the Old.

WINSTON CHURCHILL, *Speech to the*
House of Commons, 1940.*

19.   The Struggle Against Common Enemies

In your hands, my fellow citizens, more than mine, will rest the final success or failure of our course. Since this country was founded, each generation of Americans has been summoned to give testimony to its national loyalty. The graves of young Americans who answered the call to service surround the globe. Now the trumpet summons us again—not as a call to bear arms, though arms we need—not as a call to battle, though embattled we are—but a call to bear the burden of a long twilight struggle, year in and year out "rejoicing in hope, patient in tribulation"—a struggle against the common enemies of man: tyranny, poverty, disease, and war itself.

Can we forge against these enemies a grand and global alliance, North and South, East and West, that can assure a more fruitful life for all mankind? Will you join me in that historic effort?

In the long history of the world, only a few generations have been granted the role of defending freedom in its hour of maximum danger. I do not shrink from this responsibility—I welcome it. I do not believe that any of us would exchange places with any other people or any other generation. The energy, the faith, and the devotion which we bring to this endeavor will light our country and all who serve it—and the glow from that fire can truly light the world. And so, my fellow Americans: ask not what your country can do for you—ask what you can do for your country.

JOHN F. KENNEDY, *Inaugural Address,* 1961.

The selections that follow provide useful pronunciation exercises, particularly in the pronunciation of foreign proper names. Be sure you consult a dictionary for the pronunciations of which you have some doubt.

20.   The Versailles of Romance

When we think of Versailles in the full sunshine of Louis XIV, there rises in our minds the vision of a long white façade; of a terrace, so vast under the wide sky that men and women seem as beetles creeping; of clipped alleys leading down to

* Reprinted from *The World's Great Speeches,* revised edition, edited by Lewis Copeland and Lawrence W. Lamm, copyright 1942 by Copeland & Lamm, Inc., copyright 1958 by Dover Publications, Inc.

grottoes, where, from the mouths of tritons, the water splashes continuously upon the backs of dolphins, river virgins and fat frogs. We see long galleries and high saloons, with trim trees of bay and myrtle in silver tubs, with guards grouped at entrances, with footmen in white wigs and liveries of blue. When a mirrored doorway opens, it swings a reflection of painted ceilings, of great plaques of porphyry and marble, of bronze glinting, of the soft summer sky outside. At night time we picture candles guttering in the sconces, we see brocaded groups seated around gaming tables, we hear the faint sound of stringed instruments playing one of Lulli's dreamy tunes. And we imagine that, when the King has retired splendidly to bed, the courtiers will escape to their own cramped compartments and there discuss the morning's sermon by Bossuet, the latest fable by La Fontaine, the theories of Nicole, Arnauld and Pascal, the injunctions of Jean de Balsac, the impending comedy of Molière, or the haunting rhythms of Racine's careful line.

HAROLD NICOLSON, *Good Behaviour.**

21.   The Highbrow Way of Life
     The real highbrow's way of life is as intellectualized as his way of thinking, and as carefully plotted. He is likely to be either extremely self-conscious about his physical surroundings and creature comforts or else sublimely, and rather ostentatiously, indifferent to them. If he affects the former attitude, he will within the limits of his income surround himself with works of art. If he cannot afford paintings he buys drawings. Color reproductions, except as casual reminders tucked in the frame of a mirror or thrown down on a table, are beneath him. The facsimile is no substitute in his mind for the genuine, and he would rather have a slight sketch by a master, Braque or Picasso or even Jackson Pollock, than a fully realized canvas by an artist he considers not quite first-rate. Drawings by his friends he hangs in the bathroom. His furniture, if it is modern, consists of identifiable pieces by Aalto, or Breuer, or Mies van der Rohe, or Eames; it does not come from department stores. If he finds modern unsympathetic, he will tend to use Biedermeier or the more "entertaining" varieties of Victorian, which he collects piece by piece with an eye to the slightly eccentric. If he has antiques, you may be sure they are not maple; the cult of Early American is offensive to him.

RUSSELL LYNES, *The Tastemakers.*†

22.   Florentine Painters

Florentine painting between Giotto and Michelangelo contains the names of such artists as Orcagna, Masaccio, Fra Filippo, Pollaiuolo, Verrocchio, Leonardo, and Botticelli. Put besides these the greatest names in Venetian art, the Vivarini, the Bellini, Giorgione, Titian, and Tintoretto. The difference is striking. The significance of the Venetian names is exhausted with their significance as painters. Not so with the Florentines. Forget that they were painters, they remain great sculptors; forget that they were sculptors, and they still remain architects, poets, and even men of science. They left no form of expression untried, and to none could they say, "This will perfectly convey my meaning." Painting, therefore, offers but a partial and not always the most adequate manifestation of their personality, and we feel the artist as greater than his work, and the man as soaring above the artist.

BERNARD BERENSON, *Italian Painters of the Renaissance.**

In the following excerpt from Charles Dickens' novel *Our Mutual Friend,* Mr. Podsnap illustrates, in a number of ways, how not to talk to someone who doesn't understand English very well. His pomposity is that of a type of English gentleman of the nineteenth century, but we easily make some of the same errors today. As you read this selection aloud, you will realize that the capitalized words were meant to receive more than usual stress.

23.   Mr. Podsnap Assists a Frenchman with English

As a delicate concession to this unfortunately-born foreigner, Mr. Podsnap, in receiving him, had presented his wife as "Madame Podsnap;" also his daughter as "Mademoiselle Podsnap," with some inclination to add "ma fille," in which bold venture, however, he checked himself. The Veerings being at that time the only arrivals, he had added (in a condescendingly explanatory manner), "Monsieur Vey-nair-reeng," and had then subsided into English.

"How Do You Like London?" Mr. Podsnap now inquired from his station of host, as if he were administering something in the nature of a powder or potion to the deaf child; "London, Londres, London?"

The foreign gentleman admired it.

"You find it Very Large?" said Mr. Podsnap spaciously.

The foreigner found it very large.

---

* From *Italian Painters of the Renaissance* by Bernard Berenson. Published by Phaidon Press, London; distributed in the United States by the New York Graphic Society, Greenwich, Conn.

"And Very Rich?"

The foreign gentleman found it, without doubt, enormement riche.

"Enormously Rich, We say," returned Mr. Podsnap, in a condescending manner. "Our English adverbs do Not terminate in Mong, and we pronounce the "ch" as if there were a "t" before it. We say Ritch."

"Reetch," remarked the foreign gentleman.

"And Do You Find, Sir," pursued Mr. Podsnap, with dignity, "Many Evidences that Strike You, of our British Constitution in the Streets Of The World's Metropolis, London, Londres, London?"

The foreign gentleman begged to be pardoned, but did not altogether understand.

"The Constitution Britannique," Mr. Podsnap explained, as if he were teaching in an infant school. "We Say British, But You Say Britannique, You Know" (forgivingly, as if that were not his fault). "The Constitution, Sir."

The foreign gentleman said, "Mais, yees; I know eem." . . .

"I was Inquiring," said Mr. Podsnap, resuming the thread of his discourse, "Whether You Have Observed in our Streets as We would say, Upon our Pavvy as You would say, any Tokens—"

The foreign gentleman with patient courtesy entreated pardon; "But what was a tokenz?"

"Marks," said Mr. Podsnap; "Signs, you know, Appearances—Traces."

"Ah! Of a Orse?" inquired the foreign gentleman.

"We call it Horse," said Mr. Podsnap, with forbearance. "In England, Angleterre, England, We Aspirate the 'H,' and We Say 'Horse.' Only our Lower Classes say 'Orse!'"

"Pardon," said the foreign gentleman; "I am alwiz wrong!"

"Our Language," said Mr. Podsnap, with a gracious consciousness of being always right, "is Difficult. Ours is a Copious Language, and Trying to Strangers. I will not Pursue my Question." . . .

"It meerely referred," Mr. Podsnap explained, with a sense of meritorious proprietorship, "to our Constitution, Sir. We Englishmen are Very Proud of our Constitution, Sir. It Was Bestowed Upon Us By Providence. No Other Country is so Favoured as This Country."

"And ozer countries?—" the foreign gentleman was beginning, when Mr. Podsnap put him right again.

"We do not say Ozer; we say Other; the letters are 'T' and 'H;' you say Tay and Aish, You Know;" (still with clemency). "The sound is 'th'—'th!'"

CHARLES DICKENS, *Our Mutual Friend*, Book I, Chapter 11.

Chapter 5

Selections for Oral Analysis and Interpretation

ORAL ANALYSIS: EXPLANATION

32.01 The second section of this part of the book is given over to selections for oral reading that demand a thorough understanding of content on the part of the reader. While this understanding is, of course, necessary for every oral reading, in reading the selections that follow, the student must have a keen awareness of the shades of meaning implied by the words. In using all these materials, the student must work for good voice production and articulation.

SELECTIONS

32.02 The following dramatic monolog by Robert Browning demands careful analysis before being read aloud. Here are some of the questions you should be able to answer about the selection:

What sort of individual is speaking?
What is his mood?
How is this mood reflected in the tone of his voice?
Why does he have the attitude he has?
What is the setting of the poem?
What contrasts are explicit in the poem?
What does Browning seem to be saying?

1.   The Patriot

It was roses, roses, all the way,
    With myrtle mixed in my path like mad:
The house-roofs seemed to heave and sway,
    The church-spires flamed, such flags they had,
A year ago on this very day.

The air broke into a mist with bells,
    The old walls rocked with the crowd and cries.
Had I said, "Good folk, mere noise repels—
    But give me your sun from yonder skies!"
They had answered, "And afterward, what else?"

Alack, it was I who leaped at the sun
    To give it my loving friends to keep!
Naught man could do, have I left undone:
    And you see my harvest, what I reap
This very day, now a year is run.

There's nobody on the house-tops now—
    Just a palsied few at the windows set;
For the best of the sight is, all allow,
    At the Shambles' Gate—or better yet,
By the very scaffold's foot, I trow.

I go in the rain, and, more than needs,
    A rope cuts both my wrists behind;
And I think, by the feel, my forehead bleeds,
    For they fling, whoever has a mind,
Stones at me for my year's misdeeds.

Thus I entered, and thus I go!
    In triumphs people have dropped down dead.
"Paid by the world, what dost thou owe
    Me?"—God might question; now instead,
'Tis God shall repay: I am safer so.

                                   ROBERT BROWNING.

2.   The King's English

He was indeed the glass
Wherein the noble youth did dress themselves.
He had no legs, that practis'd not his gait;
And speaking thick, which nature made his blemish,

Became the accents of the valiant;
For those that could speak low and tardily
Would turn their own perfection to abuse
To seem like him; so that in speech, in gait,
In diet, in affections of delight,
In military rules, humours of blood,
He was the mark and glass, copy and book,
That fashion'd others.

  WILLIAM SHAKESPEARE, *Henry the Fourth,* Part II, II, iii.

3.   The Real Cowboy

What the cowboy was actually like has always been embellished beyond recognition by the authors of westerns. He is generally portrayed as an unsmiling, untalkative fellow, quick on the draw (and usually too quick on the trigger). He seems to have spent most of his time catching cattle thieves and other "varmints."

In reality cowboys were, as one of them said, "merely folks, just plain, every-day bow-legged humans." They carried only one revolver apiece if they carried any at all—not two to be fired from the hip simultaneously—and they would not have thought of notching the handles to keep count of the "enemies" they had "gotten."

The work of the cowboy was always hard, frequently boring, and at times dangerous. The day began at dawn with the cry, "Roll out!" Horses frequently needed to be shod; the cattle had to be branded; saddles, wagons, lariats, and harnesses had to be inspected and repaired. Then, of course, the cattle themselves were a continual responsibility.

Occasionally Indians "jumped" the reservations and clashed with the cowboys over the rustling, or stealing, of cattle. The blizzards in the winter and the hot, dry spells in the summer sometimes created extremely difficult conditions under which cowboys had to do their work.

The cowboy's special garb was not an affectation but an adaptation to the circumstances of his daily life: cowhide clothes wore better in the saddle than cotton; the bandana around the neck and the wide-brimmed hat were protection against dust and sun. For his labors, which consumed all his waking hours, the average cowboy received about twenty-five dollars a month, with a top man receiving perhaps forty.

  HENRY F. GRAFF and JOHN A. KROUT, *The Adventure
of the American People.**

---

* From *The Adventure of the American People,* copyright 1963 by Rand McNally & Co., now in its eighth printing.

4.   Heinrich Schliemann—Founder of Modern Archeology

During the seventies and eighties of the last century an old gray-haired scholar, wearing a high collar and a sun helmet, was to be seen wandering over the ruins of an obscure mound in Asia Minor. He was short and wiry, with dark brown eyes, high cheekbones, a heavy nose, and a sensual mouth; there was something of the peasant about him, something too of the Luebeck merchants who were his ancestors. He spoke in a high-pitched nervous voice, dressed shabbily, walked with a curious gliding motion, and always carried in his coat pocket a dog-eared paper-bound edition of the *Iliad* or the *Odyssey*. To the friendly inquirer he would explain that he had uncovered the ancient city of Troy and found in its walls a secret treasure hoard of gold, which he kept securely locked in his house in Athens. He believed that the ashes of Odysseus, the crown jewels of the Trojan Empire, and the golden death masks of Agamemnon and many other Greek heroes were in his possession, and it is just possible that his claims were justified. Until he was long past middle age he never touched a spade, but during the last seventeen years of his life he excavated continually. The most unscientific of archeologists, he founded the modern science of archeology.

ROBERT PAYNE, *The Gold of Troy.**

5.   The Age of Napoleon

During the wars of the Empire, while the husbands and brothers were in Germany, the anxious mothers brought forth an ardent, pale, nervous generation. Conceived between two battles, educated amidst the noises of war, thousands of children looked about them with a somber eye while testing their puny muscles. From time to time their blood-stained fathers would appear, raise them on their gold laced bosoms, and place them on the ground and remount their horses.

The life of Europe was centered in one man; all were trying to fill their lungs with the air which he had breathed. Every year France presented that man with three hundred thousand of her youth; it was the tax paid to Caesar, and, without that troop behind him, he could not follow his fortune. It was the escort he needed that he might traverse the world, and then perish in a little valley in a deserted island, under the weeping willow.

Never had there been so many sleepless nights as in the time of that man; never had there been seen, hanging over the ramparts of the cities, such a nation of desolate mothers; never was there such a silence about those who spoke of death. And

* From *The Gold of Troy* by Robert Payne, published by the Funk & Wagnalls Co., Inc.

yet there was never such joy, such life, such fanfares of war, in all hearts. Never was there such pure sunlight as that which dried all this blood. God made the sun for this man, they said, and they called it the Sun of Austerlitz. But he made this sunlight himself with his ever-thundering cannons which dispelled all clouds but those which succeed the day of battle.

ALFRED DE MUSSET, *The Confession of a Child of the Century*, translated by K. WARREN.

6.   The Parisian Type
By dint of taking interest in everything, the Parisian ends by being interested in nothing. No emotion dominating his face, which friction has rubbed away, it turns gray like the faces of those houses upon which all kinds of dust and smoke have blown. In effect, the Parisian, with his indifference on the day for what the morrow will bring forth, lives like a child, whatever may be his age. He grumbles at everything, consoles himself for everything, jests at everything, forgets, desires, and tastes everything, seizes all with passion, quits all with indifference—his kings, his conquests, his glory, his idols of bronze or glass—as he throws away his stockings, his hats, and his fortune. In Paris no sentiment can withstand the drift of things, and their current compels a struggle in which the passions are relaxed: there love is a desire, and hatred a whim; there's no true kinsman but the thousand-franc note, no better friend than the pawnbroker. This universal toleration bears its fruits, and in the salon, as in the street, there is no one *de trop*, there is no one absolutely useful, or absolutely harmful—knaves or fools, men of wit or integrity. There everything is tolerated: the government and the guillotine, religion and the cholera. You are always acceptable to this world, you will never be missed by it.

HONORÉ DE BALZAC, *The Girl with the Golden Eyes*, translated by ELLEN MARRIAGE.

7. The following group of reading selections is taken from Charles Dickens' *American Notes*, representing his impressions of some American scenes in the year 1842:

a.   Broadway—New York
The great promenade and thoroughfare, as most people know, is Broadway; a wide and bustling street, which, from the Battery Gardens to its opposite termination in a country road may be four miles long. Shall we sit down in an upper floor of the Carlton House (situated in the best part of this main artery of New York), and when we are tired of looking

upon the life below, sally forth arm-in-arm, and mingle with the stream?

Warm weather! The sun strikes upon our heads at this open window, as though its rays were concentrated through a burning-glass; but the day is in its zenith, and the season an unusual one. Was there ever such a sunny street as this Broadway! The pavement stones are polished with the tread of feet until they shine again; the red bricks of the houses might be yet in the dry, hot kilns; and the roofs of these omnibuses look as though, if water were poured on them, they would hiss and smoke and smell like half-quenched fires. No stint of omnibuses here! Half-a-dozen have gone by within as many minutes. Plenty of hackney cabs and coaches too; gigs, phaetons, large-wheeled tilburies, and private carriages—rather of a clumsy make, and not very different from the public vehicles, but built for heavy roads beyond the city pavement.

b.   Harvard

There is no doubt that much of the intellectual refinement and superiority of Boston is referable to the quiet influence of the University of Cambridge [sic] which is within three or four miles of the city. The resident professors at that university are gentlemen of learning and varied attainments; and are, without one exception that I can call to mind, men who would shed a grace upon, and do honour to, any society in the civilized world. . . . Whatever the defects of American universities may be, they disseminate no prejudices; rear no bigots; dig up the buried ashes of no old superstitions; never interpose between the people and their improvement; exclude no man because of his religious opinions; above all, in their whole course of study and instruction, recognize a world, and a broad one too, lying beyond the college walls.

c.   New York to Philadelphia—1842

The journey from New York to Philadelphia, is made by railroad, and two ferries; and usually occupies between five and six hours. It was a fine evening when we were passengers in the train: and, watching the bright sunset from a little window near the door by which we sat, my attention was attracted to a remarkable appearance issuing from the windows of the gentleman's car immediately in front of us, which I supposed for some time was occasioned by a number of industrious persons inside, ripping open feather-beds, and giving the feathers to the wind. At length it occurred to me that they were only spitting, which was indeed the case; though how any number of passengers which it was possible for the car to contain could have maintained such a playful and incessant shower of expectoration, I am still at a loss to understand . . .

8.   Dutch Courage
    For an instant the mighty Peter paused in the midst of his
career, and mounting on a stump, addressed his troops in
eloquent Low Dutch, exhorting them to fight like *duyvels*,
and assuring them that if they conquered, they should get
plenty of booty—if they fell, they should be allowed the satisfaction, while dying, of reflecting that it was in the service of
their country, and after they were dead, of seeing their names
inscribed in the temple of renown, and handed down, in company with all the other great men of the year, for the admira-
tion of posterity. Finally, he swore to them, on the word of
a governor (and they knew him too well to doubt it for a
moment), that if he caught any mother's son of them looking
pale, or playing craven, he could curry his hide till he made
him run out of it like a snake in spring-time. Then lugging
out his trusty sabre, he brandished it three times over his head,
ordered Van Corlear to sound a charge, and shouting the
words "St. Nicholas and the Manhattoes!" courageously dashed
forwards. His warlike followers, who had employed the inter-
val in lighting their pipes, instantly stuck them into their
mouths, gave a furious puff, and charged gallantly under
cover of the smoke.
    The Swedish garrison, ordered by the cunning Risingh not
to fire until they could distinguish the whites of their assail-
ants' eyes, stood in horrid silence on the covertway, until the
eager Dutchmen had ascended the glacis. Then did they pour
into them such a tremendous volley, that the very hills quaked
around, and were terrified even unto an incontinence of
water, insomuch that certain springs burst forth from their
sides, which continue to run unto the present day. Not a
Dutchman but would have bitten the dust beneath that dread-
ful fire, had not the protecting Minerva kindly taken care that
the Swedes should, one and all, observe their usual custom of
shutting their eyes and turning away their heads at the moment of discharge.
    Washington Irving, *Knickerbocker's History of New York.*

9.   National Disease
    From the reign of Anne till the beginning of the nineteenth
century gambling was a national disease among the leisured
classes of both sexes. Games of skill and games of chance,
horseracing, lotteries, and commercial speculations—all made
an irresistible appeal. While the men spent most of the day,
and sometimes of the night also, round the card-tables at the
fashionable clubs of Almack's, White's, and Boodle's, the ladies
occupied themselves in similar fashion in their own drawing-
rooms. Thousands of pounds would be won or lost at a single

sitting. It is recorded that Charles James Fox would occasionally sit for nigh twenty-four hours at play, losing £500 an hour. Before he was twenty-five he had squandered £140,000, mostly at cards. He played whist and piquet very well, but it was the element of chance that really attracted him, and it was in such a purely gambling game as the popular "faro" that he lost most of his money. Men would take wagers on anything—that X would not be made a vice-admiral by such and such a date, that Y would be found wearing a certain suit on a particular occasion, that Z would, although seriously ill, be still surviving on the first of next month, and so forth.

A. S. Turberville, *English Men and Manners in the Eighteenth Century.*[*]

10.   An Essay in Gloom
During the whole of a dull, dark and soundless day in the autumn of the year, when the clouds hung oppressively low in the heavens, I had been passing alone, on horseback, through a singularly dreary tract of country, and at length found myself, as the shades of evening drew on, within view of the melancholy House of Usher. I know not how it was, but, with the first glimpse of the building a sense of insufferable gloom pervaded my spirit. I say insufferable; for the feeling was unrelieved by any of that half-pleasurable, because poetic, sentiment with which the mind usually receives even the sternest natural images of the desolate or terrible. I looked upon the scene before me—upon the mere house, and the simple landscape features of the domain, upon the bleak walls, upon the vacant eye-like windows, upon a few rank sedges, and upon a few white trunks of decayed trees, with an utter depression of soul which I can compare to no earthly sensation more properly than to the after-dream of the reveller upon opium, the bitter lapse into every-day life, the hideous dropping off of the veil. There was an iciness, a sinking, a sickening of the heart, an unredeemed dreariness of the thought which no goading of the imagination could torture into aught of the sublime. What was it, I paused to think, what was it that so unnerved me in the contemplation of the House of Usher? It was a mystery all insoluble; nor could I grapple with the shadowy fancies that crowded upon me as I pondered.

Edgar Allan Poe, *The Fall of the House of Usher.*

---

[*] From *English Men and Manners in the Eighteenth Century* by A. S. Turberville, published by the Oxford University Press.

11.   The Oral vs. the Written Dr. Johnson
        Johnson, as Mr. Burke most justly observed, appears far
greater in Boswell's books than in his own. His conversation
appears to have been quite equal to his writings in matter,
and far superior to them in manner. When he talked, he
clothed his wit and his sense in forcible and natural expressions. As soon as he took his pen in his hand to write for the
public, his style became systematically vicious. All his books
are written in a learned language which nobody hears from
his mother or his nurse, in a language in which nobody ever
quarrels, or drives bargains, or makes love, in a language in
which nobody ever thinks. It is clear that Johnson himself did
not think in the dialect in which he wrote. The expressions
which first came to his tongue were simple, energetic, and picturesque. When he wrote for publication, he did his sentences
out of English into Johnsonese. His letters from the Hebrides
to Mrs. Thrale are the original of that work of which the
Journey to the Hebrides is the translation; and it is amusing
to compare the two versions. "When we were taken up stairs,"
he says in one of his letters, "a dirty fellow bounced out of the
bed on which one of us was to lie." This incident is recorded
in the Journey as follows: "Out of one of the beds on which
we were to repose started up at our entrance, a man as black
as a Cyclops from the forge."
            THOMAS BABINGTON MACAULAY, *Samuel Johnson.*

12.   The Charm of Distance
        A little before nine o'clock, I descended to the ground
floor of the house. The solemn man-servant of the night before met me wandering among the passages, and compas-
sionately showed me the way to the breakfast-room.
        My first glance round me, as the man opened the door, dis-
closed a well-furnished breakfast-table, standing in the middle
of a long room, with many windows in it. I looked from the
table to the window farthest from me, and saw a lady standing
at it, with her back turned towards me. The instant my eyes
rested on her, I was struck by the rare beauty of her form, and
by the unaffected grace of her attitude. Her figure was tall,
yet not too tall; comely and well-developed, yet not fat; her
head set on her shoulders with an easy pliant firmness; her
waist, perfection in the eyes of a man, for it occupied its
natural place, it filled out its natural circle, it was visibly and
delightfully undeformed by stays. She had not heard my entrance into the room; and I allowed myself the luxury of admiring her for a few moments, before I moved one of the
chairs near me, as the least embarrassing means of attracting
her attention. She turned towards me immediately. The easy

elegance of every movement of her limbs and body as soon as she began to advance from the far end of the room, set me in a flutter of expectation to see her face clearly. She left the window—and I said to myself, The lady is dark. She moved forward a few steps—and I said to myself, The lady is young. She approached nearer—and I said to myself (with a sense of surprise which words fail me to express), The lady is ugly!

WILKIE COLLINS, *The Woman in White.*

13.   The Nipping Frost
He came down the following morning a sad and thoughtful man. He was attenuated in appearance; one might almost say emaciated. I doubt whether his now grizzled locks had not palpably become more grey than on the preceding evening. At any rate he had aged materially. Years do not make a man old gradually and at an even pace. Look through the world and see if this is not so always, except in those rare cases in which the human being lives and dies without joys and without sorrows, like a vegetable. A man shall be possessed of florid youthful blooming health till, it matters not what age. Thirty—forty—fifty, then comes some nipping frost, some period of agony, that robs the fibres of the body of their succulence, and the hale and hearty man is counted among the old.

ANTHONY TROLLOPE, *Barchester Towers.*

14.   Mona Lisa
The presence that thus rose so strangely beside the waters, is expressive of what in the ways of a thousand years men had come to desire. Hers is the head upon which all "the ends of the world are come," and the eyelids are a little weary. It is a beauty wrought out from within upon the flesh, the deposit, little cell by cell, of strange thoughts and fantastic reveries and exquisite passions. Set it for a moment beside one of those white Greek goddesses or beautiful women of antiquity, and how would they be troubled by this beauty, into which the soul with all its maladies has passed! All the thoughts and experience of the world have etched and moulded there, in that which they have a power to refine and make expressive the outward form, the animalism of Greece, the lust of Rome, the mysticism of the middle age with its spiritual ambition and imaginative loves, the return of the Pagan world, the sins of the Borgias. She is older than the rocks among which she sits; like the vampire, she has been dead many times, and learned the secrets of the grave; and has been a diver in deep seas, and keeps their fallen day about her; and trafficked for strange webs with Eastern merchants, and as Leda, was the mother of Helen of Troy, and, as Saint Anne, the mother of Mary; and all this has been to her but as the sound of lyres

and flutes, and lives only in the delicacy with which it has moulded the changing lineaments, and tinged the eyelids and the hands. The fancy of a perpetual life, sweeping together ten thousand experiences, is an old one; and modern thought has conceived the idea of humanity as wrought upon by, and summing up in itself, all modes of thought and life. Certainly Lady Lisa might stand as the embodiment of the old fancy, the symbol of the modern idea.

WALTER PATER, *The Renaissance.*

15.   English Pride

The English seem as silent as the Japanese, yet vainer than the inhabitants of Siam. Upon my arrival, I attributed that reserve to modesty, which I now find has its origin in pride. Condescend to address them first, and you are sure of their acquaintance; stoop to flattery, and you conciliate their friendship and esteem.

They bear hunger, cold, fatigue, and all the miseries of life without shrinking; danger only calls forth their fortitude; they even exult in calamity; but contempt is what they cannot bear. An Englishman fears contempt more than death; he often flies to death as a refuge from its pressure, and dies when he fancies the world has ceased to esteem him.

Pride seems the source not only of their national vices, but of their national virtues also. An Englishman is taught to love his king as his friend, but to acknowledge no other master than the laws, which himself has contributed to enact. He despises those nations who, that one may be free, all are content to be slaves—who first lift a tyrant into terror, and then shrink under his power as if delegated from heaven.

"Liberty" is echoed in all their assemblies; and thousands might be found ready to offer up their lives for the sound, though perhaps not one of all the number understands its meaning. The lowest mechanic, however, looks upon it as his duty to be a watchful guardian of his country's freedom, and often uses a language that might seem haughty, even in the mouth of a great emperor who traces his ancestry to the moon.

OLIVER GOLDSMITH, *The Citizen of the World.*

16. The following collection of anecdotes should provide you with material for oral reading during which you can demonstrate your flexibility of tone and intonation in bringing out the flavor of the humor:

a.   Mixed Signals

"Mark Twain" became a lecturer in California in 1869, after he had returned to San Francisco from the Sandwich

Islands. He had written from there a series of picturesque and humorous letters for the Sacramento "Union," a California journal, and was asked to lecture about the islands. He tells of his first experience with great glee. He had written the lecture and committed it to memory, and was satisfied with it. Still, he dreaded a failure on the first night, as he had had no experience in addressing audiences. Accordingly, he made an arrangement with a woman friend, whose family was to occupy one of the boxes, to start the applause if he should give her the sign by looking in her direction and stroking his mustache. He thought that if he failed to "strike" the audience he would be encouraged by a round of applause, if anyone would start it after he had made a good point.

Instead of failure his lecture was a boundless success. The audience rapturously applauded every point, and "Mark" forgot all about his instructions to the lady. Finally, as he was thinking of some new point that occurred to him as he was talking, without a thought of the lady at all, he unconsciously put his hand up to his mustache, and happened to turn in the direction of the box. He had said nothing just then to cause even his appreciative audience to applaud; but the lady took his action for the signal, and nearly broke her fan in striking it against the edge of the box. The whole house joined her applause.

JAMES BURTON POND, Memories of the Lyceum.

b.   An American journalist, addressing an audience of Chinese students in Peking [some years ago], found his address being interpreted to the audience by writing in Chinese upon a blackboard. The novelty of the interpretation attracted his interest. He watched the writing upon the blackboard as he continued his address. The writing grew gradually slow and finally was discontinued altogether, although the speaker continued his address for some minutes thereafter. Leaving the stage, he asked the presiding officer what the interpreter put upon the blackboard in the Chinese language. "He was reporting your speech," was the reply.

"And then why did he stop before the speech was finished?"

"Oh," smilingly said the Chinese, who presided, "he only wrote the ideas upon the blackboard."

DEAN WALTER WILLIAMS, "Condensed Speech,"
Modern Eloquence, Vol. XII.

c.   Plutarch, relating the story of a Roman divorced from his wife, observes: "This person, being highly blamed by his friends, who demanded: 'Was she not chaste? was she not fair?' holding out his shoe, asked them whether it was not new and well made. 'Yet,' added he, 'none of you can tell me where it pinches me.' "

ANONYMOUS, *Modern Eloquence*, Vol. X.

d.   Two men, disputing about the pronunciation of the word "either"—one saying it ee-ther, the other i-ther—agreed to refer the matter to the first person they met, who happened to be from Ireland. He confounded both by declaring: "It's nay-ther, for it's aye-ther."

ANONYMOUS, *Modern Eloquence*, Vol. X.

e.   "Waiter!" called the Englishman, "What is this?"
"It's bean soup," the waiter responded.
"I don't care what it's been;" the Englishman thundered, "the question is, what is it now?"

f.   A physician was called upon to see a seamstress who felt indisposed. He inquired as to her health, and she responded very appropriately: "Well, it's about sew sew, doctor, but seams worse today, and I have frequently stitches in the side." The doctor hemmed as he felt her pulse, and said she would mend soon, and that he would patch her up.

ANONYMOUS, *Modern Eloquence*, Vol. X.

g.   Zimmerman, who was very eminent as a physician, went from Hanover to attend Frederick the Great in his last sickness. One day the king said to him: "You have, I presume, sir, helped many a man into another world?" This was rather a bitter pill for the doctor; but the dose he gave the king in return was a judicious mixture of truth and flattery. "Not so many as your majesty, nor with so much honor to myself."

ANONYMOUS, *Modern Eloquence*, Vol. X.

h.   A gentleman, once of a fair and sober character, in the city of Philadelphia, for many years drank toddy as his constant drink. From this he proceeded to drink grog—after awhile nothing would satisfy him but slings, made of equal parts of rum and water, with a little sugar. From slings he advanced to raw rum—and from common rum to Jamaica spirits. Here he rested for a few months; but at last he found even Jamaica spirits were not strong enough to warm his stomach, and he made it a constant practice to throw a tablespoonful of ground pepper into each glass of his spirits (in order, to use his own expression), "to take off their coldness." It is hardly necessary to add, that he soon afterwards died a martyr to his intemperance.

BENJAMIN RUSH, *The Gentleman's Magazine*,
September, 1785.

i.   A conversation between the famous orator Henley and an attorney of Clement's Inn in an eighteenth century chop house:

Attorney: I remember the man well, but I don't know what became of him. I think they say he went to the West Indies, and settled at Ceylon, or somewhere thereabouts; in one of our islands, however.

Orator: In the first place, Ceylon is no island of ours; and in the second place, it is not in the West Indies, but in the East.

Attorney: I deny that.

Orator: The more shame for you. I'll bring you a boy ten years old who shall prove it to you.

Attorney: Well, I thank God, I know nothing about East or West either. I am no great geographer.

Orator: So then, you thank God for your ignorance, do you?

Attorney: (Looking very angry) Yes, I do, Sir.

Orator: (Making him a low bow) Then, Sir, you have much to be thankful for.

The Gentleman's Magazine, July, 1786.

17.   Reading the Human Face

There is an old story that Matthews, the actor, was once lauding the ability of the human face to express the passions and emotions hidden in the breast. He said the countenance could disclose what was passing in the heart plainer than the tongue could.

"Now," he said, "observe my face—what does it express?"
"Despair!"
"Bah, it expresses peaceful resignation! What does *this* express?"
"Rage!"
"Stuff! it means terror! *This!*"
"Imbecility."
"Fool! It is smothered ferocity! Now this!"
"Joy!"
"Oh, perdition! Any ass can see it means insanity."

Expression! People coolly pretend to read it who would think themselves presumptuous if they pretended to interpret the hieroglyphics on the obelisk of Luxor—yet they are fully as competent to do the one thing as the other.

MARK TWAIN, The Innocents Abroad.

18. A Hare-raising Tale

A panting and perspiring hunter ran up to a youngster leaning on a split rail fence. "Boy," he said, "did you see a hare run across the fields a minute ago?"

"You mean, a rabbit, sir?"

"Yes, yes," gasped the man with the shotgun.

"A thing which runs and jumps along with big ears?"

"Yes, yes," said the hunter impatiently. "Did you see it come out of the woods and run over the field?"

"You mean the thing with a white tail that goes loppety lop, loppety lop?"

"Yes, you fool," said the man impatiently. "Did you see it?"

"Very long ears?"

"Yes, you idiot."

"Oh, then," said the farmer boy chewing a straw, "I didn't see it."

HENRY MANDEVILLE, Third Reader.

19. The following scene from Sheridan's famous comedy *The Rivals* provides a vocabulary as well as a reading exercise. What did Mrs. Malaprop mean to say?

Mrs. Malaprop.	There's a little intricate hussy for you!
Sir Anthony.	It is not to be wondered at, ma'am—all this is the natural consequences of teaching girls to read. Had I a thousand daughters, by Heaven! I'd as soon have them taught the black art as their alphabet!
Mrs. Malaprop.	Nay, nay, Sir Anthony, you are an absolute misanthropy.
Sir Anthony.	In my way hither, Mrs. Malaprop, I observed your niece's maid coming forth from a circulating library! —She had a book in each hand—they were half-bound volumes, with marble covers! —From that moment I guessed how full of duty I should see her mistress!
Mrs. Malaprop.	Those are vile places, indeed!
Sir Anthony.	Madam, a circulating library in a town is as an evergreen tree of diabolical knowledge! It blossoms through the

year! —and depend on it, Mrs. Malaprop, that they who are so fond of handling the leaves, will long for the fruit at last.

Mrs. Malaprop.   Fy, fy, Sir Anthony, you surely speak laconically.

Sir Anthony.   Why, Mrs. Malaprop, in moderation now, what would you have a woman know?

Mrs. Malaprop.   Observe me, Sir Anthony. I would by no means wish a daughter of mine to be a progeny of learning; I don't think so much learning becomes a young woman; for instance, I would never let her meddle with Greek, or Hebrew, or algebra, or simony, or fluxions, or paradoxes, or such inflammatory branches of learning —neither would it be necessary for her to handle any of your mathematical, astronomical, diabolical instruments. —But, Sir Anthony, I would send her, at nine years old, to a boarding school, in order to learn a little ingenuity and artifice. Then, sir, she should have a supercilious knowledge in accounts;—and as she grew up, I would have her instructed in geometry, that she might know something of contagious countries;—but above all, Sir Anthony, she should be mistress of orthodoxy, that she might not mis-spell, and mis-pronounce words so shamefully as girls usually do; and likewise that she might reprehend the true meaning of what she is saying. This, Sir Anthony, is what I would have a woman know; —and I don't think there is a superstitious article in it.

RICHARD BRINSLEY SHERIDAN, The Rivals, I, ii.

20. The following selection is from Molière's famous farce The Would-be Gentleman. (In reading it aloud, to get the full flavor of the fun, pronounce the vowels in the French way: a /a/, e /e/, i /i/, o /o/, u /u/.) How accurate is the Philosophy Master in describing the vowels and consonants?

Philosophy Master.   In order to carry out your wishes properly and treat the matter philosophically, we must begin, in strict order, with an exact knowledge of the nature of the letters of the alphabet and their correct pronunciation. And, on this question, I should tell you that the letters are divided into vowels, called such because they are open sounds made with the voice (Latin, *vox*), and consonants, called this because they are sounded with (*con-sonant*) the vowels and thus make the various articulations of the voice in syllables. There are five vowels: A, E, I, O, U.

M. Jourdain.	Yes, yes, I follow you.
Philosophy Master.	The vowel A is formed by opening the mouth very wide. A.
M. Jourdain.	A, A. Right.
Philosophy Master.	Now the vowel E is formed by bringing the lower jaw up towards the upper jaw, so. A, E.
M. Jourdain.	A, E. A, E. You're absolutely right!
Philosophy Master.	And the vowel I is made by bringing the jaws still closer together and stretching the corners of the mouth up towards the ears. A, E, I.
M. Jourdain.	A, E, I. I, I, I. That's quite true. What a great thing knowledge is!
Philosophy Master.	The vowel O is formed by opening the jaws again, and bringing the corners of the mouth together, thus. O.
M. Jourdain.	O, O. It's just as you say. A, E, I, O, U. Wonderful! Really wonderful! I, O; I, O.
Philosophy Master.	You see, the opening of the mouth makes a perfect little circle, just like an O.
M. Jourdain.	O, O, O. You are so right. O. Oh, this education is a great thing—a great thing.
Philosophy Master.	The vowel U is formed by bringing the teeth closer together, but without letting them touch, and shooting out the lips which at the same time are also brought closer together but without being completely shut. U.

M. Jourdain.	Nothing could be truer. U, U.
Philosophy Master.	The lips should shoot out just as if you were making a pout. And if you want to make fun of someone, you've only to say U to him.
M. Jourdain.	U, U. That's exactly right. Oh, why didn't I begin my studies earlier in life? Then I would have known all this.
Philosophy Master.	Tomorrow we will have a look at the other letters, which, as you will recall, are called consonants.
M. Jourdain.	And is there fascinating information to be had about them too?
Philosophy Master.	Certainly. The consonant D, for example, is formed by placing the tip of the tongue just inside the upper teeth. DA.
M. Jourdain.	DA, DA. Yes, you're right. Amazing!
Philosophy Master.	F is made by closing the upper teeth on the lower lip, like this. FA, FA.
M. Jourdain.	FA, FA. Why it's just as you say. Oh, my father and mother, why did you deny me an education!
Philosophy Master.	Now the R is formed by bringing the tip of the tongue to the top of the palate. There it is gently set in motion by the forcible expulsion of breath. It drops and returns again to the same place, making a sort of trembling. R, RA.
M. Jourdain.	R, R, RA, R, R, R, R, RA. True enough! True enough! What a clever man you are, Professor. And what a lot of time I have lost! R, R, R, RA.
Philosophy Master.	You will see that I will instruct you in the heart of all these matters in our future lessons.

MOLIÈRE, *The Would-be Gentleman,* II, iv.

21. The Dauphiness

It is now sixteen or seventeen years since I saw the Queen of France, then the Dauphiness, at Versailles; and surely never lighted on this orb, which she hardly seemed to touch, a more delightful vision. I saw her just above the horizon, decorating and cheering the elevated sphere she just began to move in—glittering like the morning-star, full of life and splendour and joy! Oh! what a revolution! and what a heart must I have to contemplate without emotion that elevation and that fall! Little did I dream when she added titles of veneration to those of enthusiastic, distant, respectful love, that she should ever be obliged to carry the sharp antidote against disgrace concealed in that bosom; little did I dream that I should have lived to see such disasters fallen upon her in a nation of gallant men, in a nation of men of honour, and of cavaliers. I thought ten thousand swords must have leaped from their scabbards to avenge even a look that threatened her with insult. But the age of chivalry is gone. That of sophisters, economists, and calculators has succeeded; and the glory of Europe is extinguished for ever. Never, never more shall we behold that generous loyalty to rank and sex, that proud submission, that dignified obedience, that subordination of the heart which kept alive, even in servitude itself, the spirit of an exalted freedom. The unbought grace of life, the cheap defence of nations, the nurse of manly sentiment and heroic enterprise is gone! It is gone, that sensibility of principle, that chastity of honour, which felt a stain like a wound, which inspired courage whilst it mitigated ferocity, which ennobled whatever it touched, and under which vice itself lost half its evil by losing all its grossness.

EDMUND BURKE, *Reflections on the Revolution in France.*

22. Count the Bottles Before You Are Sunk

I had 18 bottles of whisky in my cellar and was told by my wife to empty the contents of each and every bottle down the sink or else!

I said I would and proceeded with the unpleasant task.

I withdrew the cork from the first bottle and poured the contents down the sink, with the exception of one glass, which I drank. I extracted the cork from the second bottle and did likewise, with the exception of one glass which I drank. I then withdrew the cork from the third bottle and poured the whisky down the sink which I drank.

I pulled the cork from the fourth bottle down the sink and poured the bottle down the glass, which I drank. I pulled the bottle from the cork of the next and drank one sink and then threw the rest down the glass. I pulled the sink from the next glass and poured the cork down the bottle. Then I corked the sink with the next glass, bottled the drink and drank the pour.

When I had everything emptied, I steadied the house with one hand, counted the glasses, bottles and sinks with the other which were 21 and as the house came by I counted them again and finally I had all the houses in one bottle which I drank.

I'm not under the affluence of incohol as some theople pink I am. I am not half as thunk as you might drink. I fool so feelish that I don't know who is me, and the drunker I stand here the longer I get.

ANONYMOUS, American and Scottish folk tale.

Chapter 6

Selections on Language and Usage for Oral Reading and Discussion

EXPLANATION

33.01 The third chapter of Part II contains excerpts from writings about language and its use. Many of these selections will be helpful both as practice material for speech improvement and for discussion in class. The subject matter of the selections will provide the student with increased information about language and may help to form the basis for a disciplined attitude toward its proper use.

SELECTIONS

33.02

1.   English Spelling an Instance of Conspicuous Waste

As felicitous an instance of futile classicism as can be found, outside of the Far East, is the conventional spelling of the English language. A breach of proprieties in spelling is extremely annoying and will discredit any writer in the eyes of all persons who are possessed of a developed sense of the true and beautiful. English orthography satisfies all the requirements of the canons of reputability under the law of conspicuous waste. It is archaic, cumbrous, and ineffective; its acquisition consumes much time and effort; failure to acquire it is easy of detection. Therefore it is the first and

readiest test of reputability in learning, and conformity to its
ritual is indispensable to a blameless scholastic life.

THORSTEIN VEBLEN, *The Theory of the Leisure Class.**

Why does Veblen call English orthography archaic? Do
you agree that it is also cumbrous and ineffective? Why?
Are you shocked or annoyed by breaches of the proprieties
in spelling?

2.   The Alphabet

The invention of the phonetic alphabet must rank with
that of the wheel among the great landmarks of human culture. It is so fundamental that one is astonished at its still
primitive form. It is as though we had advanced from the
oxcart to jet propulsion without ever modernizing the con-
struction of the wheel. Other written languages preceded it
by thousands of years but, like Chinese, they had all started
as picture-writing. A symbol expressed an idea rather than a
sound. While such a language, if it develops enough ideo-
grams and a system of combining them into compound ideas,
may in time become richly expressive, it will also become
more and more difficult to learn and so tend to become restricted in use to a small group of scholars. And because an
ideographical language is totally unrelated to the spoken
language, it is not precise in its meaning and can only be
used with great difficulty in expressing new ideas.

FRANK DENMAN, *The Shaping of Our Alphabet.*†

Why does Denman call the phonetic alphabet still a primitive form? (He does not refer, of course, to the International
Phonetic Alphabet.) What would be the advantages of a
new English alphabet, based on modern phonetic principles?
Can you foresee any disadvantages? Compare English as a
phonetic language with any other languages of which you
have knowledge.

The sixteenth-century rhetorician Thomas Wilson was
explicit in his criticism of the affectations of speech of his
day and of the great vogue for importing foreign words into
English.

* From *The Theory of the Leisure Class* by Thorstein Veblen, published
by The Viking Press, Inc.

† From *The Shaping of Our Alphabet* by Frank Denman, published by
Alfred A. Knopf, Inc.

3.   Inkhorn Terms

Among all other lessons this should first be learned, that we never affect any strange inkhorn terms, but so speak as is commonly received, neither seeking to be over fine, nor yet living over careless, using our speech as most men do, and ordering our wits as the fewest have done. Some seek so far for outlandish English, that they forget altogether their mother's language. And I dare swear this, if some of their mothers were alive, they would no be able to tell what they say; and yet these fine English clerks will say, they speak in their mother-tongue if a man should charge them for counterfeiting the King's English. Some far-journeyed gentlemen at their return home, like as they love to go in foreign apparel, so they will powder their talk with oversea language. He that cometh lately out of France will talk French English and never blush at the matter . . . The unlearned or foolish fantastical, that smells but of learning (such fellows as have seen learned men in their days) will so Latin their tongues, that the simple cannot but wonder at their talk, and think surely they speak by some Revelation. I know them that think *Rhetoric* to stand wholly upon dark words, and he that can catch an inkhorn term by the tail, him they count to be a fine Englishman, and a good *Rhetorician*.

THOMAS WILSON, *The Art of Rhetorique.*

In spite of the archaic constructions and some obsolete words, the purport of Wilson's thought is evident. Paraphrase the selection. When is it appropriate to use foreign words and expressions in your own speech? When do you like to hear them in the speech of others?

4.   Manners and Speech

The existence of different manners of speech for persons in various ranks is a familiar fact. We are constantly sorting and classifying people according to them. A variation of any national language according to social levels is called a *class dialect*. Even within the class dialect there may be many variations and minor divisions. For instance, the younger members of a privileged class who attend special schools sometimes develop a special jargon among themselves which is almost incomprehensible to outsiders. Yet it is clearly an offshoot of the general "upper-class" dialect of their parents. Poorer youngsters also develop a kind of tribal jargon as local and esoteric as the other. Even families and other restricted groups develop special jargons mystifying to an outsider. But these are even more clearly recognized and assigned to the general class of dialects to which they belong.

MARGARET SCHLAUCH, *The Gift of Tongues.**

Do you find any evidence of class dialects in your community? Have you discovered any differences between the speech of a college professor, for example, and that of a taxi-cab driver? Have you assumed that such differences exist?

5.   The Affinity of Words

If we know English and French and begin a sentence in French, all the later words that come are French; we hardly ever drop into English. And this affinity of the French words for each other is not something merely operating mechanically as a brain-law, it is something we feel at the time. Our understanding of a French sentence heard never falls to so low an ebb that we are not aware that the words linguistically belong together. Our attention can hardly so wander that if an English word be suddenly introduced we shall not start at the change. Such a vague sense as this of the words belonging together is the very minimum of fringe that can accompany them, if "thought" at all. Usually the vague perception that all the words we hear belong to the same language and to the same special vocabulary in that language, and that the grammatical sequence is familiar, is practically equivalent to an admission that what we hear is sense. But if an unusual foreign word be introduced, if the grammar trip, or if a term from an incongruous vocabulary suddenly appear, such as "rat trap" or "plumber's bill" in a philosophical discourse, the sentence detonates as it were, we receive a shock from the incongruity, and the drowsy assent is gone. The feeling of rationality in these cases seems rather a negative than a positive thing, being the mere absence of shock, or sense of discord, between the terms of thought.

Conversely, if words do belong to the same vocabulary, and if the grammatical structure is correct, sentences with absolutely no meaning may be uttered in good faith and pass unchallenged. Discourses at prayer-meetings, reshuffling the same collection of cant phrases, and the whole genus of penny-a-line-isms and newspaper-reporter's flourishes give illustrations of this. "The birds filled the tree-tops with their morning song, making the air moist, cool, and pleasant," is a sentence I remember reading once in a report of some athletic exercises in Jerome Park. It was probably written uncon-

---

* From *The Gift of Tongues* by Margaret Schlauch, published by The Viking Press, Inc.

sciously by the hurried reporter and read uncritically by many readers.

WILLIAM JAMES, *Psychology.*

Summarize the preceding selection. What is the central idea of James's statement?

6.   For Lack of Ideas

The latest blight to afflict the spoken word in the United States is the rapidly spreading reiteration of the phrase "you know." I don't know just when it began moving like a rainstorm through the language, but I tremble at its increasing garbling of meaning, ruining of rhythm, and drumming upon my hapless ears. One man, in a phone conversation with me last summer, used the phrase thirty-four times in about five minutes, by my own count; a young matron in Chicago got seven "you knows" into one wavy sentence, and I have also heard it as far west as Denver, where an otherwise charming woman at a garden party in August said it almost as often as a whippoorwill says "Whippoorwill." . . .

This curse may have originated simultaneously on Broadway and in Hollywood, where such curses often originate. About twenty-five years ago, or perhaps longer, theatre and movie people jammed their sentences with "you know what I mean?" which was soon shortened to "you know?" That had followed the over-use, in the 1920's, of "you see?" or just plain "see?" These blights often disappear finally, but a few have stayed and will continue to stay, such as "Well" and "I mean to say" and "I mean" and "the fact is." Others seem to have mercifully passed out of lingo into limbo, such as, to go back a long way, "Twenty-three, skidoo" and "So's your old man" and "I don't know nothin' from nothin'" and "Believe you me." About five years ago both men and women were saying things like "He has a new Cadillac job with a built-in bar deal in the back seat" and in 1958 almost everything anybody mentioned, or even wrote about, was "triggered." Arguments were triggered, and allergies, and divorces, and even love affairs. This gun-and-bomb verb seemed to make the jumpiest of the jumpy even jumpier, but it has almost died out now, and I trust that I have not triggered its revival.

JAMES THURBER, "The Spreading 'You Know,'"
*Lanterns and Lances.**

What current expressions annoy you? Why do you feel this way? Why are such expressions as "you know" so often heard? Can we do without them entirely?

* Copyright © 1960 James Thurber. Originally in *The New Yorker.*

Do you share any of the opinions expressed by the writers of the preceding selections? Which points of view seem to you to be without basis in fact?

7.   Society and Speech

In France, to talk the language well is still the indispensable accomplishment of a gentleman. Society preserves the happy diction, and the graceful phrase, which literature has stamped with its authority: and the Court may be considered as the Master of Ceremonies to the Muses. But in England, people in the best and most fastidious society, are not remarkable for cultivating the more pure or brilliant order of conversation, as the evidence of *ton*, and the attribute of rank. . . . Our rational conversation is for the most part carried on in a series of the most extraordinary and rugged abbreviations—a species of talking shorthand. Hesitating, Humming, and Drawling are the three Graces of our Conversation.

We are at dinner: a gentleman, "a man about town," is informing us of a misfortune that has befallen his friend: "No—I assure you—now err—err—that—er—it was the most shocking accident possible—er—poor Chester was riding in the Park—er—you know that grey—er (substantive dropped, hand a little flourished instead)—of his—splendid creature!—er—well sir, and by Jove—er—the—er—(no substantive, flourish again) —took fright, and—e—er—" here the gentleman throws up his chin and eyes, sinks back exhausted into his chair, and after a pause adds, "Well, they took him into—the shop—there—you know—with the mahogany sashes—just by the Park—er—and the—er—man there—set his—what d'ye call it—er—collar-bone; *but* he was—er—ter-ri-bly—terribly"—a full stop. The gentleman shakes his head,—and the sentence is suspended to eternity.

EDWARD BULWER-LYTTON, *England and the English.*

The hesitation, repetitions, vocalized pauses (uh-er), and filler phrases in speech are sometimes called "non-fluencies." Does there seem to be any difference in type or degree between their occurrence in American speech and their occurrence in British speech?

Other commentaries on English speech are contained in the following selections from *The Spectator*, by Joseph Addison. Remember that they were written to apply to eighteenth-century speech in southeastern England. Would you be able to say that some of the speech characteristics of that day and place can also be found at the present time in the United States? Do Americans use less gesture than Italians or Frenchmen? What is the present validity of Addison's remarks about the desire for brevity and speed among speakers of English? Are there any evidences of naïveté in his attitude toward language matters?

8.   How To Keep an Audience Awake

Most Foreign Writers who have given any Character of the English Nation, whatever Vices they ascribe to it, allow in general, that the People are naturally Modest. It proceeds perhaps from this our National Virtue, that our Orators are observed to make use of less Gesture or Action than those of other Countries. Our Preachers stand stock-still in the Pulpit, and will not so much as move a Finger to set off the best Sermons in the World. We meet with the same speaking Statues at our Bars, and in all Publick places of Debate. Our Words flow from us in a smooth continued Stream, without those Strainings of the Voice, Motions of the Body, and Majesty of the Hand which are so much celebrated in the Orators of Greece and Rome. We can talk of Life and Death in cold Blood, and keep our Temper in a Discourse which turns upon everything that is dear to us. Though our Zeal breaks out in the finest Tropes and Figures, it is not able to stir a Limb about us. . . .

It is certain that proper Gestures and vehement Exertions of the Voice cannot be too much studied by a publick Orator. They are a kind of Comment to what he utters, and enforce everything he says, with weak Hearers, better than the strongest Argument he can make use of. They keep the Audience awake, and fix their Attention to what is delivered to them, at the same time that they shew the Speaker is in earnest, and affected himself with what he so passionately recommends to others. Violent Gesture and Vociferation naturally shake the Hearts of the Ignorant, and fill them with a kind of Religious Horror. Nothing is more frequent than to see Women weep and tremble at the Sight of a moving Preacher, though he is placed quite out of their Hearing; as in England we very frequently see People lulled Asleep with solid and elaborate Discourses of Piety, who would be warmed and transported out of themselves by the Bellowings and Distortions of Enthusiasm.

If Nonsense, when accompanied with such an Emotion of Voice and Body, has such an influence on Men's Minds, what might we not expect from many of those admirable Discourses which are printed in our Tongue, were they delivered with a becoming Fervour, and with the most agreeable Graces of Voice and Gesture?

JOSEPH ADDISON, "No. 407," *The Spectator.*

9.   English Speech Ways

a.   Hem and Haw

The English delight in Silence more than any other European Nation, if the Remarks which are made on us by Foreigners are true. Our Discourse is not kept up in Conversation, but falls into more Pauses and Intervals than in our Neighboring Countries; as it is observed, that in the matter of our Writings is thrown much closer together, and lies in a narrower Compass than is usual in the Works of Foreign Authors: For, to favor our Natural Taciturnity, when we are obliged to utter our Thoughts, we do it in the shortest way we are able, and give as quick a Birth to our Conceptions as possible.

b.   The English Voice

This Humour shews itself in several Remarks that we may make upon the English Language. At first of all by its abounding in Monosyllables, which gives us an Opportunity of delivering our Thoughts in a few Sounds. This indeed takes off from the Elegance of our Tongue, but at the same time expresses our Ideas in the readiest manner, and consequently answers the first Design of Speech better than the Multitude of Syllables, which make the Words of other Languages more Tunable and Sonorous. The Sounds of our English Words are commonly like those of String Musick, short and transient, which rise and perish upon a single Touch; those of other Languages are like the Notes of Wind Instruments, sweet and swelling, and lengthen'd out into variety of Modulation.

c.   Lack of Vowels in English

The same natural Aversion to Loquacity has of late Years made a very considerable Alteration in our Language, by closing in one Syllable the Termination of our Praeterperfect Tense, as in these Words, *drown'd, walk'd, arriv'd,* for *drowned, walked, arrived,* which has very much disfigured the Tongue, and turned a tenth part of our smoothest Words into so many Clusters of Consonants. This is the more remarkable, because the want of Vowels in our Language has been the general Complaint of our politest Authors, who nevertheless are the Men that have made these Retrenchements, and consequently very much increased our former Scarcity.

d.   Hiss or Hith

This Reflection on the Words that end in *ed,* I have heard
in Conversation from one of the Greatest Geniuses this Age
has produced. I think we may add to the foregoing Observation, the Change which has happened in our Language, by
the Abbreviation of several Words that are terminated in *eth,*
by substituting an *s* in the room of the last Syllable, as in
drowns, walks, arrives, and innumerable other Words, which
in the Pronunciation of our Fore-fathers were *drowneth,*
walketh, arriveth. This has wonderfully multiplied a Letter
which was before too frequent in the English Tongue, and
added to that *hissing* in our Language, which is taken so much
notice of by Foreigners; but at the same time humours our
Taciturnity, and eases us of many superfluous Syllables.

JOSEPH ADDISON, "No. 135," *The Spectator.*

10.   Ears or Tongue

The most fruitful and natural exercise of our mind, in my
opinion, is conversation. I find the practice of it more pleasant than that of any other action of our life; and that is the
reason why, if I were right now compelled to choose, I should
sooner, I believe, consent to lose my sight than my hearing or
speech. The Athenians, and also the Romans, kept this exercise in great honor in their academies. In our times the Italians retain some traces of it to their great advantage, as it is
manifest in a comparison of our intelligence with theirs. The
study of books is a languishing and feeble activity that produces no heat, whereas conversation teaches and exercises at
the same time. If I converse with a man of strong mind and
a stiff jouster, he presses hard upon me and digs at me right
and left, his ideas spur on mine. Rivalry, glory, and contention thrust and lift me above myself. And agreement is a
very tiresome quality in conversation.

MICHEL DE MONTAIGNE, *Of the Art of Conversing,* translated by WILLIAM HAZLITT.

Do you agree with Montaigne that you would rather lose
your sight than your hearing or speech? Comment on the
statement "agreement is a very tiresome quality in conversation."

11.   Liberty of the Tongue for Women

We next went to the school of languages, where three
professors sat in consultation upon improving that of their own
country.

The first project was to shorten discourse by cutting poly-

syllables into one, and leaving out verbs and participles; because in reality all things imaginable are but nouns.

The other project was a scheme for entirely abolishing
all words whatsoever; and this was urged as a great advantage
in point of health as well as brevity. For it is plain, that every
word we speak is in some degree a diminution of our lungs
by corrosion; and consequently contributes to the shortening
of our lives. An expedient was therefore offered, that since
words are only names for *things*, it would be much more convenient for all men to carry about them, such things as were
necessary to express the particular business they are to discourse on. And this invention would certainly have taken
place, to the great ease as well as health of the subject, if the
women, in conjunction with the vulgar and illiterate, had not
threatened to raise a rebellion, unless they might be allowed
the liberty to speak with their tongues, after the manner of
their ancestors; such constant irreconcilable enemies to science are the common people. However, many of the most
learned and wise adhere to the new scheme of expressing
themselves by things; which hath only this inconvenience at-
tending it—that if a man's business be very great, and of various kinds, he must be obliged in proportion to carry a greater
bundle of things upon his back, unless he can afford one or
two strong servants to attend him. I have often beheld two
of those sages almost sinking under the weight of their packs,
like pedlars among us; who, when they met in the streets,
would lay down their loads, open their sacks, and hold conversation for an hour together; then put up their implements,
help each other to resume their burthens, and take their leave.
JONATHAN SWIFT, *Gulliver's Travels.*

Is Dean Swift's proposal completely absurd, or does the
concept have any possible merit? What principle of language
does it seem to illustrate? The following selection from one
of his works seems to advocate that the standards of pronunciation and spelling be established by "fine ladies and
gentlemen," and not by scholars. Is Swift serious in this
proposal? How are present standards of pronunciation and
spelling achieved?

12.   Pedants and Speech
It would be another infinite advantage, that, by cultivating
this science [of conversation], we should wholly avoid the
vexations and impertinence of pedants, who affect to talk in
a language not to be understood; and whenever a polite person offers accidentally to use any of their jargon terms, have

the presumption to laugh at us for pronouncing those words in a genteeler manner. Whereas, I do here affirm, that, whenever any fine gentleman or lady condescends to let a hard word pass out of their mouths, every syllable is smoothed and polished in the passage; and it is a true mark of politeness, both in writing and reading, to vary the orthography as well as the sound; because we are infinitely better judges of what will please a distinguishing ear than those, who call themselves scholars, can possibly be; who, consequently, ought to correct their books, and manner of pronouncing, by the authority of our example, from whose lips they proceed with infinitely more beauty and significancy.

JONATHAN SWIFT, "Introduction," *A Complete Collection of Genteel and Ingenious Conversation.*

13.   Advice to Writers

To write a genuine familiar or truly English style is to write as any one would speak in common conversation who had a thorough command and choice of words, or who could discourse with ease, force, and perspicuity, setting aside all pedantic and oratorical flourishes. Or, to give another illustration, to write naturally is the same thing in regard to common conversation as to read naturally is in regard to common speech. It does not follow that it is an easy thing to give the true accent and inflection to the words you utter, because you do not attempt to rise above the level of ordinary life and colloquial speaking. You do not assume, indeed, the solemnity of the pulpit, or the tone of stage-declamation; neither are you at liberty to gabble on at a venture, without emphasis or discretion, or to resort to vulgar dialect or clownish pronunciation. You must steer a middle course. You are tied down to a given and appropriate articulation, which is determined by the habitual associations between sense and sound, and which you can only hit by entering into the author's meaning, as you must find the proper words and style to express yourself by fixing your thoughts on the subject you have to write about. Anyone may mouth out a passage with a theatrical cadence, or get upon stilts to tell his thoughts; but to write or speak with propriety and simplicity is a more difficult task. Thus it is easy to affect a pompous style, to use a word twice as big as the thing you want to express: it is not so easy to pitch upon the very word that exactly fits it. Out of eight or ten words equally common, equally intelligible, with nearly equal pretensions, it is a matter of some nicety and discrimination to pick out the very one, the preferableness of which is scarcely perceptible, but decisive.

WILLIAM HAZLITT, *On Familiar Style.*

Have you ever heard an old-fashioned orator? What are the characteristics of that type of speaking? Here is what Nicholas Murray Butler, a former president of Columbia University, had to say on the same general subject:

14.   Correct, Pedantic, and "Elegant" English

One's hold upon the English tongue is measured by his choice of words and by his use of idiom. The composite character of modern English offers a wide field for apt and happy choice of expression. The educated man, at home with his mother tongue, moves easily about in its Saxon, Romanic, and Latin elements, and has gained by long experience and wide reading a knowledge of the mental incidence of words as well as of their artistic effect. He is hampered by no set formulas, but manifests in his speech, spoken and written, the characteristic powers and appreciation of his nature. The educated man is of necessity, therefore, a constant reader of the best written English. He reads not for conscious imitation, but for unconscious absorption and reflection. He knows the wide distinction between correct English on the one hand, and pedantic, or, as it is sometimes called, "elegant" English on the other. He is more likely to "go to bed" than to "retire," to "get up" than to "arise," to have "legs" rather than "limbs," to "dress" than to "clothe himself," and to "make a speech" rather than to "deliver an oration." He knows that "if you hear poor English and read poor English, you will pretty surely speak poor English and write poor English," and governs himself accordingly. He realizes the power and place of idiom and its relation to grammar, and shows his skill by preserving a balance between the two in his style. . . . In short, in his use of his mother tongue he would give sure evidence of an education.

NICHOLAS MURRAY BUTLER, "Five Evidences of an Education," *The Meaning of Education.*

15.   Truth and Understanding

There is very great necessity indeed of getting a little more silent than we are. It seems to me as if the finest nations of the world,—the English and the American, in chief,—were going all off into wind and tongue. . . . There is a time to speak, and a time to be silent. Silence, withal is the eternal duty of a man. He won't get to any real understanding of what is complex, and what is more than aught else pertinent to his interests, without keeping silence too. "Watch the tongue," is a very old precept, and a most true one.

I don't want to discourage any of you from your Demosthenes, and your studies of the niceties of language, and all that.

Believe me, I value that as much as any one of you. I consider it a very graceful thing, and a most proper, for every human creature to know what the implement which he uses in communicating his thoughts is, and how to make the very utmost of it. I want you to study Demosthenes, and to know all his excellences. At the same time, I must say that speech, in the case even of Demosthenes, does not seem, on the whole, to have turned to almost any good account. He advised next to nothing that proved practicable; much of the reverse. Why tell me that a man is a fine speaker, if it is not the truth that he is speaking?

It is not the speech, but the things spoken, that I am anxious about! I really care very little how a man said it, provided I understand him, and it be true. Excellent speaker? But what if he is telling me things that are contrary to the fact; what if he has formed a wrong judgment about the fact —if he has in his mind . . . no power to form a right judgment in regard to the matter? An excellent speaker of that kind is, as it were, saying, "Ho, every one that wants to be persuaded of the thing that is not true; here is the man for you!" I recommend you to be very chary of that kind of excellent speech.

Well, all that sad stuff being the too well-known product of our method of vocal education,—the teacher merely operating on the tongue of the pupil, and teaching him to wag it in a particular way,—it has made various thinking men entertain a distrust of this not very salutary way of procedure; and they have longed for some less theoretic, and more practical and concrete way of working out the problems of education; in effect, for an education not vocal at all, but mute except where speaking was strictly needful.

THOMAS CARLYLE, *Inaugural Address at Edinburgh*, 1866.

Can you indicate some situations in which men need to be more silent? What are the advantages of silence compared to speech? Give examples of speakers who were powerful in effect but who distorted truth to gain their effects.

Thomas Carlyle's remarks have a bearing on our subject. He spoke, of course, in a day when certain teachers emphasized manner to the exclusion of matter and when speakers were often admired merely for their display of oratorical tricks (trumpeting voices, exaggerated pitch range, elaborate gestures, extravagant language, etc.). We should continue to keep in mind that what we say is of primary importance. However, when the way we say something interferes with the effectiveness of what we are saying, the manner of speaking is a subject for improvement.

The following excerpt from a letter to Henry James by John J. Chapman represents a rather unusual point of view. Do you agree with it?

16.   John J. Chapman to Henry James
There are lots of people who can't think seriously without injuring their minds. Their minds were not meant for this use, and so the more they think the feebler they grow.

The cure is simple.

Speak out opinions before you think—and before the other fellow speaks. Thus you will give your mind some chance of forming them in a natural way—unconsciously. Accustom yourself to not knowing what your opinions are till you have blurted them out and thus find what they are. That's what talk is for—and it doesn't prevent the careful summarizing of ideas upon occasion when this is in order. Your valued father went the limit in the expression of things in writing in this improvised way, for he never knew quite what was in his mind—as he told me himself—till he wrote; and it was by this course that he made his most telling cracks: for it is only in the poetic element that truth is told. For truth to be truth must be new.

If one is dealing with such simple matters as making an engine—adding a cog to it—or finding a microbe—you may reason and ratiocinate to good ends. But if you're dealing with human nature in any form, you go broke if you reason— you're an ass to reason—you must put the thing off your mind and allow the probabilities to occur to you—and never be sure then.

                              "John J. Chapman and His Letters,"
                                   The Practical Cogitator.＊

17.   The Writing of Speech
The demand for realism has inveigled dramatists into a naturalism even greater and greater, a style that has been cultivated to its utmost limit, as we know, by Noel Coward. Not only is the "literary" avoided, but actuality has been so much sought after that grammar is eschewed, sentences are broken, for it is said that in ordinary life people speak ungrammatically and in short or unfinished sentences, and a vocabulary has been employed in which only the simplest and most ordinary words are allowed. This dialogue is eked out

＊ From *The Practical Cogitator,* selected and edited by Charles P. Curtis, Jr., and Ferris Greenslet, published by the Houghton Mifflin Co.

with shrugs, waves of the hand and grimaces. In thus yield-
ing to the fashion it seems to me that dramatists have gravely
handicapped themselves. For this slangy, clipped, broken
speech they reproduce is only the speech of a class, the
speech of the young, ill-educated well-to-do, who are de-
scribed in the papers as the smart set. . . . The present
mode, which forces a judge or an eminent physician to express himself as inadequately as a bar-lounger, grossly misrep-
resents the truth. It has narrowed the range of character that
the dramatist can deal with, for he can only show this by
speech, and it is impossible to portray people of any subtlety
of mind or intricacy of emotion when his dialogue is but a
sort of spoken hieroglyph. He is insensibly led to choose as
his characters persons who talk naturally in the way his audience have come to think natural and these inevitably are very
simple and obvious. It has restricted his themes since it is
hard to deal with the fundamental issues of human life. It is
impossible to analyze the complexities of human nature (dramatic subjects both) when you confine yourself to a naturalis-
tic dialogue. It has killed comedy, which depends on verbal
wit, which in turn depends on the well-turned phrase. It has
thus knocked another nail in the coffin of prose drama.

W. SOMERSET MAUGHAM, *The Summing Up.**

Can you think of examples and analogies to support or
oppose Maugham's point? Do you believe that Shakespeare's
dialog represents very accurately the common speech of his
day? Are you disconcerted by dialog in books and plays in
which the characters "talk like books"?

18.   Prolix
I sat lately at dinner with a notoriously witty person (a
really witty man) whom our hostess had introduced to provide the entertainment. I had read many of his reviews of
books and plays, and while I confess their wit and brilliancy,
I had thought them to be hard and intellectual and lacking in
all that broader base of humor which aims at truth. His writing—catching the bad habit of the time—is too ready to pro-
claim a paradox and to assert the unusual, to throw aside in
contempt the valuable haystack in a fine search for a paltry
needle. His reviews are seldom right—as most of us see the
right—but they sparkle and hold one's interest for their
perversity and unexpected turns.

In conversation I found him much as I had found him in his writing—although, strictly speaking, it was not a conversation, which requires an interchange of word and idea and is a turn about. A conversation should not be a market where one sells and another buys. Rather, it should be a bargaining back and forth, and each person should be both merchant and buyer. My rubber plant for your victrola, each offering what he has and seeking his deficiency. It was my friend B_____ who fairly put the case when he said that he liked so much to talk that he was willing to pay for his audience by listening in his turn.

But this was a speech and a lecture. He loosed on us from the cold spigot of his intellect a steady flow of literary allusion—a practice which he professes to hold in scorn—and wit and epigram. He seemed torn from the page of Meredith. He talked like ink. I had believed before that only people in books could talk as he did, and then only when their author had blotted and scratched their performance for the seventh time before he sent it to the printer. To me it was an entirely new experience, for my usual acquaintances are good, common, honest, daytime, woolen folk and they seldom average better than one bright thing in an evening.

At first I feared that there might be a break in his flow of speech which I should be obliged to fill. Once, when there was a slight pause—a truffle was engaging him—I launched a frail remark; but it was swept off at once in the renewed torrent. And seriously it does not seem fair. If one speaker insists—to change the figure—on laying all the cobbles of a conversation, he should at least allow another to carry the tarpot and fill in the chinks. When the evening was over, although I recalled two or three clever stories, which I shall botch in the telling, I came away tired and dissatisfied, my tongue dry with disuse.

CHARLES S. BROOKS, "On the Difference Between Wit and
Humor," *Chimney-Pot Papers.**

Have you had disappointments similar to the one Mr. Brooks experienced? How does what he said relate to what has been said about conversation in previous essays?

19.   As or Like

I guess it is farewell to grammatical compunction,
I guess a preposition is the same as a conjunction,
I guess an adjective is the same as an adverb,

* From *Chimney-Pot Papers* by Charles S. Brooks, published by Yale University Press.

And "to pause" is a bad verb.
Blow, blow, thou winter wind,
Thou are not that unkind
Like man's ingratitude to his ancestors who left him the
  English language for an inheritance;
This is a chromium world in which even the Copley Plazas
  and the Blackstones and the Book Cadillacs are simplified
  into Sheratons.
I guess our ancient speech has gone so flat that we have to
  spike it;
Like the hart panteth for the water brooks I pant for a revival
  of Shakespeare's *Like You Like It.*
I can see the tense draftees relax and purr
When the sergeant barks, "Like you were."
—And don't try to tell me that our well has been defiled by
  immigration;
Like goes Madison Avenue, like so goes the nation.

    OGDEN NASH, "Oafishness Sells Good, Like an Advertise-
    ment Should," *Verses from 1929 On.* *

20.   Who Speaks Better?

The inferior orders of society in America certainly speak
more accurately than the inferior orders of Britain, and those
local peculiarities of accent which abound so amazingly in
our native country, and which a foreigner travelling among us
must detect much more readily than a native, are totally unknown here. There is a great degree of uniformity in the
style of conversation throughout that portion of the country
which I have visited; and a very considerable degree of what
is called in Scotland the English pronunciation. . . . The
educated classes of society, do not speak by any means so
accurately in America as in Britain; there are more deficiencies
in grammar, in accent, in pronunciation; there is a mixture of
unauthorized phrases of which we know nothing; and were
a casual conversation between a well educated native of
America, and a well educated native of Britain, faithfully
committed to writing, that of the American, would I think in
a large majority of cases be found deficient.

    JOHN M. DUNCAN, *Travels Through Part of the United
    States and Canada in 1818 and 1819.*

21.   84.5 Per Cent

I find that 84.5 per cent of Americans of both sexes stretch
into three syllables such words as "sparkling," "struggling,"

* Copyright © 1956 by Ogden Nash. Originally appeared in *The New
Yorker.*

and "battling." The bastard sound of "sparkeling" is heard, day in and night out, in radio and television commercials, and even trained actors are afflicted by these three-syllable enormities. In trying to figure it all out, I began with an impossible assumption—namely, that 84.5 per cent of American men and women were sick in bed on the day when the formation of the present participle from words ending in "le" was taken up in school. We are much too healthy a nation for that. The chief culprit, it now seems to me, is, and always has been, the writer of lyrics for popular songs. Fifty years ago, one of thém came up with "We'll be cuddle-in' soon" (by the light of the silvery moon, of course), and only a little later everybody was singing, from "Waiting for the Robert E. Lee," the memorable "Join that shuffle-in' throng." Then the lyricist of "The tumble-in' tumbleweeds," and many others, joined the shuffle-in' throng.

JAMES THURBER, "Friends, Romans, Countrymen, Lend
Me Your Ear Muffs," *Lanterns and Lances.**

22.   A Living Language and a Dying People

But what I have most at heart, is, that some method should be thought on for ascertaining and fixing our language for ever, after such alterations are made in it as shall be thought requisite. For I am of opinion, it is better a language should not be wholly perfect, than that it should be perpetually changing; and we must give over at one time, or at length infallibly change for the worse; as the Romans did, when they began to quit their simplicity of style, for affected refinements, such as we meet in Tacitus and other authors; which ended by degrees in many barbarities, even before the Goths had invaded Italy.

JONATHAN SWIFT, *A Proposal for Correcting, Improving,
and Ascertaining the English Tongue.*

What is Swift really proposing in this statement? What seems important to you about the proposal? Why do you think he referred to the Late Latin authors as having written "barbarities"?

23.   A Dictionary Without Pronunciations

Boswell. "It may be of use, Sir, to have a Dictionary to ascertain the pronunciation."

Johnson. "Why, Sir, my Dictionary shows you the accents of words, if you can but remember them."

* Copyright © 1959 James Thurber. Originally in *The New Yorker.*

Boswell. "But, Sir, we want marks to ascertain the pronunciation of the vowels. Sheridan, I believe, has finished such a work."

Johnson. "Why, Sir, consider how much easier it is to learn a language by the ear, than by any marks. Sheridan's Dictionary may do very well; but you cannot always carry it about with you: and, when you want the word, you have not the Dictionary. It is like a man who has a sword that will not draw. It is an admirable sword, to be sure: but while your enemy is cutting your throat, you are unable to us it."

JAMES BOSWELL, *Life of Samuel Johnson,* Vol. II.

Does Dr. Johnson's logic seem sound to you? What reservations do you have about it? What is the standard of acceptable pronunciation in the United States? How do the dictionaries reflect that standard?

24. Youth and Language

Several young men at the universities, terribly possessed with the fear of pedantry, run into a worse extreme, and think all politeness to consist in reading the daily trash sent down to them from hence; this they call knowing the world and reading men and manners. Thus furnished, they come up to town, reckon all their errors for accomplishments, borrow the newest set of phrases; and if they take a pen into their hands, all the odd words they have picked up in a coffee house, or a gaming ordinary, are produced as flowers of style; and the orthography refined to the utmost.

JONATHAN SWIFT, *A Proposal for Correcting, Improving, and Ascertaining the English Tongue.*

Have you ever inquired into the slang used by your parents when they were in college? Ask them to use some of it, and see if you understand it. What about the slang words used by the present-day high school students: do you know and use it? What generalizations can you make about the use of slang from your observations? To what is Swift objecting in this passage?

25. Word Count

Shakespeare's vocabulary is often stated to be the richest ever employed by a single man. It has been calculated to comprise 21,000 words . . . or, according to others, 24,000 or 15,000. In order to appreciate what that means we must look a little at the various statements that have been given of the number of words used by other authors and by ordinary beings, educated and not educated. Unfortunately these statements are in many cases given and repeated without any indication of the manner in which they have been arrived at. Milton's vocabulary is said to comprise 7,000 or 8,000 words, that of the Iliad and Odyssey taken together 9,000, that of the Old Testament 5,642 and that of the New Testament 4,800; A. S. Cook (in *The Nation*, Sept. 12, 1912) computes the vocabulary of the Authorized Version at 6,568 words, or at 9,884, if inflected forms of nouns, pronouns, or verbs are included.

OTTO JESPERSEN, Growth and Structure of the
English Language.*

What reservation does Mr. Jespersen have about statements of word counts? How much do they indicate as to the value of a writer's work or an individual's intelligence?

26.   Evaluating the Sentence

The unit of speech is neither the individual sound nor the individual word, but the sentence, i.e., a word or group of words expressing a complete concept, each word composed of individual sounds, and the meaning of the single word (when the sentence consists of only one word) or the combination of meanings of the group of words conveying a unitary idea. Since the sentence is the oral expression of a mental concept, the relationship of its constituent words is largely determined by psychological factors. The speaker speaks, and the hearer hears, sentences, not words (except when the single sentence conveys a complete concept), and still less sounds. The hearer, in particular, has his attention concentrated on getting the meaning of the sentence as a whole; he normally hears (i.e., specifically recognizes) only those individual words or sounds which he feels necessary for understanding the force of the sentence collectively.

LOUIS H. GRAY, Foundations of Language.†

How does the meaning of this selection relate to the work you have been doing in speech improvement?

27   The Pedant

For rhetoric he could not ope
His mouth, but out there flew a trope:
And when he happened to break off

---

* From *Growth and Structure of the English Language* by Otto Jespersen, published by The Macmillan Co.

† From *Foundations of Language* by Louis H. Gray, published by The Macmillan Co.

I'th'middle of his speech or cough
H' had hard words, ready to show why,
And tell what rules he did it by.
Else when with greatest art he spoke,
You'd think he talk'd like other folk,
For all a rhetorician's rules,
Teach nothing but to name his tools,
His ordinary rate of speech
In loftiness of sound was rich,
A Babylonish dialect,
Which learned pedants much affect.
It was a parti-colour'd dress
Of patch'd and pybal'd languages:
'Twas English cut on Greek and Latin,
Like fustian heretofore on satin.
It had an odd promiscuous tone,
As if h'had talk'd three parts in one.
Which made some think when he did gabble,
Th' had heard three laborers of Babel;
Or Cerberus himself pronounce
A leash of languages at once.
This he as volubly would vent
As if his stock would ne'er be spent.
And truly to support that charge
He had supplies as vast and large.
For he could coin or counterfeit
New words with little or no wit:
Words so debas'd and hard, no stone
Was hard enought to touch them on.
And when with hasty noise he spoke 'em
The ignorant for current took 'em.
That had the orator who once,
Did fill his mouth with pebble stones
When he harangu'd, but known his phrase,
He would have us'd no other ways.

SAMUEL BUTLER, Hudibras.

Here are several observations on dialect as spoken in Maine and in South Carolina:

28.   Dialect or Vernacular

a.   What commonly passes for the Maine vernacular in print and on stage, screen and radio is a libel on the

"Down-Easter's" manner of speaking. In reality, there are as many Maine dialects as there are States in the Union. A skilled listener acquainted with Maine speech should be able to identify the community to which any Maine person speaking his home dialect belongs. Variations in the vernacular between one community or region and another do not lie in the use or misuse of words, but in changes in inflection and timbre. Thus it is next to impossible accurately to reproduce the Maine vernacular in printed words. The common speech of Maine people of English-Scottish-Irish stock is probably as nearly pure, in being free from corruptions and in retaining old forms intact, as any of this country, with the possible exception of that of the Carolina and Kentucky mountaineers. The peculiarities of Maine speech are its nasal qualities, slurred enunciation, and dropped syllables, with a hesitancy in delivery.

"Maine: A Guide to Down East," *
American Guide Series.

b.   The South Carolinian is a Low Countryman or an Up Countryman, with the native of the mid-section having characteristics of both. This classification occurs within the State and outsiders are probably unaware of it. To a certain extent the same principles that produced the Roundhead-Cavalier antagonism in England persist even now in South Carolina. In the Low Country the South Carolinian has one sort of personality, in the Up Country another, and in the middle of the State he becomes a somewhat unamalgamated combination of both. Such is the case, regardless of class or color or creed.

c.   The Low Countryman's social life, his habits of speech and dress, are all an outgrowth of his decades of association with the geography and history of his section. Camp meetings, surviving from ancient itinerary Methodism, and tournaments smacking of ante-bellum grandeur are occasions for religion, sport, and social converse. The St. Cecelia balls, rigidly restricted, still attempt to preserve the old attitude of Charleston society when tradesmen were scorned and members of the upper class acted as lords and barons.

The Low Countryman speaks in a special intonation, softens his "r's," and slurs his words, which may be slowly drawled or fired with startling rapidity—especially the lat-

* From "Maine: A Guide to Down East," published by the Houghton Mifflin Co.

ter if he lives in Charleston. On the sea islands, his speech changes; he will talk Gullah if he is a Negro and if he is white there will be evidences of this unique dialect in his conversation. . . .

The Low Countryman himself, however, will not change. He will still have his afternoon nap, eat his rice, revere his ancestors, go hunting and fishing in season, and take time out from his labors to entertain friends and guests with courtesy, ease, and graceful hospitality.

The Up Country South Carolinian, on the other hand, while possessing many qualities of the Low Countryman, will exhibit more physical energy and a greater desire to accumulate a bank account. His forebears were largely Scotch-Irish or German, who in the Old World had to struggle for existence and in the New World chose an isolated inland region. He has worked his own small farm for generations, and the few slaves he once had were of scant economic significance.

"South Carolina: A Guide to the Palmetto State," *

American Guide Series.

Prepare a short, informal talk on the dialect of your own area. What pronunciations and expressions seem to be distinctive in your area?

29.   The Reverend Micah Sowls

The Reverend Micah Sowls,
He shouts and yells and howls,
He screams, he mouths, he bumps,
He foams, he rants, he thumps.

His armour he has buckled on, to wage
The regulation war against the Stage;
And warns his congregation all to shun
"The Presence-Chamber of the Evil One."

The subject's sad enough
To make him rant and puff,
And fortunately, too
His Bishop's in a pew.

So Reverend Micah claps on extra steam,
His eyes are flashing with superior gleam,
He is as energetic as can be,
For there are fatter livings in that see.

* Published by Oxford University Press.

The Bishop, when it's o'er,
Goes through the vestry door,
Where Micah, very red,
Is mopping of his head.

"Pardon, my Lord, your Sowls' excessive zeal,
It is a theme on which I strongly feel."
(The sermon somebody had sent him down
From London, at a charge of half-a-crown.)

The Bishop bowed his head,
And, acquiescing said,
"I've heard your well-meant rage
Against the Modern Stage.

"A modern Theatre, as I heard you say,
Sows seeds of evil broadcast—well it may;
But let me ask you, my respected son,
Pray, have you ever ventured into one?"

"My Lord," said Micah, "no!
I never, never go!
What! Go and see a play?
My goodness, gracious, nay!"

The worthy Bishop said, "My friend, no doubt
The Stage may be the place you make it out;
But if, my Reverend Sowls, you never go,
I don't quite understand how you're to know."

"Well, really," Micah said,
"I've often heard and read,
But never go—do you?"
The Bishop said, "I do."

"That proves me wrong," said Micah, in a trice:
"I thought it all frivolity and vice."
The Bishop handed him a printed card:
"Go to a theatre where they play our Bard."

The Bishop took his leave,
Rejoicing in his sleeve.

The next ensuing day
Sowls went and heard a play.

He saw a dreary person on the stage,
Who mouthed and mugged in simulated rage,
Who growled and spluttered in a mode absurd,
And spoke an English Sowls had never heard.

    For "gaunt" was spoken "garnt,"
    And "haunt" transformed to "harnt,"
    And "wrath" pronounced as "rath,"
    And "death" was changed to "dath."

For hours and hours and hours that dismal actor walked,
And talked, and talked, and talked, and talked,
Till lethargy upon the parson crept,
And sleepy Micah Sowls serenely slept.

    He slept away until
    The farce that closed the bill
    Had warned him not to stay,
    And then he went away.

"I thought *my* gait ridiculous," said he—
"My elocution faulty as could be;
I thought *I* mumbled on a matchless plan—
I had not seen our great Tragedian!

    "Forgive me, if you can,
    O great Tragedian!
    I own it with a sigh—
    You're drearier than I!"

                W. S. GILBERT, *The Bab Ballads.*

Do the present-day actors in Shakespearean productions
have some of the same faults detailed in the previous account
of Victorian England? What speech characteristics of actors
have you found annoying?

30.   What Do We Say for It?
    The details of speech which occasion this feeling of dif-
ference are usually details of pronunciation and intonation,
less often details of vocabulary. So far as vocabulary is concerned, the speech of all educated persons in America is re-

markably uniform. One may occasionally observe a word which by its meaning reveals a local custom, as when one gives the words *evening* or *gallery* the Southern senses of *afternoon* or *porch*, or when one calls the enclosure around a house, as they do in New England, a *door-yard*, or calls a *farm* a *ranch*, as they do in the Far West. But occasions for expressing the ideas which may call for the use of peculiarly local words are obviously less frequent and therefore less revealing than pronunciations, or cadences, which affect all words, whether they are local or not. Moreover, the conventional spelling of modern English, though it is adequate to universalize vocabulary through the printed pages of books, magazines, and newspapers, by the very fact that it is conventional is made powerless to normalize pronunciation or to prevent increasing differentiation in it.

GEORGE PHILIP KRAPP, *The English Language in America.**

Have you any dialectal words in your vocabulary? Can you distinguish between a *spider* and a *skillet*, a *pail* and a *bucket*, a *run* and a *creek*, a *seesaw* and a *teeter-totter*? Certainly there are some words in your area that are not in those of other students in your class. Try to collect such a list.

31.   Call Me No Names
In every language, sounds convey emotional impressions, partly because of their intrinsic quality, partly because of their suggestions and alliances. Take the hypocritical villain in Dickens: Uriah Heep. Quite apart from its Biblical background, Uriah seems to writhe, and Heep seems to creep and to peer and to sneak meanly. Another of Dickens' novels is named after an important commercial firm: *Dombey and Son.* Dombey sounds pompous and rather dumb, and it has a weak ending: DOMbey. The helpless optimistic bankrupt in *David Copperfield* is named Micawber: his name begins weakly, swells out into a bubble of empty sound, and then disintegrates again: MiCAWber. Elsewhere in Dickens there is a splendidly empty-headed society lady whose name sounds like empty-headed conversation: Julia Wititterly . . .

GILBERT HIGHET, from a radio talk, "What's in a Name?" †

Think of some of the names of your friends. Do some names "fit" and others "not fit"? Can you work out any reason

* From *The English Language in America* by George Philip Krapp, published by the Frederick Ungar Publishing Co., Inc.

† This and the two following selections appear by courtesy of Oxford University Press.

for this? What about the names of Tom Sawyer and Huck Finn? Look at the names of characters in the plays of Ben Jonson to find out the system by which he devised their naming.

32.   Words Are Canny

Then there is a second group of words which are known throughout the English-speaking world, but which were originally pure Scots. For instance, *tartan, plaid, clan* and probably *porridge.* (Yet only the Scots know that *porridge* is not singular, but plural; you say "these are good porridge.") *Whisky* came into English from the Gaelic of Ireland. But *slogan,* meaning "a war cry," and now much debased, is Scottish. Everyone knows *canny* and *uncanny,* although the difference between them is not simply the difference between "wise" and "unwise"; *uncanny* seems to mean "incomprehensible" and therefore "unsafe." Most of us know *daft,* which is old English, but survives only in the North. And surely everyone uses the affectionate little adjective *wee;* it is somehow more natural to say "a wee baby" than "a small infant," and to wait "a wee while" rather than "a short time."

        GILBERT HIGHET, from a radio talk, "Scottish Words."

Do you recall any Scottish words still current in your dialectal area? What about the words *bairn, cutty, mickle,* and *sark?* Look them up in your dictionary, and discover their derivations. Have you experienced any difficulty reading the poetry of Robert Burns? How do you account for the comparatively few Scottish words in our current speech, when German, French, and even Spanish words are so frequent?

33.   It's True. I Saw It in the Movies.

In movies about ancient Greece and Rome, the static parts often look quite real and convincing—no doubt because they have been modeled on pictures and statues. It is the active parts which are usually so funny. Almost every motion picture about ancient Rome I have ever seen showed somebody driving through the streets of the city in a chariot, trr, trr, trr, while the citizens cringed away from his mad career. This is as absurd as showing a cowboy on horseback galloping along the sidewalk of Fifth Avenue, New York. Chariots and such things were absolutely prohibited in the streets of Rome; they were kept for war or else for hot-pole driving on the highways outside the cities. Everybody walked. The average

Roman never rode in a chariot from the day of his birth to the day of his death.

GILBERT HIGHET, from a radio talk, "History on the Silver Screen."

Verisimilitude is a term used to identify the attempt to give a semblance of truth or of probability to something. Is verisimilitude always possible in the movies? Is it always desirable in stage speech? What would be your reaction to a performance of a Shakespearean play given with the pronunciation of the early seventeenth century?

Index of Authors

Index of Topics